I0824826

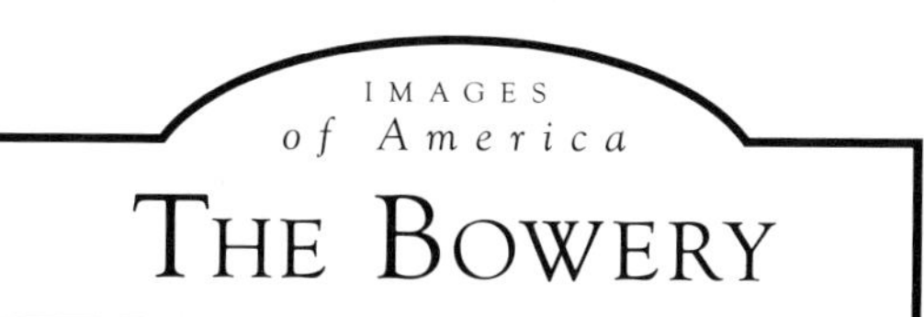
IMAGES
of America
THE BOWERY

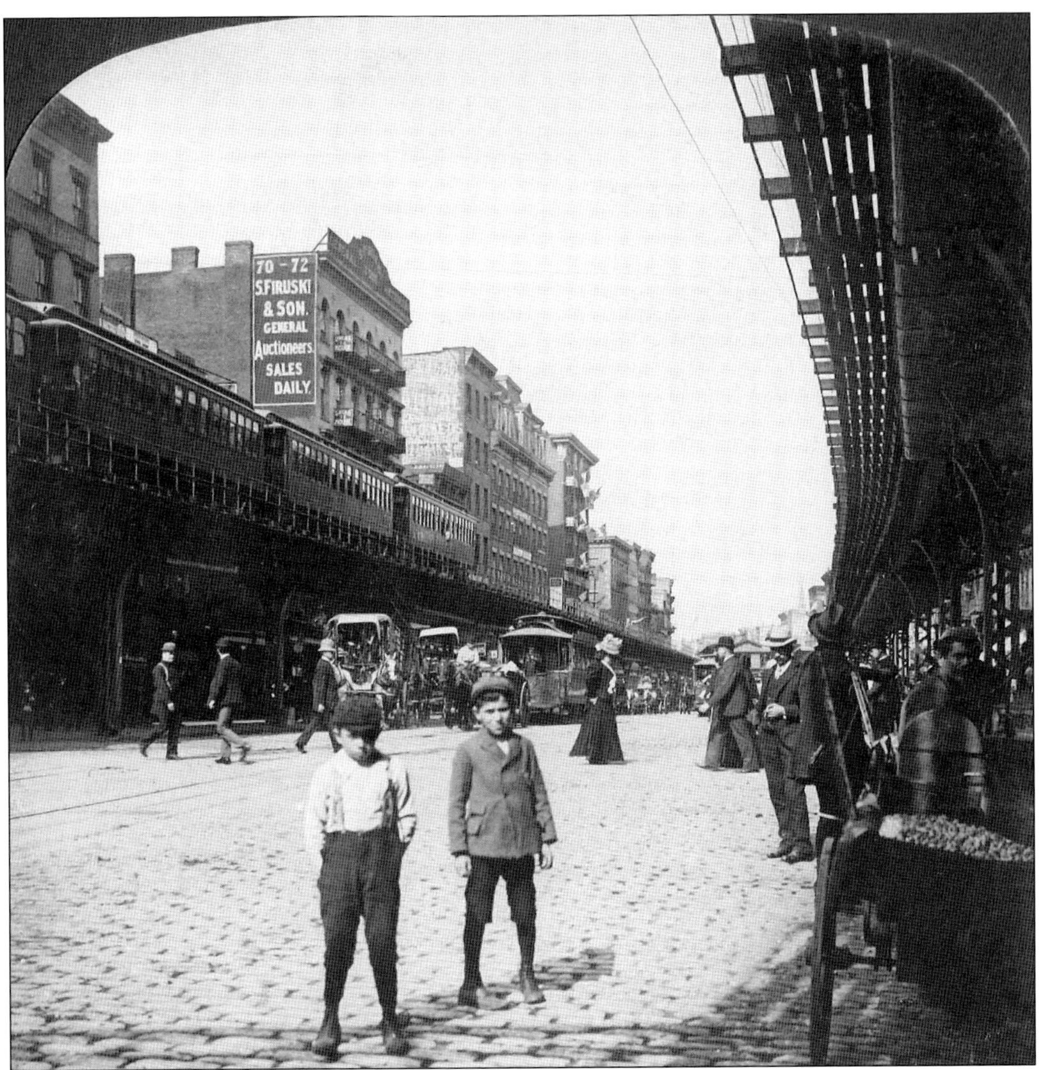

This bustling Bowery street scene, looking north from Canal Street, shows the Third Avenue Elevated train, horse-drawn carriages and streetcars, and an ad for an auction house at 70-72 Bowery. In addition to the boys, there are a roughneck in a derby hat, a policeman, an elegant lady, and a peanut vendor in the shadow of the "El." This scene is from a 1901 stereoscope 3-D viewing card by H.C. White Co. (David Mulkins.)

On the Cover: This c. 1905 Brown Brothers photograph shows 142-190 Bowery, including a diamond and watch store, at 144; the Occidental Hotel, at 146; clothing stores, a German restaurant, and the Germania Bank Building (with flag), at 190. The elevated train tracks are above the sidewalk on both sides of the street—downtown on the west side, uptown on the east. (Adam Woodward Collection.)

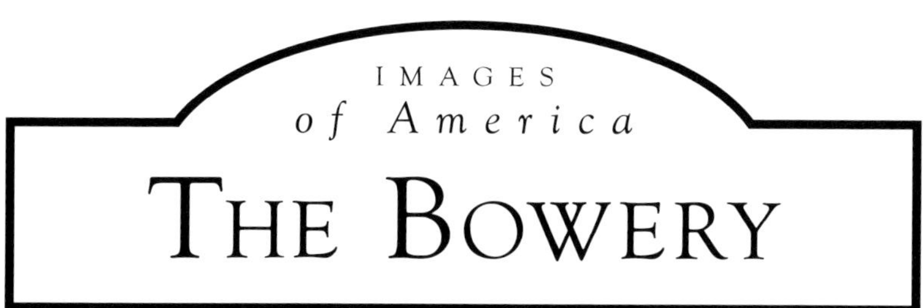

David Mulkins
Foreword by Kerri Culhane, PhD

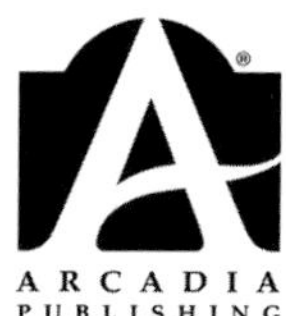

ISBN 9781-4671-6206-7

Published by Arcadia Publishing
Charleston, South Carolina

Printed in the United States of America

Library of Congress Control Number: 2024952729

For all general information, please contact Arcadia Publishing:
Telephone 843-853-2070
Fax 843-853-0044
E-mail sales@arcadiapublishing.com

Visit us on the Internet at www.arcadiapublishing.com

To my wife, Louise Millmann, for her support and help; to friend Frankie Holbrook, and to the mothers Lola Mulkins, Sue Clous, and Mary Harris Jones

Contents

Foreword

"Save the Bowery!" is not a rallying cry you would have heard a century ago—or even 50 years ago. In 1916, real estate interests even tried to rename the Bowery "Central Broadway" to disassociate themselves from its then-seedy reputation. Yet, since 2007, a dedicated group of local residents—among them artists, educators, historians, and even magicians—have banded together as the Bowery Alliance of Neighbors with a mission to do just that. As volunteers, they work tirelessly to Save the Bowery, in all its complexity, not from the vice and sin of the 19th-century sort, but from the predators of private equity, rampant overdevelopment, half-baked city planning decisions that zoned each side of the Bowery differently, and New York City's Landmarks Preservation Commission inaction that hastened the loss of some of the city's oldest and most important buildings.

Walk down the wide Bowery, along this crooked arc that cuts through the regularity of the various grids that crowd around it, and you will see a palimpsest—a history written and rewritten over the centuries. The Bowery's architectural diversity and historical breadth—its "disjointed beauty," in the words of preservationist Anthony Tung—means it is not famous for a dominant style or one historical moment, but a collection of styles, momentous events, and cultural phenomena that together attest to four centuries of New York and American history.

Despite the recent "blandification" by hotel chains and glassy condos, so many architectural marvels, modest and grand, remain legible, even if the histories that played out within and around them are less so. That is why this book is so important. The images and histories assembled so thoughtfully here by Bowery Alliance cofounder and longtime president David Mulkins is a prodigious feat of research. It demonstrates a dedication to this place, and to the lives, histories, legends, and folklore that lend the Bowery its grit, its power, and its peculiar charm. This Lenape footpath became both geographically and culturally central to the growth of New Amsterdam and New York City, and to American popular culture at large. It is a place and a history worth knowing and saving.

—Kerri Culhane, PhD
architectural historian
author of the National Register of Historic Places nominations
of Chinatown and Little Italy (2010) and the Bowery (2013)

Acknowledgments

The idea for this book was suggested both to me and the publisher by kindly James A. Beckman, historian/tour guide at Harper's Ferry, West Virginia. My deepest appreciation to Dr. Kerri Culhane—leading authority on the Bowery—for fact checks, edits, and sage advice. A shoutout to Frankie Holbrook for early proofreading, Jean Standish, Derek Kulnis, and Carol Puttre-Czyz for occasional feedback, and Louise Millmann for image advice and invaluable technical assistance. Many thanks to musician David Amram, musicologists Leni Sloan and Mick Moloney; historians Tom Miller and Paul Mateyunas, magic historian Tom Klem, prize-ring historian Tony Gee, ArtBridge founder Hannah Byers, Arcadia Publishing's acquisitions editor Jeff Ruetsche, Vicki Weiner at Pratt University, and Cooper Union archivist Mary Mann. Deep gratitude to multiple archives for their help and generosity, especially the New York Public Library, Harvard Theatre Collection, New-York Historical Society, Museum of the City of New York, the Ross Morgan Collection, and Adam Woodward's Collection, which the *New York Times* rightly considers a de facto Bowery Museum. A big thanks goes to photographers Carin Drechsler-Marx, David Godlis, Lisa J. Kristal, Bob Gruen, Cynthia MacAdams, Sophie Keir, Sally Young, and Erika Stone. My deepest gratitude to the Bowery Alliance of Neighbors and its benefactor La Vida Feliz Foundation for special funding.

Multiple image use from archives and individuals is abbreviated as follows:

AWC	Adam Woodward Collection
CDM	Carin Drechsler-Marx
CM	Cynthia MacAdams/New York Public Library Photography Collection
CUA	Cooper Union Archive
DG	David Godlis
DM	David Mulkins
FALH	Fine Arts Library, Harvard
HTC	Harvard Theatre Collection
LJK	Lisa J. Kristal
LOC	Library of Congress
MCNY	Museum of the City of New York
MHL	Margaret Herrick Library, AMPAS (Academy of Motion Picture Arts and Sciences
NYHS	New-York Historical Society
NYPL	New York Public Library
NYPL-BRC	NYPL Billy Rose Collection
NYPL-DC	NYPL Digital Collection
NYPL-MD	NYPL Milstein Division
NYPL-PC	NYPL Photography Collection
NYPL-Pic	NYPL Picture Collection
RHI	Rogosin Heritage, Inc.
RMC	Ross Morgan Collection
SANA	Salvation Army National Archive
WC	Wikimedia Commons

INTRODUCTION

Stephen Crane called the Bowery "the most interesting place in New York." Comparing it to the upscale Broadway, Walt Whitman found the Bowery "more democratic, with a broader, jauntier swing." Theodore Roosevelt called it "one of the great highways of humanity," but also felt it was "haunted by demons as evil as any" found in Dante's *Inferno*. With seminal links to tap dance, vaudeville, Yiddish theater, American song and slang, modern tattooing, community gardening, Abstract Expressionism, Beat literature, jazz, and punk rock, the Bowery is also the cradle of American popular culture. Complex, colorful, and gritty to be sure, with a history far older than the city itself, the Bowery is not only the city's oldest but arguably its most impactful street.

Bordering Chinatown, Little Italy, NoHo, the East Village, and Lower East Side, the Bowery stretches 1.25 miles from Chatham Square to Cooper Square. Originally extending south along present-day Park Row, and north up Fourth Avenue to Union Square, the route's curvature reflects its origin as a Native American footpath. The Lenape hunted and cultivated the land, especially at Werpoes, their settlement beside the freshwater Collect Pond, which was west of the Bowery near present-day Centre Street. The area of present-day Astor Place was a powwow site known as Kintecoying, the Crossroads of Three Nations.

During the Dutch colonial period (1624–1664), the Lenape footpath became the colonists' most important land route. Widened as a wagon road in 1626, it connected New Amsterdam's fur trading post at Manhattan's southern tip with the farms (*bouwerijs*) to the north. After 1647, the largest farm along the Bowery, in what is now the East Village, was that of Peter Stuyvesant, the colony's peg-legged governor. During the early 1640s, hostilities between the Dutch and Lenape prompted the Dutch to grant conditional freedom and small Bowery farms to several older African slaves of the Dutch West India Company. Serving as buffer, they were expected to alert New Amsterdam of a possible attack. In 1712, under British rule, their lands were taken away.

After New Amsterdam gave way to New York in 1664, the Bowery remained a major thoroughfare during the English colonial period. As Bowery Lane, it formed a lower stretch of the Boston Post Road, one of America's first highways. Still rural, it was home to landed gentry like the Bayards and De Lanceys. After 1750, when a public slaughterhouse opened on Bayard land near what is today Columbus Park in Chinatown, the lower Bowery became a butcher's district, a scene of cattle drives and drovers pubs like the legendary Bull's Head Tavern, just south of Canal Street. It was there, on November 25, 1783, that Gen. George Washington's Continental Army stopped during their triumphal march down Bowery as the British fled the city, a date celebrated for a century after as Evacuation Day. The Bull's Head's last owner was German émigré butcher Henrich Astor who, along with brother John Jacob Astor, a furrier and real estate baron, founded an American dynasty. The namesakes of Bayard and Pell Street recall the butchers era, as does the c. 1785 Edward Mooney House at 18 Bowery, Manhattan's oldest surviving brick townhouse.

Transformative changes came to the Bowery in the first half of the 19th century. By the early 1800s, the estates of the landed gentry were fast disappearing along with the Bowery's pastoral character. There were now subdivided lots in place of farm fields, and in 1813, city officials changed its name from the bucolic Bowery Lane to simply: the Bowery. While most of its commerce—especially taverns and hotels—remained confined to lower Bowery, the gentry were still enjoying the Bowery north of Houston Street. The popular Vauxhall Garden appeared at present-day Cooper Square, and the upper Bowery remained a fashionable residential district, including the 349 Bowery townhouse of Gov. Daniel D. Tompkins (1774–1825), the US vice president under James Monroe. In the early 1800s, the city's oldest still-operating hotel began life at 146-148 Bowery. In 1830, the New York Marble Cemetery, the city's first nondenominational cemetery opened on the upper Bowery, and in 1832, America's first streetcar began its run up the Bowery from Prince Street to Union Square. Though assumed to be a Civil War or labor reference, the term "Union Square" originally referenced the conjunction of Broadway and Bowery, early New York's main thoroughfares.

By the second half of the 19th century, things got more exciting. The Bowery, adjacent to the notorious Five Points ghetto and various immigrant enclaves, became a thriving social and commercial hub for the poor and the working class; the stomping ground for sailors, shopgirls, gangs, gays, sporting men, and waves of Irish, Italian, German, Jewish, and Chinese immigrants. During the day, its banks, cheap clothing stores, and pawn shops did brisk business, and at night its countless restaurants and saloons were packed. The city's first entertainment district, it boasted immense German beer gardens, 3,000-seat theaters, dime museums, dance halls, concert saloons, and a lively street scene that in itself was an attraction. When the elevated train arrived in 1878, the influx of sightseers soared, as it did in 1882 after Edison's electricity illuminated the busy thoroughfare. James D. McCabe wrote that at night the Bowery was a glorious "blaze of light from one end to the other." H.C. Bunner wrote in 1896 that this internationally famous street was "the aliviest mile on the face of the earth."

But the proliferation of saloons, tattoo parlors, gambling dens, whorehouses, and low-rent lodging houses, combined with the presence of gangs, roughnecks, the destitute, and criminal elements also brought notoriety. This included the Bowery B'hoys' two-day war with the Dead Rabbits gang, which left 8 dead in 1857, and the Astor Place Riot of 1849, which left at least 26 dead. When the elevated train arrived in 1878, it cast the entire street in shadow and brought noise and soot around the clock. The hugely popular 1891 song "The Bowery" cemented the street's dicey reputation with its sardonic refrain, "I'll never go there anymore." By the early 1900s, the theater world had moved uptown, and the Bowery devolved into America's skid row, a situation later aggravated by Prohibition and the Great Depression. Because of its ill-repute, Bowery businesses tried several times to get the street's name changed.

In 1956, the elevated train was dismantled, and light returned to the Bowery. That same year, the street resumed its influence on the music world when the Five Spot jazz club, "the hippest place on earth," opened at 5 Cooper Square. It saw some of Billie Holiday's last performances and witnessed the birth of Ornette Coleman's ground-breaking "free jazz" movement. Though the Bowery still had plenty of bars and men's shelters, its jewelry, lighting, and restaurant supply districts helped redefine the street.

In the 1960s, many of the Bowery's spacious upper-floor lofts—formerly zoned for commerce and industry—were transformed into live-work spaces by a community of cutting-edge artists, poets, filmmakers, photographers, and musicians. Legislation made artist occupancy legal, and the Bowery's depressed real estate value made it affordable. (Low loft prices were due to manufacturing decline and because the Lower Manhattan Expressway was expected to bring widespread demolition). The Immigration and Nationality Act of 1965 caused a surge in Chinatown's population, which prompted the construction of the 44-story Confucius Plaza (1975), the Bowery's largest structure. In 1973, another kind of transformation occurred at Bowery and Houston Street when gardening activists turned a vacant lot into the city's first community garden. The 1970s saw additional music history made when CBGB opened at 315 Bowery, giving birth to punk rock; from its beginning through 2006, it was a laboratory for musical experimentation and innovation.

Recent decades have seen a surge of overdevelopment. As historic buildings have come down, most are replaced by out-of-scale, ill-conceived structures without a thought about historic context, character, or the safety of their surroundings. In 2009, a high-rise construction at 91-93 Bowery caused the destabilization and forced demolition of two adjacent tenement buildings; displacing 29 low-income Chinatown residents. In 2006, multiple 1830s row houses on Cooper Square's east side were replaced by an out-of-scale 21-story boutique hotel. In 2011, after a protracted fight to save it, 35 Cooper Square, a 186-year-old Federal-era townhouse built by the Stuyvesants, was demolished.

Architectural historian Kerri Culhane considers the Bowery "among the most architecturally and historically diverse streets in the city," with buildings representing every decade from the 1780s to the present. As noted in the National Register nomination, the Bowery is "an indispensable resource," reflecting "centuries of American social, economic, political, immigrant, labor, underground, criminal, deviant, marginal, counter-cultural, literary, musical, dramatic and artistic history." Sadly, the ferocious pace of recent real estate speculation has hastened gentrification and the destruction of many of the Bowery's oldest structures. Though the Bowery Historic District was added to both the State and National Registers of Historic Places in 2013, the city has thus far not moved to recognize or protect its unique character. Sensible cities like Paris preserve their oldest streets, but much of the Bowery—especially its east side—remains unprotected by height caps or special zoning. As historian Mike Wallace warned in a 2013 letter to the City Planning Commission, if the city fails to enact protections, the Bowery will get "bulldozed out of existence."

The photographs, illustrations, ephemera, and stories in the pages ahead attempt to capture the extraordinary, often dramatic, but largely forgotten history of the oldest street in New York City (NYC). This one-time stomping ground of the poor, the working class, and immigrants possesses an international, multi-cultural character that is uniquely American, but could only have happened here on the Bowery.

One

The Architecture, Commerce, and People

The Bowery Historic District has the longest "period of significance" of any historic district in New York, stretching from the colonial Dutch period of the 1600s to the birth of punk rock in the 1970s. Native American footpath, Dutch wagon road, site of the city's first free Black homesteads, part of the Boston Post Road under the English, Washington's march route during the British evacuation, the Bowery is the city's oldest street. Over time, its mile-long stretch has been home to the landed gentry; a butcher's district, the city's first entertainment district, the main street of the working class and immigrants; and an iconic skid row. In more recent times, it has been known for its jewelry, lighting, and restaurant supply districts; music clubs; a proliferation of galleries and hotels; and an important live-work artists community.

With buildings representing every decade from the 1780s to the present, the Bowery's architecturally and historically diverse streetscape includes 3½-story Federal-era townhouses, Beaux-Arts bank buildings, cast-iron structures, the Italianate Cooper Union building, and the Neo-classical arch and colonnade of the Manhattan Bridge Plaza. While no structures survive from the colonial Dutch and English periods, intersecting street names—such as Delancey and Bayard—recall colonial landowners. The early American period is reflected in the Georgian-style Edward Mooney House at 18 Bowery, New York's oldest brick townhouse, built by a prosperous butcher.

This storied streetscape saw America's first streetcars (1832) and the first free university (1859) and dazzlingly became one of the first streets electrified by Thomas Edison (1882). It has been home to one of NYC's first pleasure gardens (1805), the first non-denominational cemetery (1830), the first community garden (1973), and the oldest continuously operating hotel (around 1805).

Over the centuries, the Bowery's streetscape—its architecture, commerce, and people—has changed many times, for many reasons. While its surviving architecture evokes part of the story, the historical records, illustrations, photographs, and ephemera in the pages ahead help visualize the street and bring its remarkable, largely forgotten history back into focus.

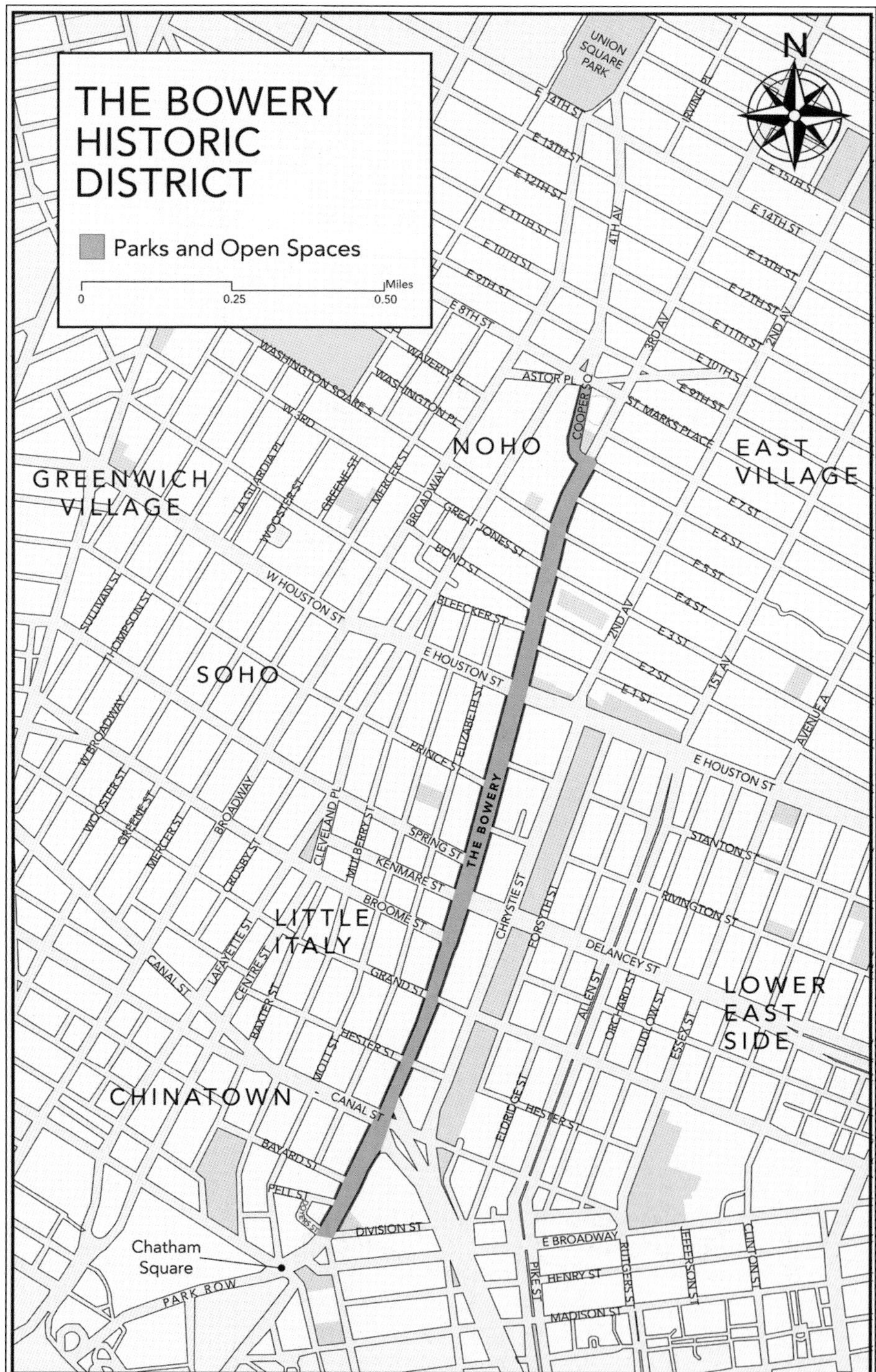

The Bowery runs from Chatham Square to Cooper Square at Astor Place. It originally extended farther south, along present-day Park Row, and farther north along the west side of present-day Cooper Square and up present-day Fourth Avenue. This map was prepared in 2024 by Deniz Cavdir, BArch, MSc. (Bowery Alliance of Neighbors.)

Petrus Stuyvesant (1610–1672) was New Netherland's director-general from 1647 until the British takeover in 1664. The namesake of schools, streets, and neighborhoods, as governor he strengthened the colony, but was pro-slavery and opposed religious freedom, especially for Lutherans, Quakers, and Jews. In exchange for securing a peace settlement with Britain, he got to keep his 62-acre slave-run farm. He is buried at St. Marks Church in-the-Bowery. (NYPL-DC.)

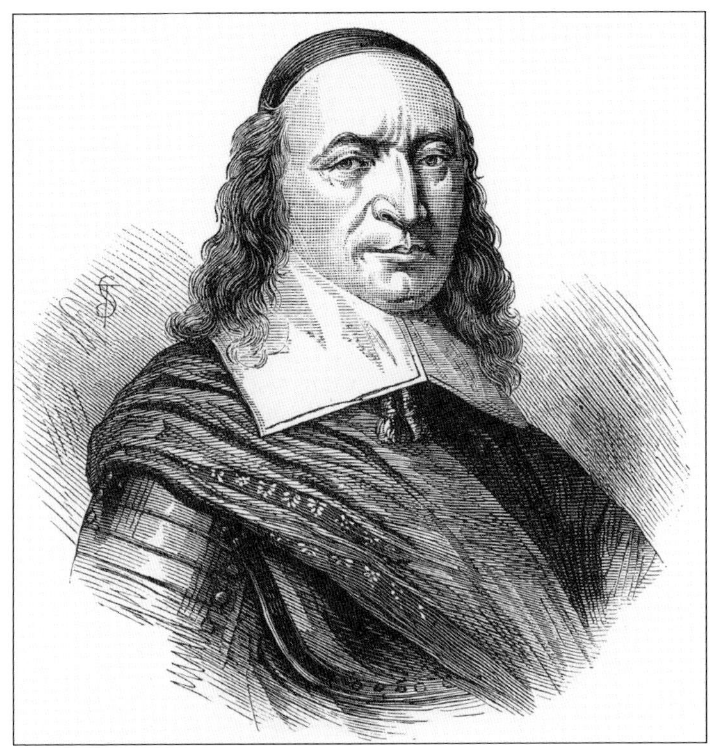

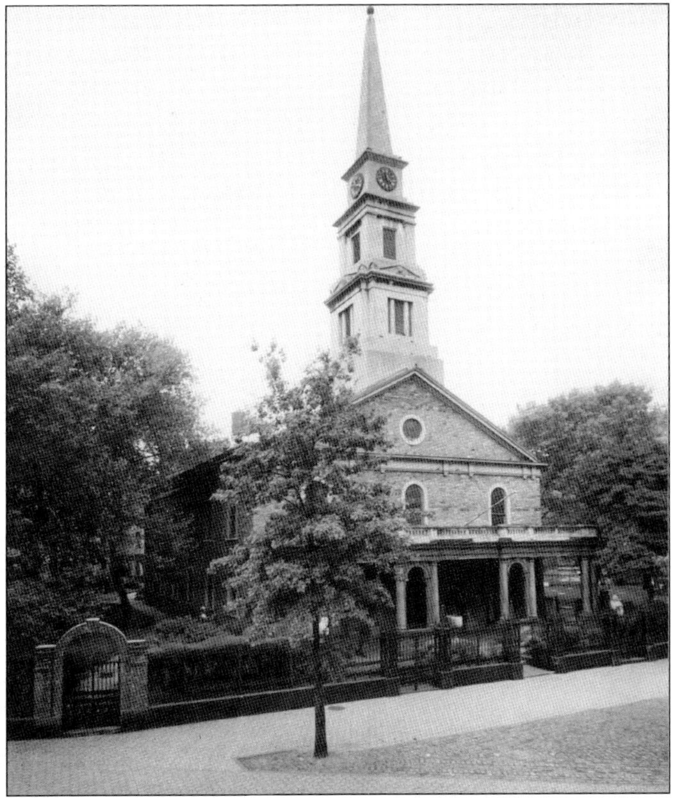

Visitors are perplexed that St. Marks Church in-the-Bowery is on Second Avenue rather than on Bowery. The Dutch word *bouwerij* means farm, and the church name references its location on Peter Stuyvesant's farm. His 1660 chapel, replaced by a larger church in 1799, is New York's oldest church site still occupied by a church. This 1957 photograph is by Angelo Rizzuto. (LOC.)

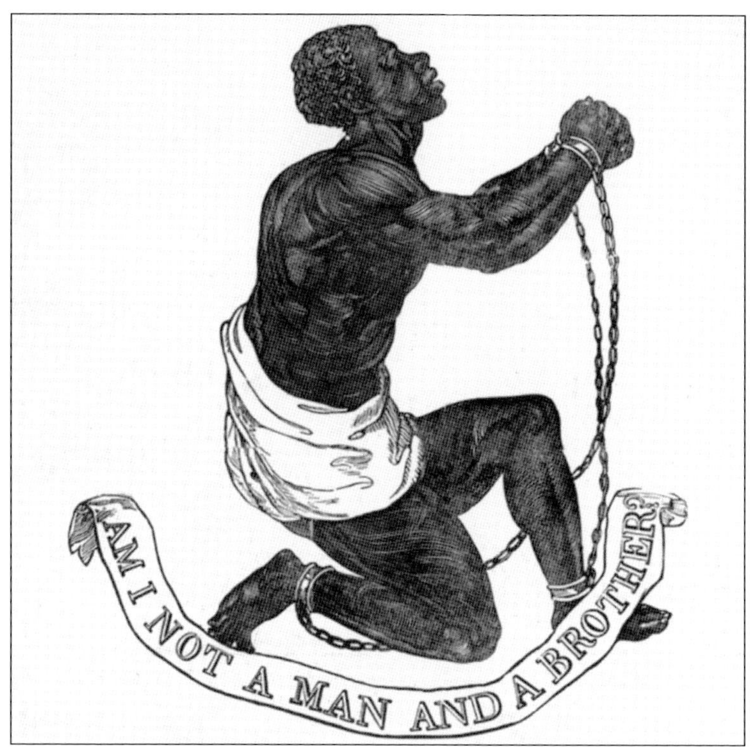

In the mid-1600s, the Dutch West India Company freed some older African slaves and gave them small Bowery farms, which served as a buffer zone between New Amsterdam and Native American tribes further north. In 1712, under English rule, those lands were taken away. This anti-slavery image was produced in 1787 by English inventor-potter Josiah Wedgwood, grandfather of Charles Darwin.

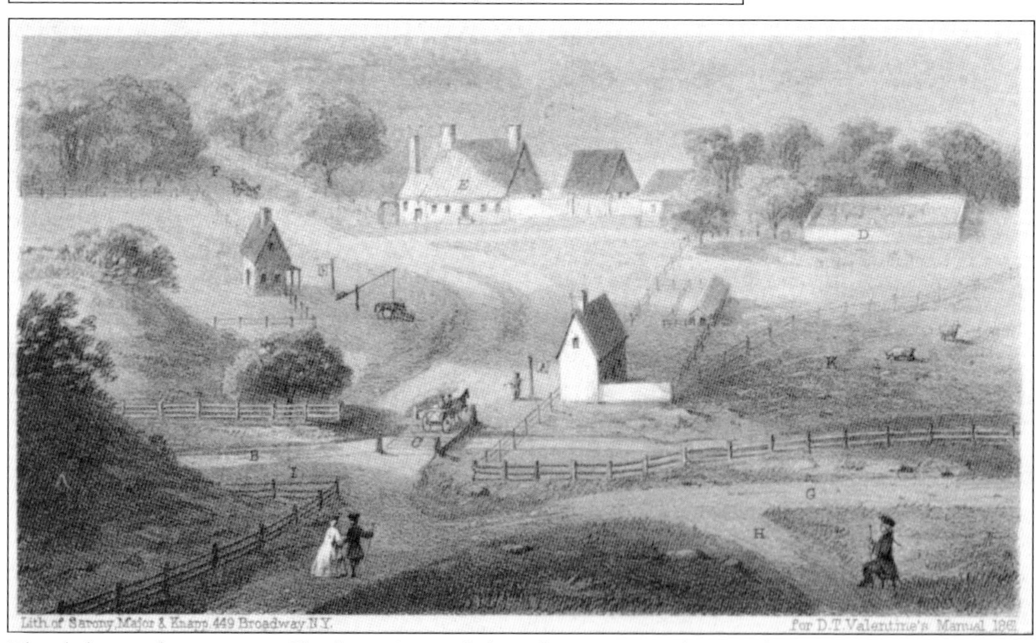

This lithograph imagines Chatham Square's bucolic environs during the 1700s English period. The Bowery snakes from the upper left to the lower right. Its lower stretch, later renamed Chatham Street, is now Park Row. At the top center is Rutgers Farm, and to its right, the extant Chatham Square Cemetery (1682), New York City's second oldest cemetery, established by First Shearith Israel, America's oldest Jewish congregation. The illustration is from *Valentine's Manual*, 1861. (NYPL-MD.)

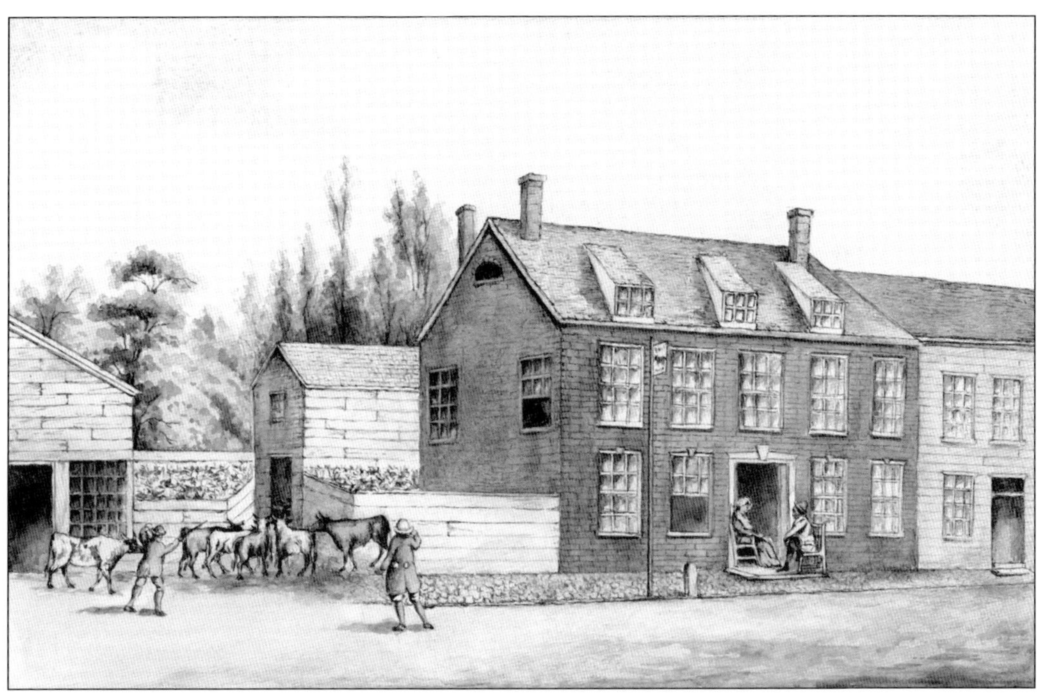

This 1783 illustration shows the legendary Bull's Head Tavern (50 Bowery), an inn, pub, and stagecoach stop during the Bowery's era as a butcher's district. From about 1755 to 1826, it witnessed cattle drives, horse races, and a visit from General Washington's troops during their triumphal march down Bowery as the British evacuated at the end of the American Revolution. The tavern's last owner was butcher/land baron Heinrich Astor. (AWC.)

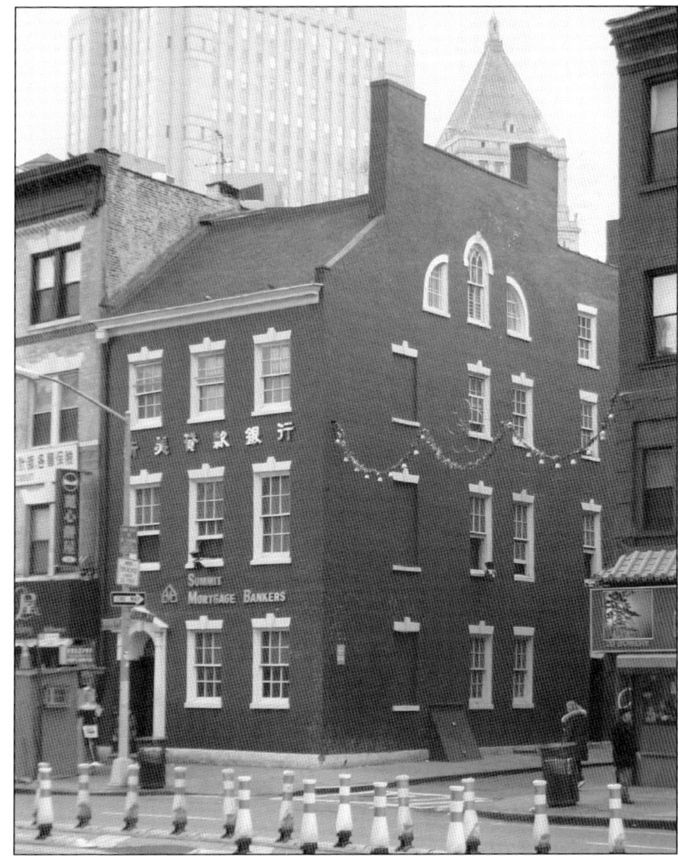

The c. 1785 Georgian-style Edward Mooney House at 18 Bowery, a NYC Landmark, is New York's oldest brick townhouse. A prosperous butcher and horse breeder, Mooney built it when the American Republic was new, on land confiscated from the Loyalist James De Lancey. This 2012 photograph is by Janine and Jim Eden.

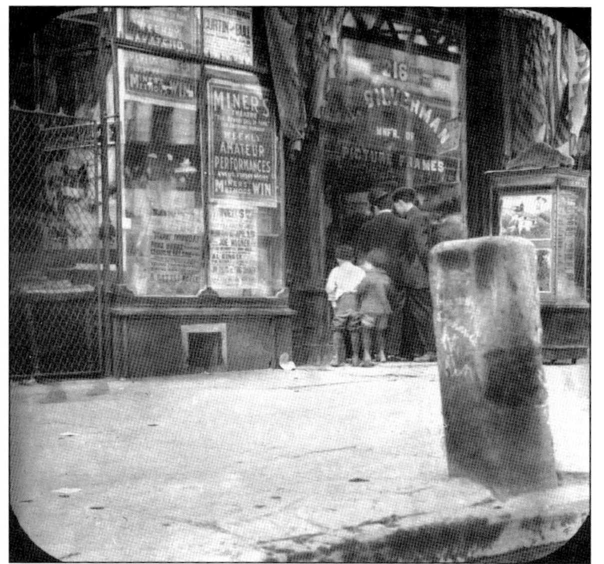

In the early 1800s, a network of carefully spaced milestones marked distance along the Bowery and the old Boston Post Road. This One Mile stone outside 214-216 Bowery, was erected in 1822, signifying one mile north of the city hall. This c. 1890s image shows I. Silverman's frame shop and placards advertising boxing matches and amateur night at Bowery theaters. (Greenwood Historic Fund.)

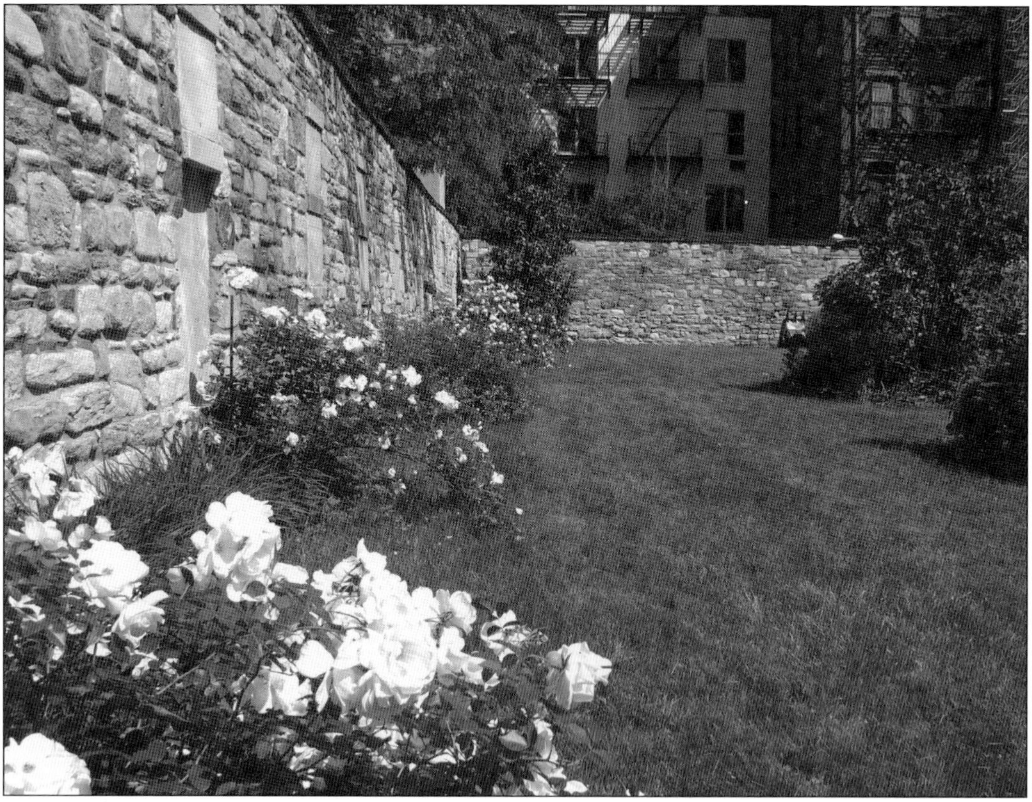

The landmark New York Marble Cemetery (1830) is one of the Bowery's best-kept secrets, a block-long urban green space hidden in the courtyard shared by Bowery, Second Avenue, Second Street, and Third Street. New York City's oldest nondenominational cemetery, interments include New York University (NYU) founder and abolitionist Congressman James Tallmadge, New-York Historical Society founder Luman Reed, Erie Canal engineer Benjamin Wright, and briefly, Pres. James Monroe. This photograph is from 2023. (DM.)

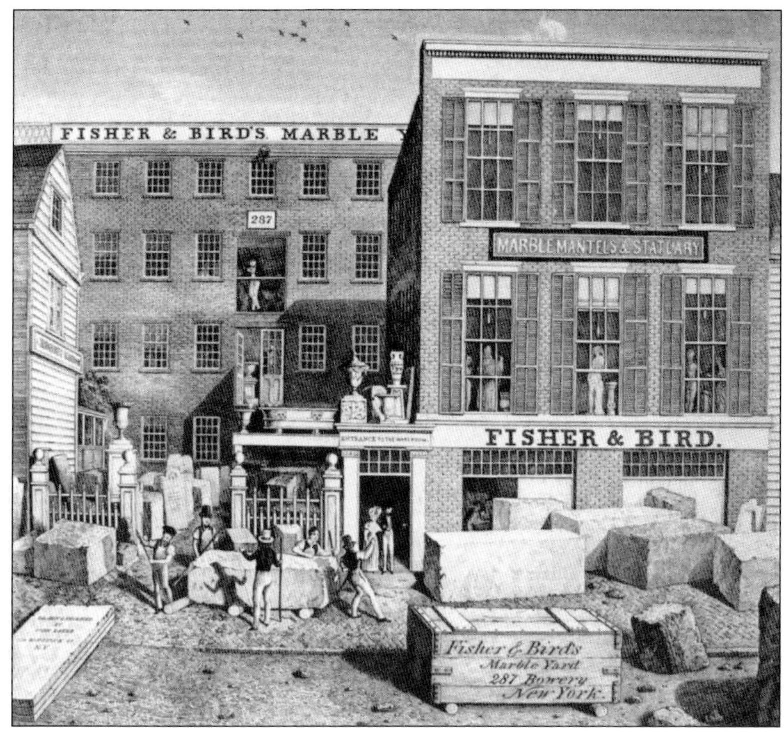

Fisher and Bird's at 287 Bowery was for decades New York's leading marble company. Ornate mantels, prepared for Secretary of State Hamilton Fish and architect Alexander Jackson Davis, were installed in homes like the Lyndhurst Mansion in Tarrytown. The business was established in 1832 by Irish immigrant John Thomas Fisher and brothers-in-law Clinton and Michael Bird. The etching is from about 1836. (Metropolitan Museum of Art.)

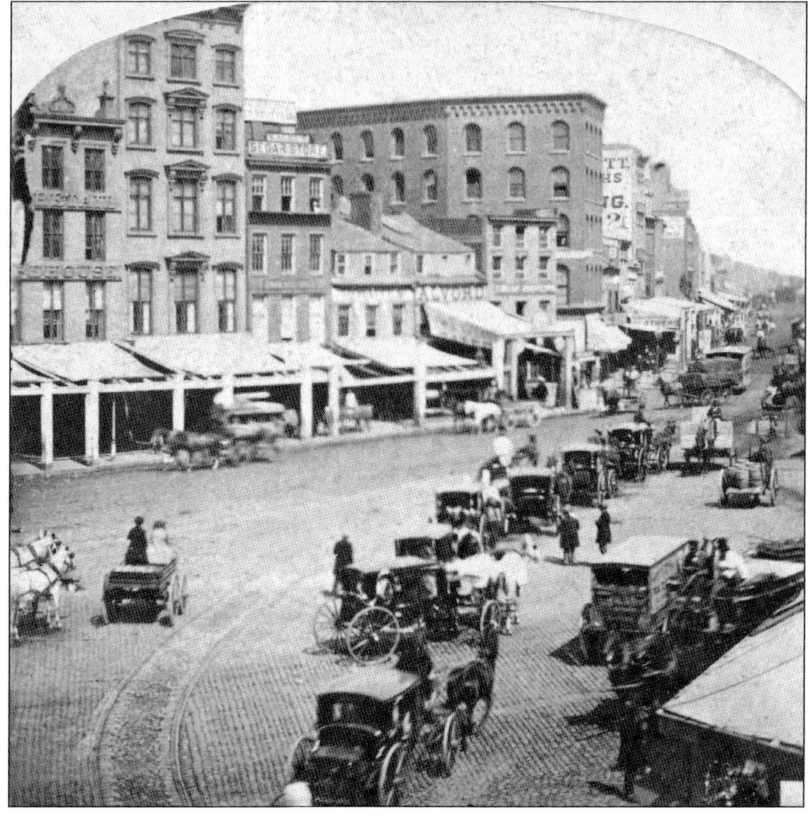

This 1860 view of Chatham Square looks north up the Bowery. The darkish building in the center, which still stands at 2 Bowery, on the corner of Doyers Street, later housed old Chinatown's popular Tuxedo Restaurant. (NYPL-PC.)

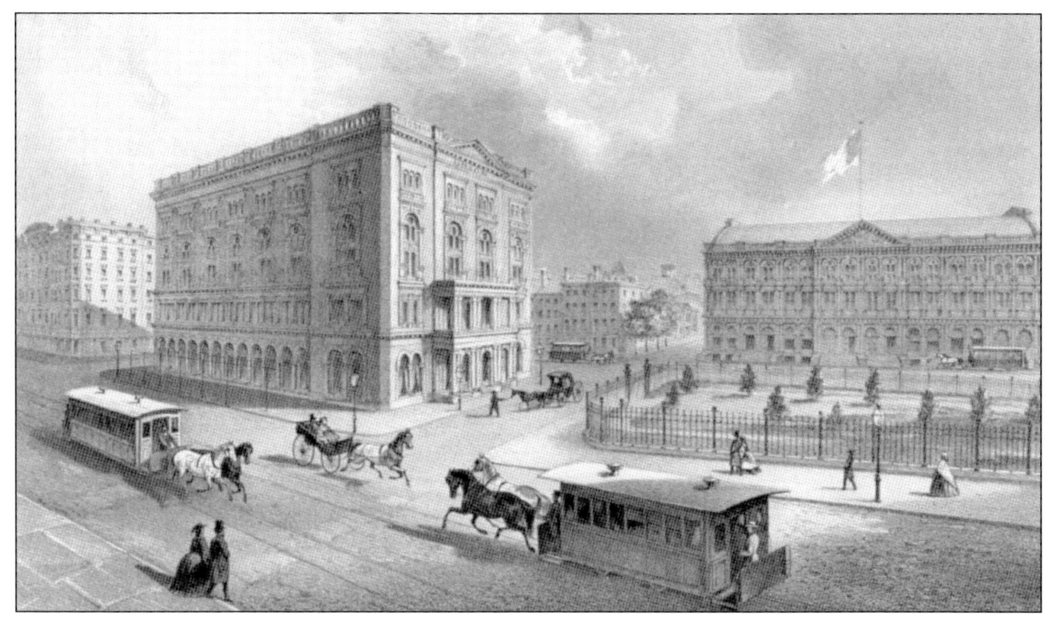

This lithograph from the 1861 *Valentine's Manual*, shows the Bible House, a printer and worldwide distributor of Bibles, and the Foundation Building of Cooper Union (1859), America's first free university, fronted by a park later named Cooper Triangle. At right is the Tompkins Market building, which housed a food market and an upstairs armory and drill room for New York's 7th Regiment. (NYPL-MD.)

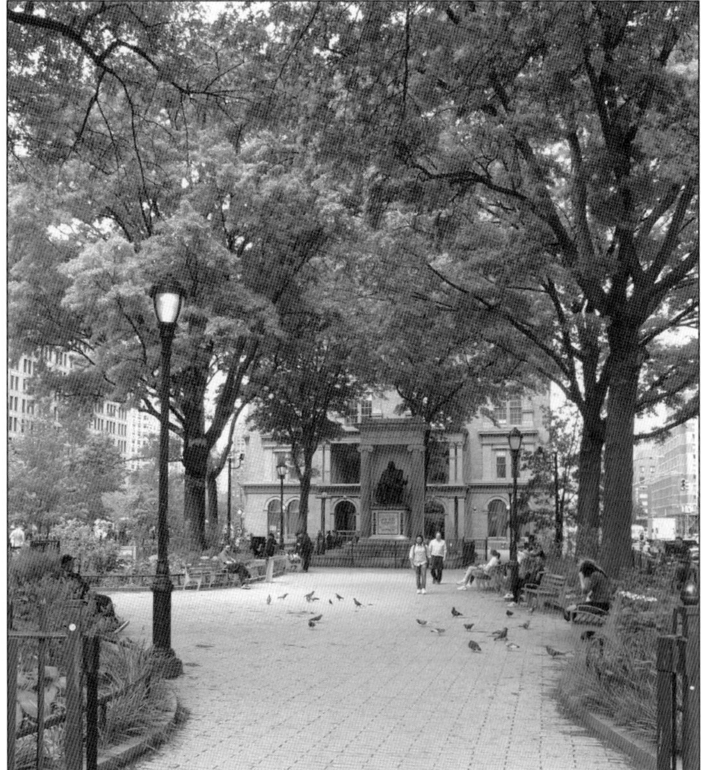

Donated to the city in 1828 by a descendant of Peter Stuyvesant, this tiny park was originally called Stuyvesant Square, but in 1883 it was renamed Cooper Triangle in honor of industrialist-inventor-philanthropist Peter Cooper. Located just south of Cooper Union, it contains an 1897 Saint-Gaudens sculpture of Cooper. This photograph is from 2024. (DM.)

New York's 7th Regiment is pictured here assembled for departure to the Civil War on April 19, 1861. The buildings behind are 363-379 Bowery, between Fourth and Fifth Streets. The regiment's armory and drill rooms were upstairs in the Tompkins Market, one block north at Sixth Street. The market's namesake is Daniel D. Tompkins, a Bowery resident (349 Bowery) and the sixth vice president of the United States. (AWC.)

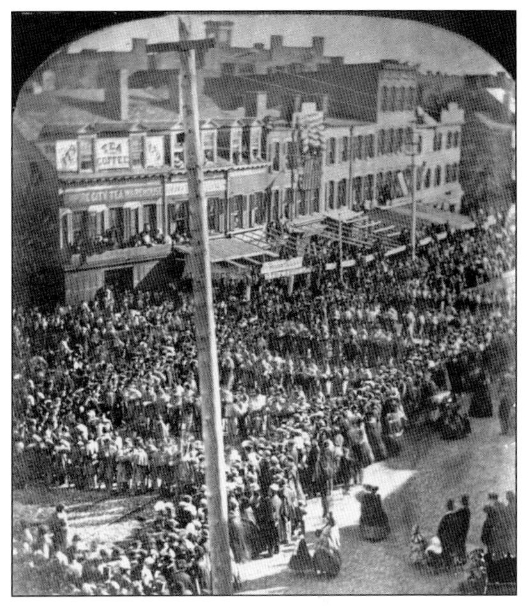

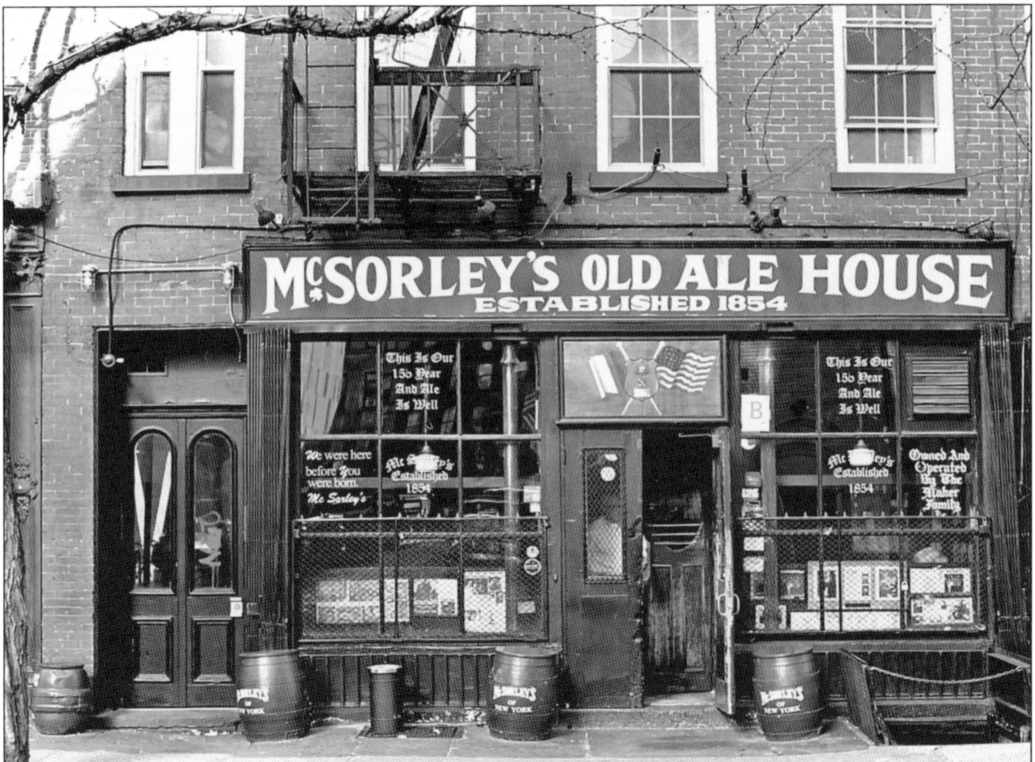

McSorley's Old Ale House at 15 East Seventh, just off Bowery, is New York City's oldest continuously operating saloon. Opening in 1854, its motto was "Good Ale, Raw Onions and No Ladies." Women were admitted in 1970, but sawdust-covered floors, Irish waiters, and Houdini's handcuffs remain. Patrons included Peter Cooper and poet e.e. cummings, who wrote of its "ale that never lets you grow old." This 2014 photograph is by John Tebeau. (John Tebeau.)

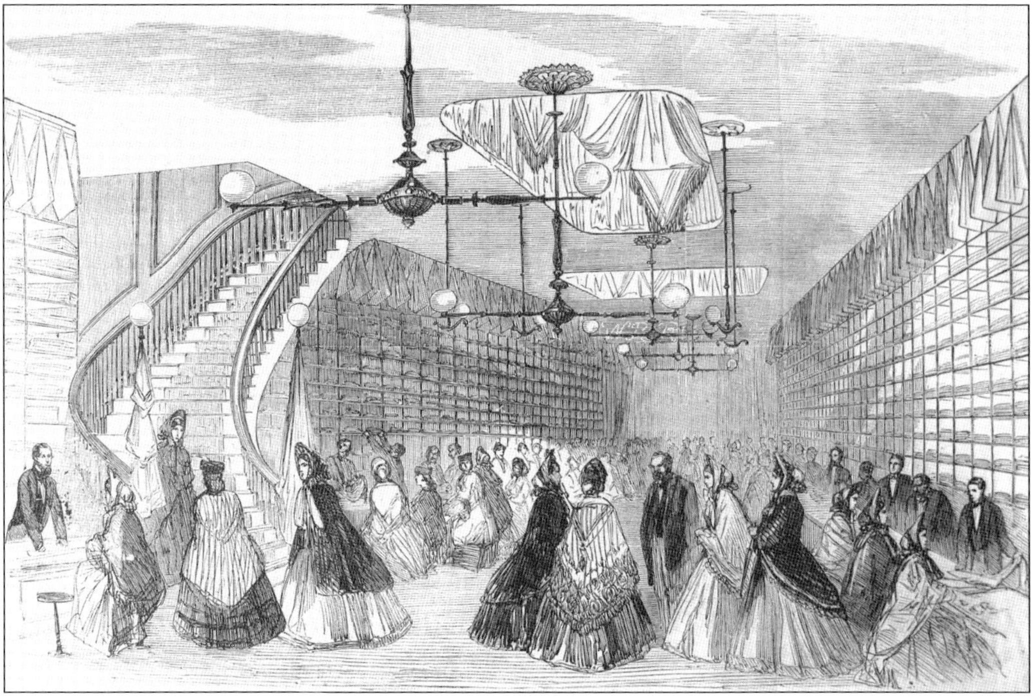

The elegant Crystal Palace Emporium at 252 Bowery specialized in silks, laces, veils, shawls, and cloaks. Its first two floors were glass-fronted retail spaces, with a cloak and mantilla manufactory employing 150 young women on floors three and four. An 1863 *New York Illustrated News* article praised owner W.B. Roberts, who supported reducing work hours from 15 to 10 hours. Bowery stores, it felt, might soon rival those of Broadway. (NYPL-MD.)

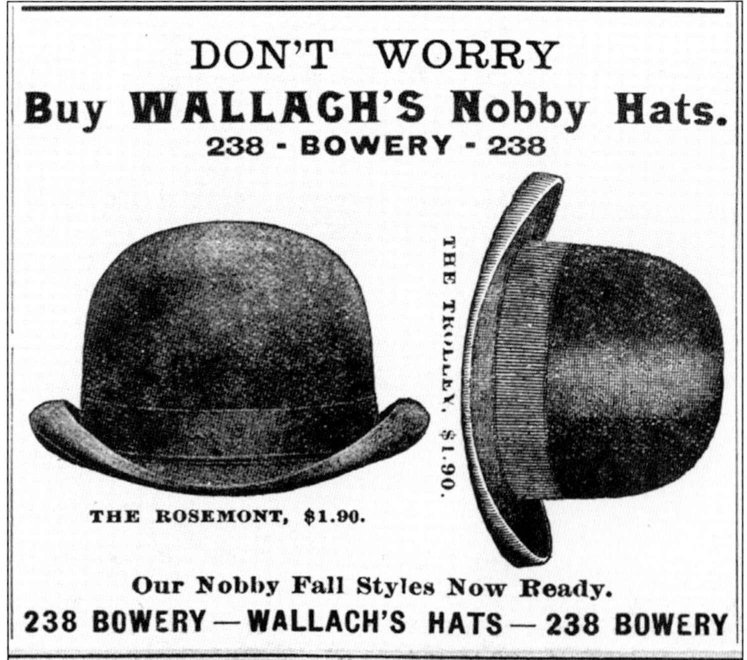

Haberdasheries were popular on the Bowery, especially the hat stores. This ad for Wallach's Hats at 238 Bowery, appeared in an 1894 Miner's Bowery Theatre program. (NYPL-BRC.)

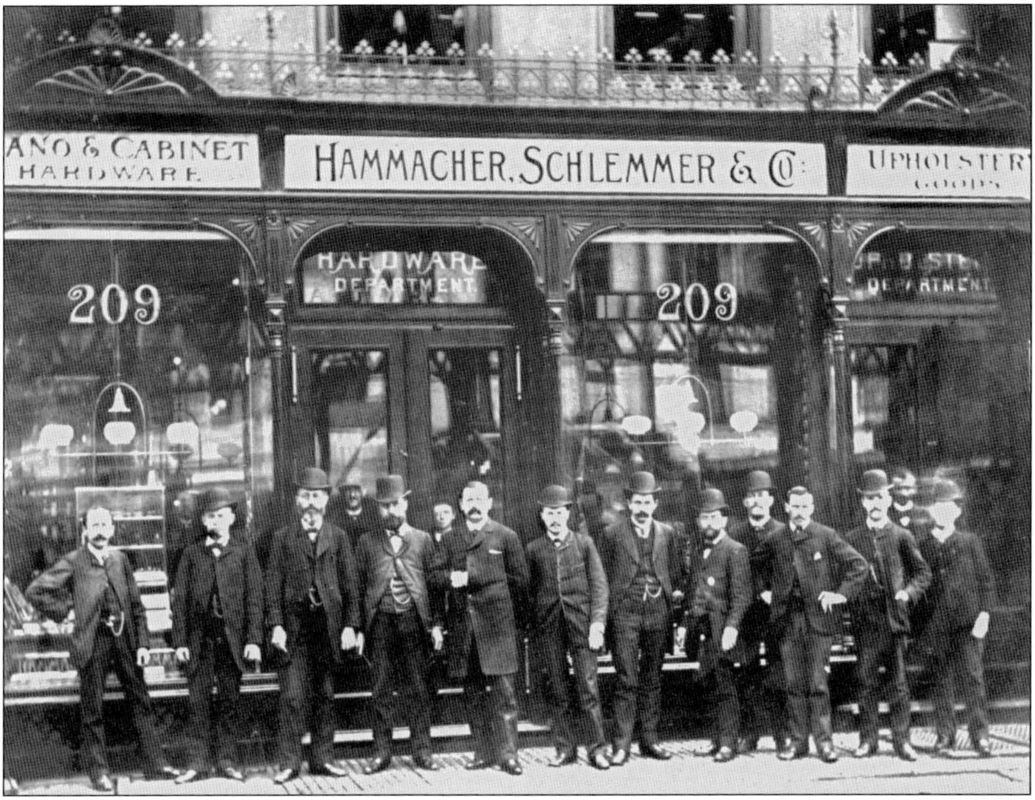

Founded by German-born immigrants, America's longest-running catalog, Hammacher Schlemmer, began life on the Bowery in 1848. Initially specializing in hard-to-find hardware, it started at 221 Bowery, and from 1857 to 1904 was at 209 Bowery. Innovative gadgetry has included the first steam irons, pop-up toasters, answering machines, and cordless phones. Customers have included Queen Elizabeth, Howard Hughes, JFK, and The Beatles. This 1890s photograph shows employees outside 209 Bowery. (Hammacher Schlemmer Archive.)

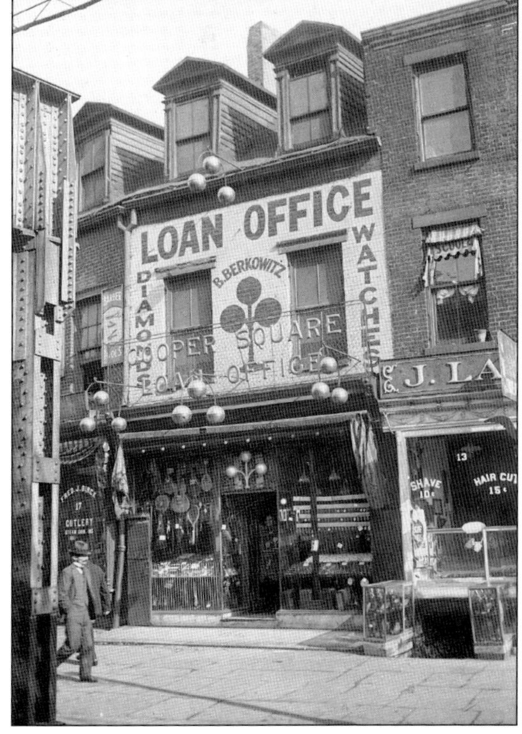

Pawn Shops were prevalent on the Bowery due to its destitute men and the working poor of the surrounding tenements. This c. 1920 Bain News Service photograph of 15 Cooper Square shows Berel Berkowitz's pawn shop, which was adjacent to a barbershop and Fred J. Birck's cutlery store. Like most of the city's Federal-era townhouses, 15 Cooper Square (375 Bowery) was later demolished. (LOC.)

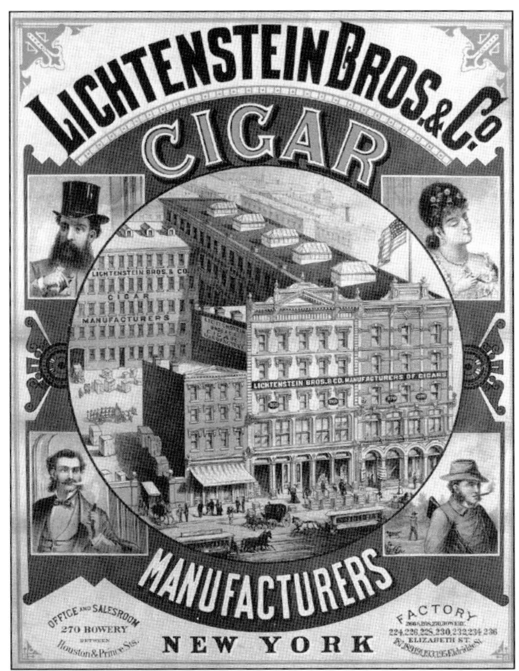

In the 1870s, the Lichtenstein Brothers cigar factory was a huge complex at 266-270 Bowery and adjacent buildings on Elizabeth Street. Unlike the hectic conditions in most sweatshops, cigar rollers' work was sedentary, which labor leader and former cigar-roller Samuel Gompers remembered "left us free to think, talk, listen, or sing." Sometimes cigar workers hired one of their own to read aloud to them. As payment, the reader got a percentage of their rolled cigars. (AWC.)

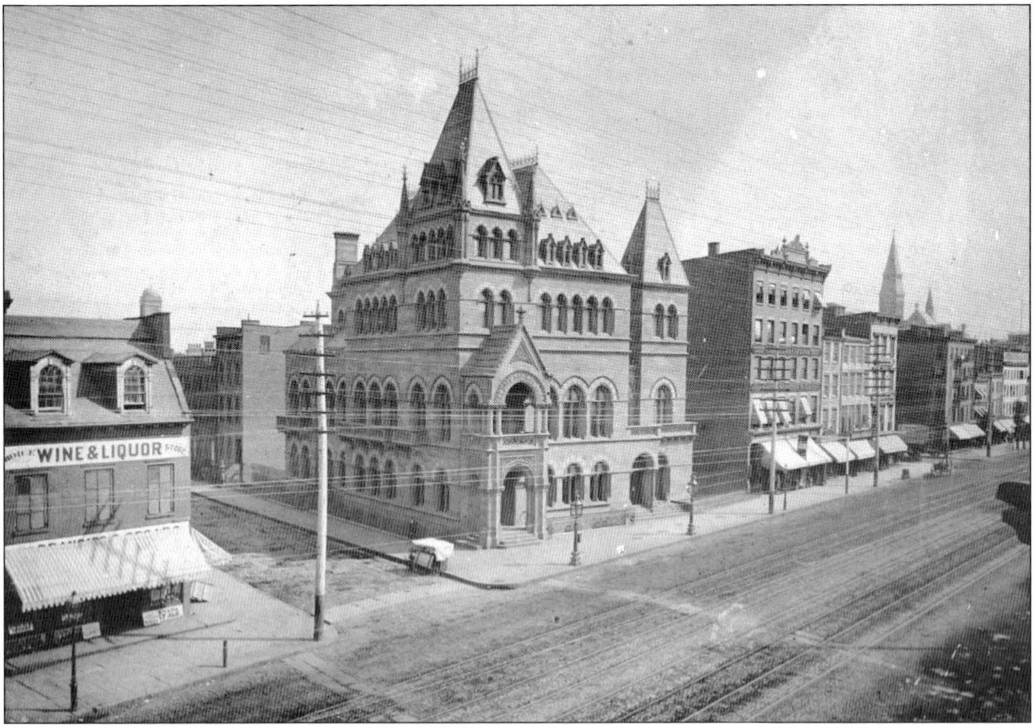

This c. 1876 photograph shows 313-347 Bowery just before elevated train tracks darkened the street. The High Victorian Gothic structure is the Dry Dock Savings Bank (1875), designed by Czech-born Leopold Eidlitz. From 1875 to 1954, it stood at 335-343 Bowery. It was replaced by a gas station in 1954, which itself was replaced in 2002 by the swank Bowery Hotel. The four buildings to the right of the bank are still standing today. (NYHS.)

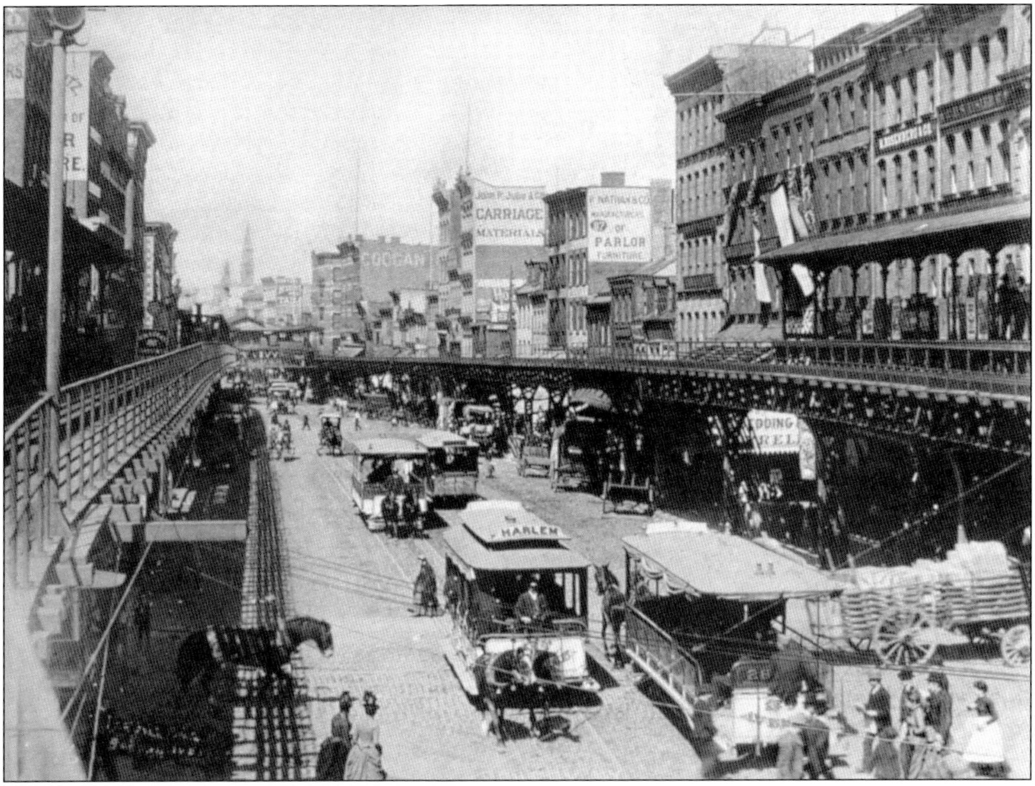

In 1832, America's first streetcars began runs on the Bowery, starting at Prince Street and traveling seven miles north to Harlem. In what must have been unbearably strenuous work, they were drawn by horses. In 1878, the Third Avenue elevated train line began to run up Park Row, Bowery, and Third Avenue. Bringing shadows, soot, and noise, it made an already gritty street even more so. This 1888 photograph looks north from Canal Street. (NYHS.)

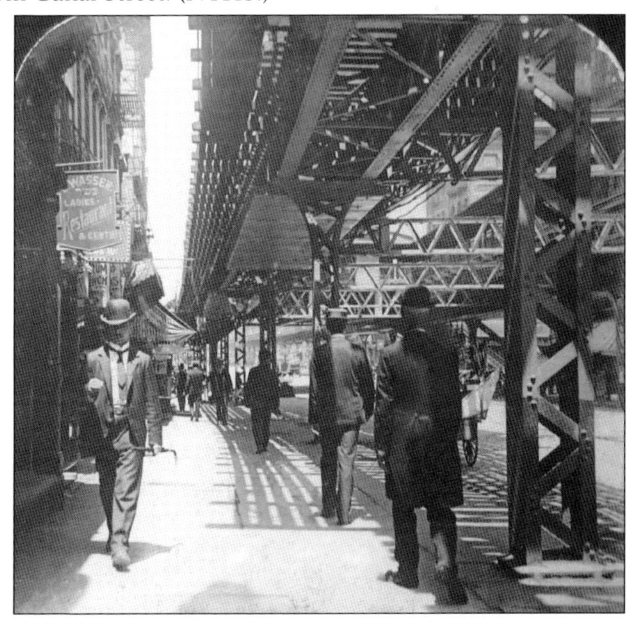

The elevated train was by all accounts a curse; darkening the street, raining down soot and cinders, and bringing regular intervals of deafening noise. The negative impact on businesses and the residents' ability to sleep can only be imagined. This 1903 view shows pedestrians and a kosher restaurant. (Phillip Van Aver.)

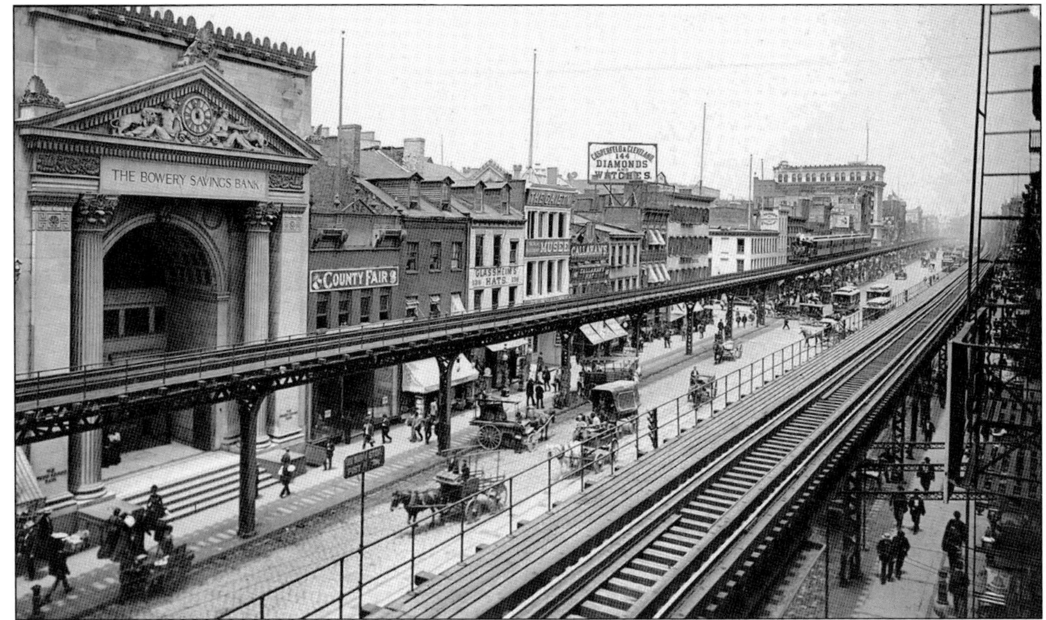

This c. 1900 streetscape shows 130-190 Bowery. The Bowery Savings Bank (1894) is a Beaux Arts masterwork of architect Stanford White. The extant dormered buildings are 134-136 Bowery, Federal-era townhouses that for 65 years were a hotbed of anti-slavery activity. The block includes hat stores, a jewelry store, the Gaiety dime museum, and the city's oldest operating hotel. The tall building further down is the Germania Bank building (1898). (LOC.)

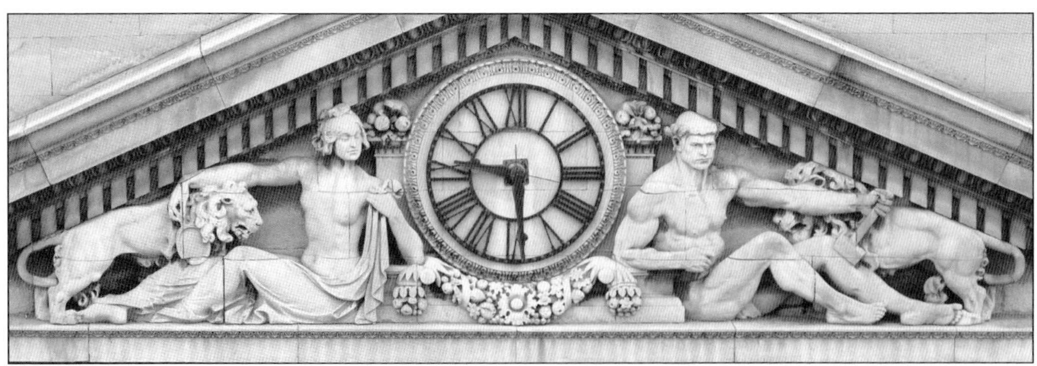

The Bowery Savings Bank's grand Corinthian columned entrances on both Bowery and Grand Street are crowned by pediments containing a clock and classical figures sculpted by Frederick MacMonnies. This 2016 photograph shows the pediment above the Bowery entrance. (DM.)

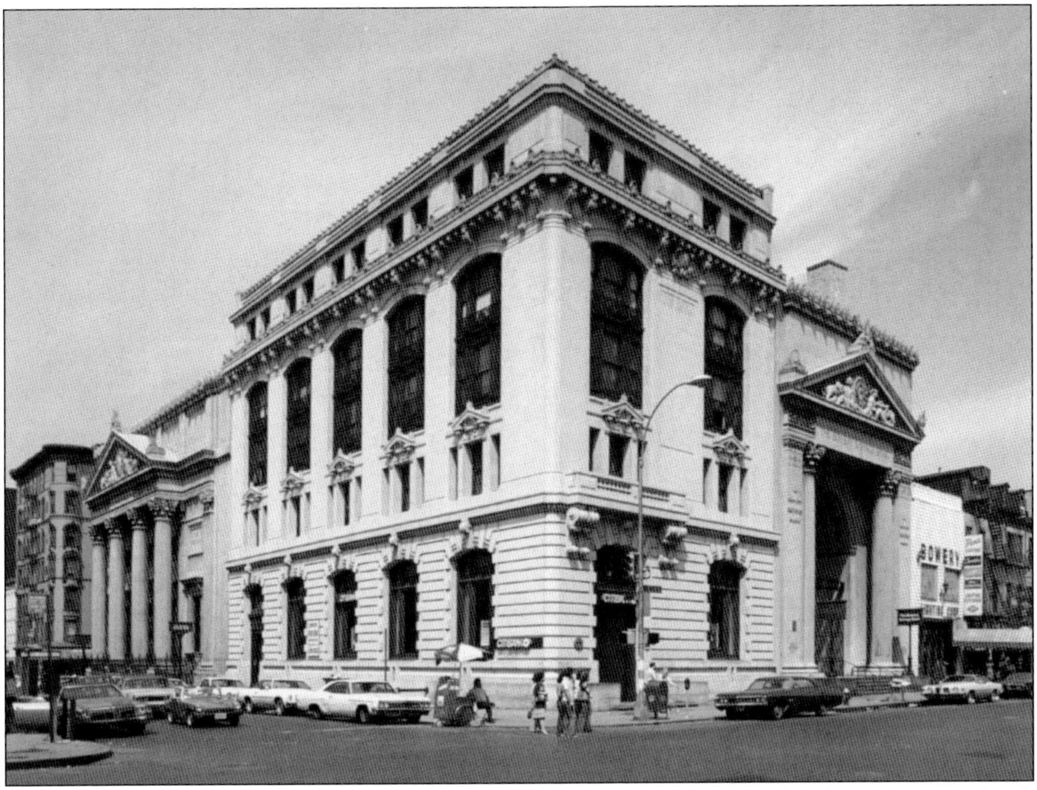

The Stanford White–designed Bowery Savings Bank at 130 Bowery is the first American bank styled after a Roman temple. With Corinthian-columned entrances on both Bowery and Grand Street, it was built L-shaped because it could not acquire the adjacent corner lot. In 1902, that lot—124 Bowery—became the Bowery Bank, designed by York & Sawyer in the Beaux Arts style to blend with its neighbor. Both are NYC landmarks. This 1975 photograph is by Edmund V. Gillon. (MCNY.)

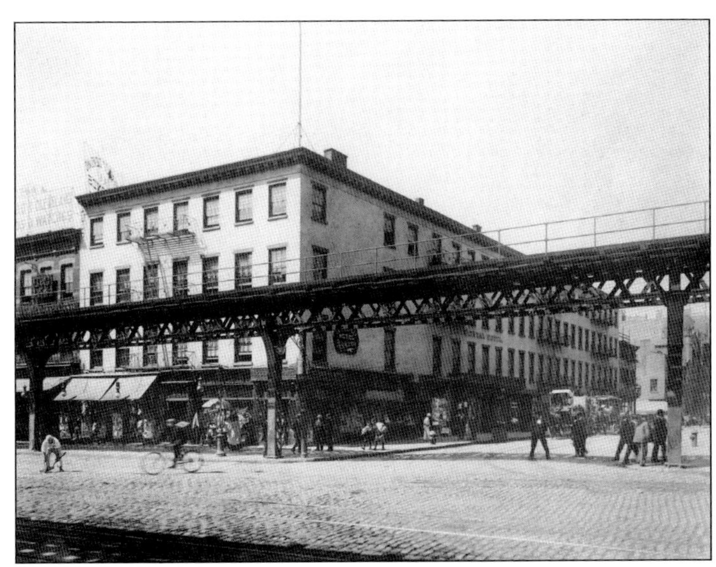

Built around 1805, the Occidental Hotel (now SoHotel) at 148 Bowery, seen here in about 1900, is New York's oldest operating hotel. It was a hangout for boxers John L. Sullivan, James Jeffries, Bob Fitzsimmons, and politicos Theodore Roosevelt, Al Smith, and the infamous William "Boss" Tweed. Its famous barroom ceiling had an immense nude bathing scene. The hotel was home and poker game headquarters for "Big Tim" Sullivan. (NYHS.)

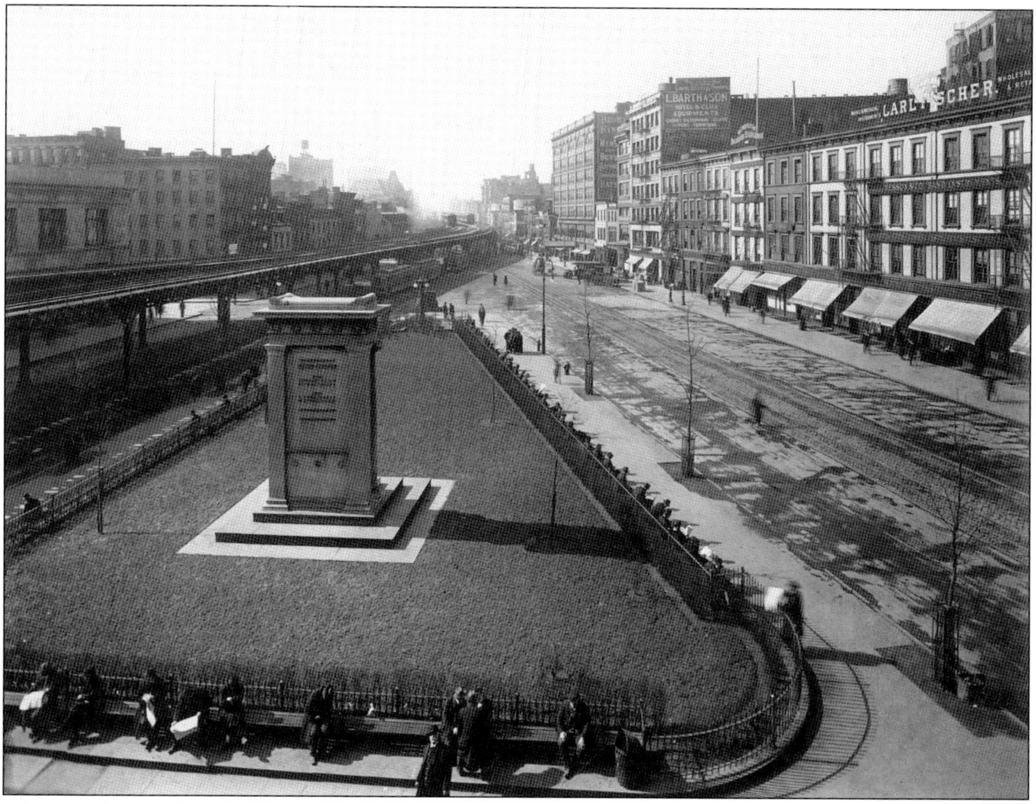

This 1915 view from atop Cooper Union's Foundation Building looks south onto Bowery, with a treeless Cooper Triangle Park and the Peter Cooper monument in the foreground. The elevated train at left continued up Third Avenue, while the Bowery on the right—called Cooper Square from Fourth Street to Astor Place—continues up Fourth Avenue to Fourteenth Street. The same view below, seen in 2024, shows a few tall buildings and a canopy of trees. (Above, AWC.; below, DM.)

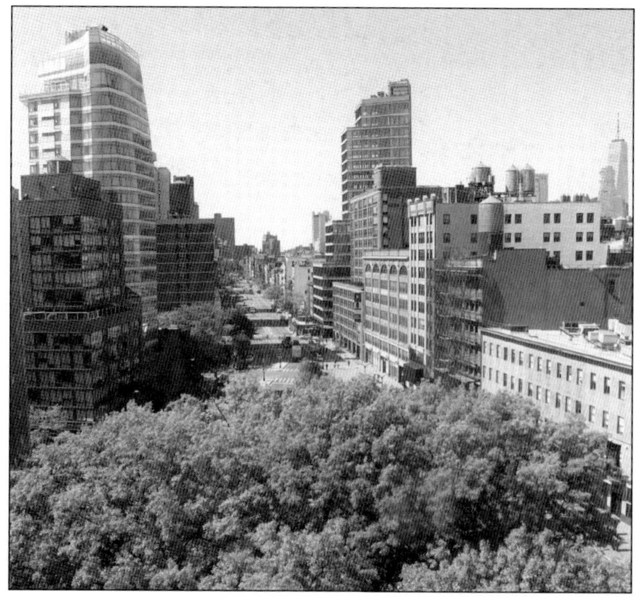

When the Manhattan Bridge Plaza opened in 1915, it was considered one of America's most beautiful bridge portals. Designed by Carrere and Hastings, its triumphal Beaux Arts arch and colonnades were patterned after the Porte St. Denis in Paris and the Bernini colonnades at the Vatican. Located at Bowery and Canal, the plaza construction destroyed four city blocks and several Bowery landmarks and displaced scores of families. This photograph is from 1940. (LOC.)

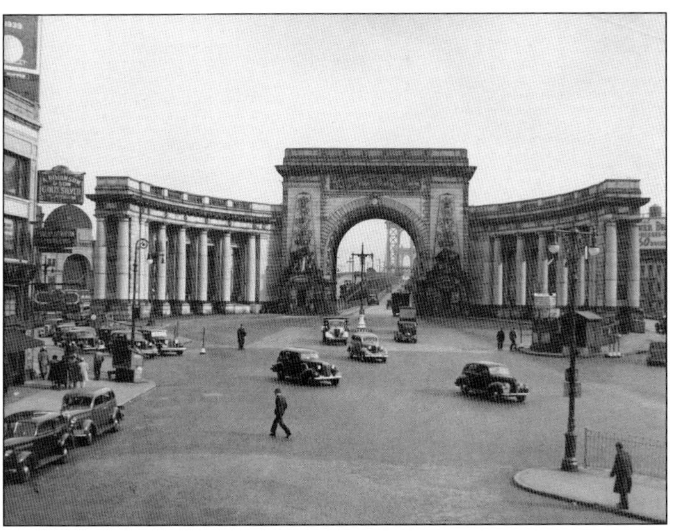

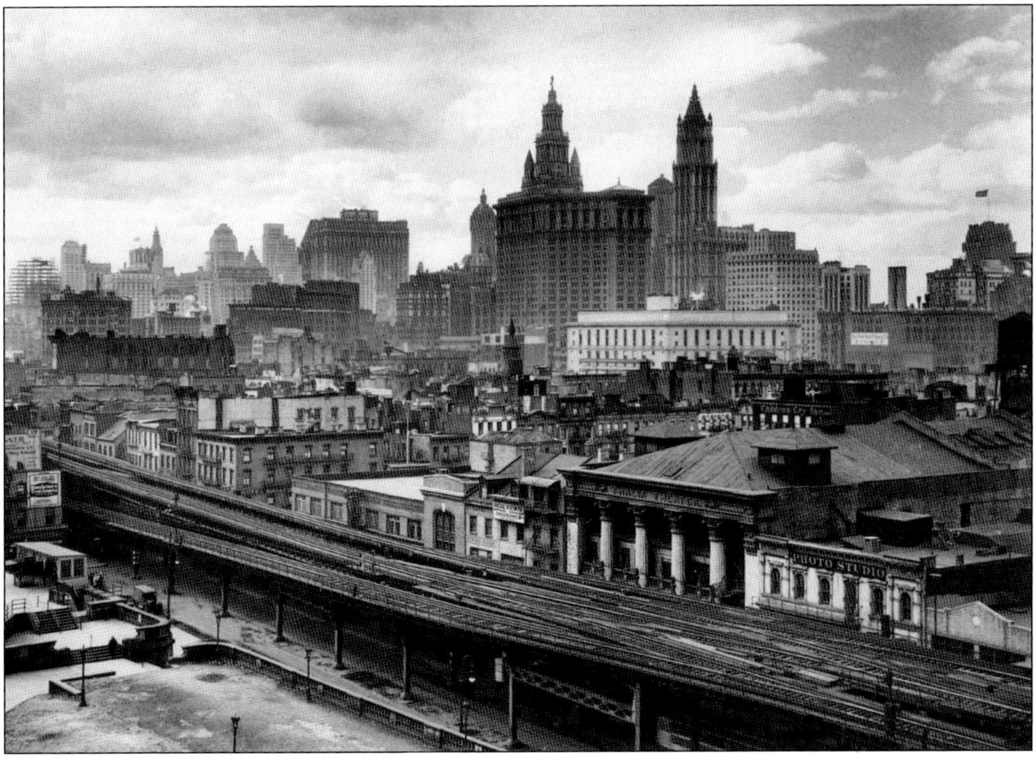

This 1927 photograph by Ewing Galloway, looking west from the Manhattan Bridge Plaza, shows the elevated train gut punching the Bowery's west side below Canal Street, with the tall Municipal Building and Woolworth Building in the distance. Visible on the right is the Thalia (formerly Bowery) Theatre, at 46 Bowery. The building to its right was formerly Atlantic Garden, the famous German beer hall. (NYPL-PC.)

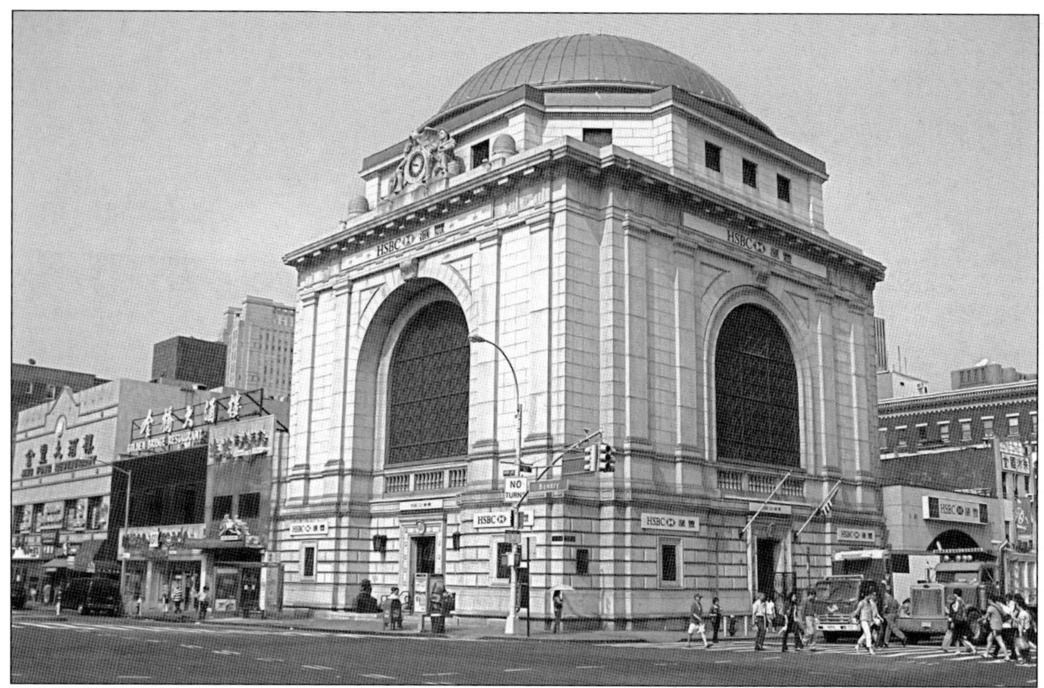

Unlike the fly-by-night storefront bank branches of today, banks in earlier eras built grand structures to suggest strength, permanence, and civic pride. The domed Beaux Arts–style Citizens Savings Bank at 58 Bowery is one of them. A New York City Landmark designed in 1922 by Clarence Brazer as a bank for the working class, its immense arched windows bring light into its 70-foot-high banking hall. This photograph was taken by Sally Young in 2010. (Sally Young.)

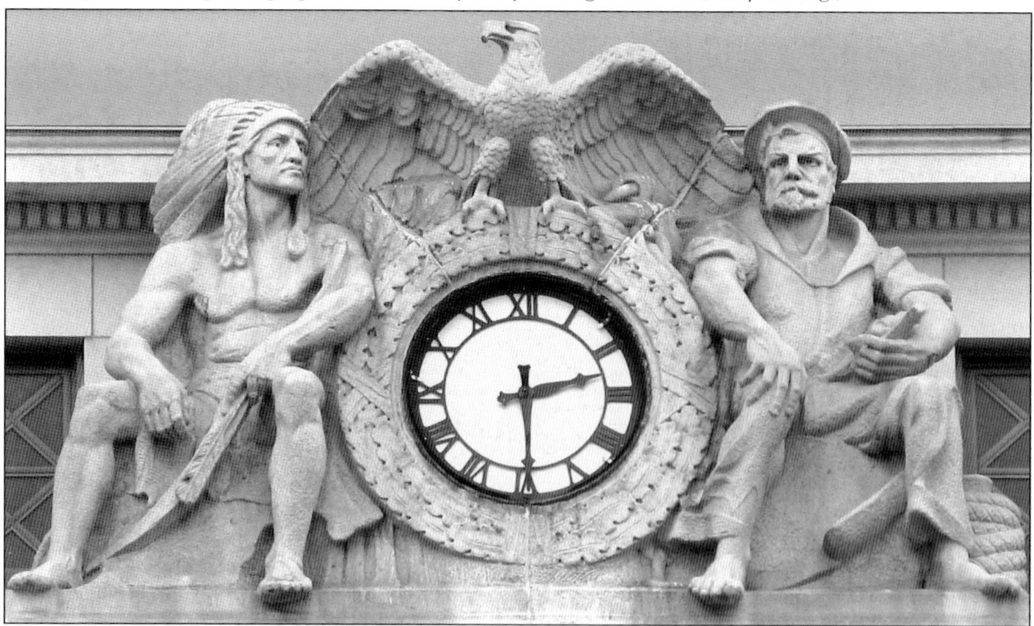

Atop the Citizen's Savings Bank on the Bowery side sits this powerful Charles Keck sculpture depicting a Native American, a Dutch sailor, and an eagle—figures from the NYC seal—surrounding a clock. This image is from 2016. (DM.)

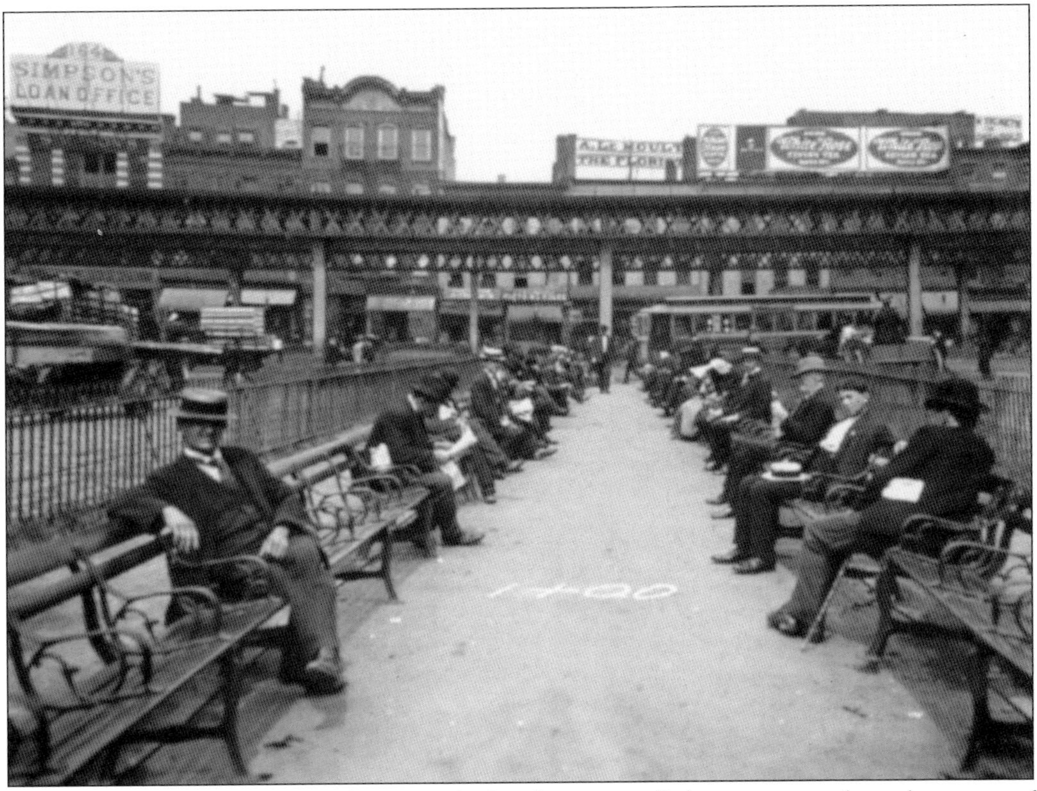

This 1907 photograph shows a long-vanished pedestrian mall that once ran along the center of Delancey Street. In the distance are the elevated train and 164-180 Bowery, including Simpson's pawn shop. Some of those buildings, including the clothing store and florist were demolished when Kenmare Street was cut through in 1911. The mall was removed in 1909 when the subway was built. (Merlis—Old NYC Photos.)

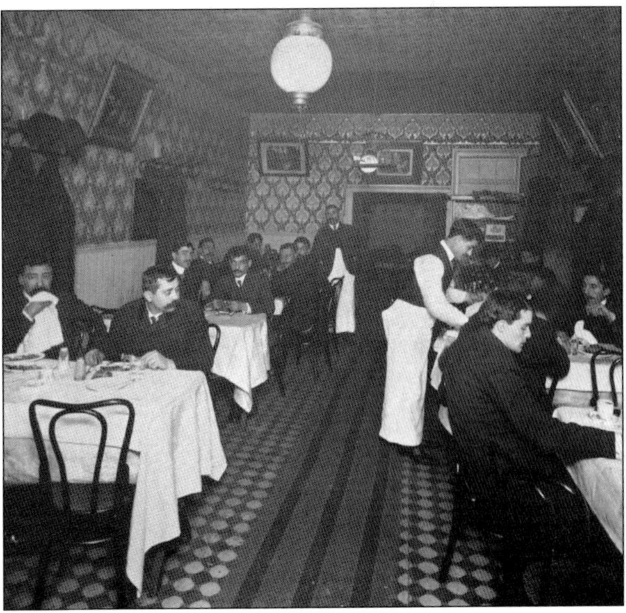

There was a culinary aspect to the Bowery's allure, since by the late 1800s there were restaurants with food from all over the globe, including this unidentified Greek restaurant, photographed in 1904. The most famous eatery, Mike Lyon's (259-261 Bowery), specialized in corned beef and cabbage. From 1872 to 1907, it was the "center of the East Side Bohemia." Tourists, politicos, boxers, gangsters, and thuggish police chief Thomas Byrnes all broke bread there. (Dover Publications.)

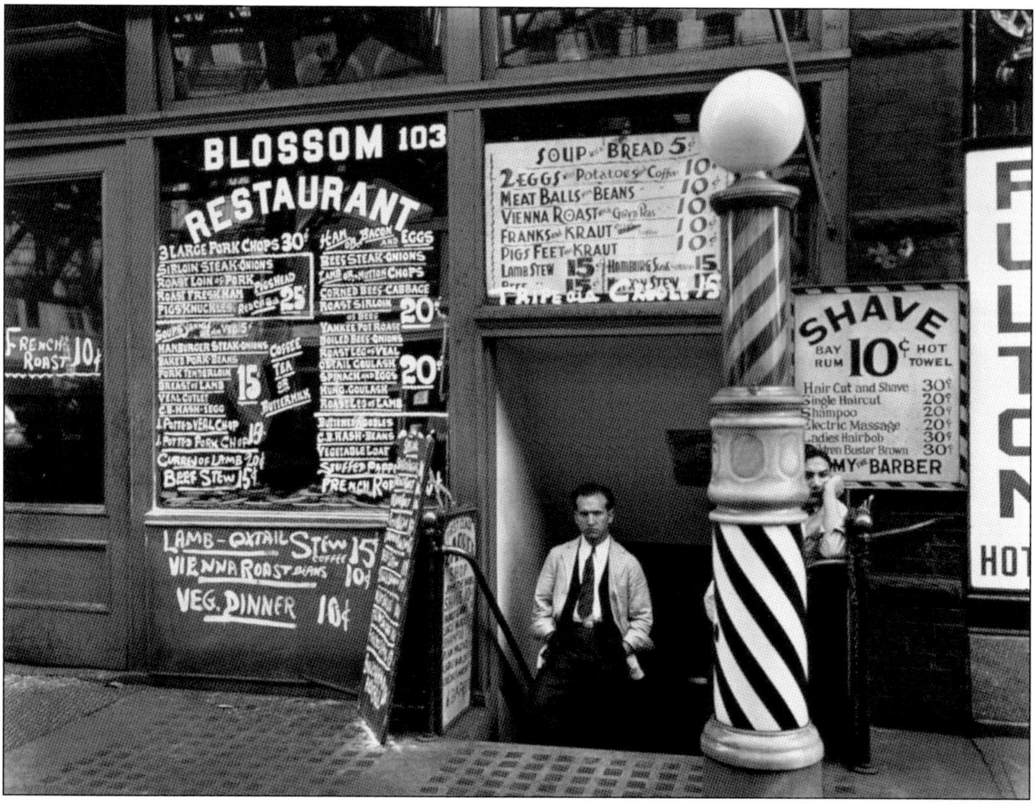

This iconic 1935 Berenice Abbott (1898–1991) photograph shows the Blossom Restaurant and a basement barbershop at 103 Bowery. When a WPA Federal Arts Project official cautioned her that "nice girls" do not go to the Bowery, Abbott retorted, "I'm not a nice girl. I'm a photographer." Her important photographic study, *Changing New York* (1939), includes the Bowery. (NYPL-DC.)

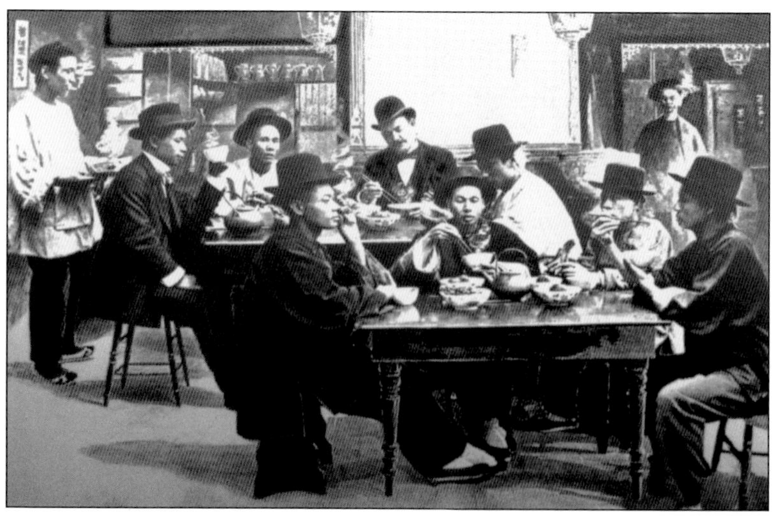

By the late 1800s, Chinese restaurants were wildly popular with local residents, tourists, and "slumming parties." This image of an unidentified Chinatown restaurant is from 1896. (NYPL-Pic.)

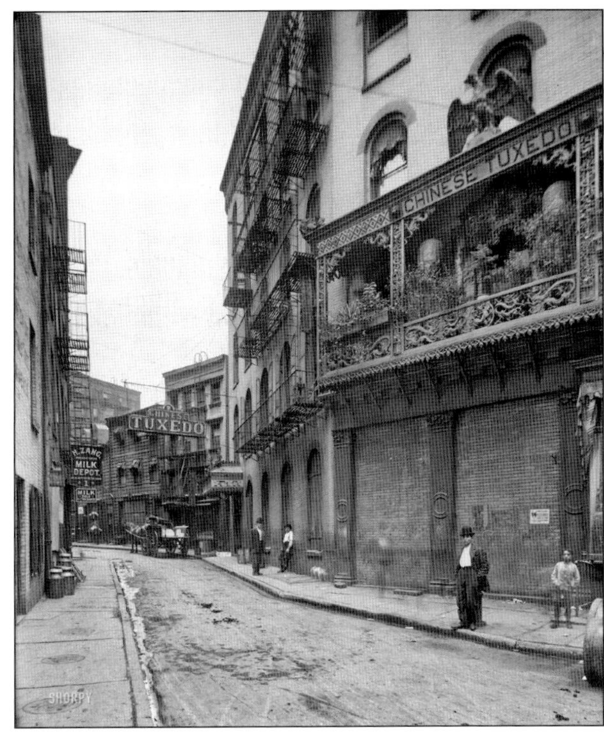

A main arrival point for Chinatown visitors was the elevated train's Chatham Square station which dropped them off at Bowery and Doyers Street. Visitors thronged to the Chinese Opera House on Doyers and the Tuxedo Restaurant whose ornate balcony at 2 Bowery was visible from the El. Zang's Milk Depot sold milk by the glass. Sometimes the scene of gangland conflict, Doyers Street was also known as "the Bloody Angle." This photograph is from around the early 1900s. (WC.)

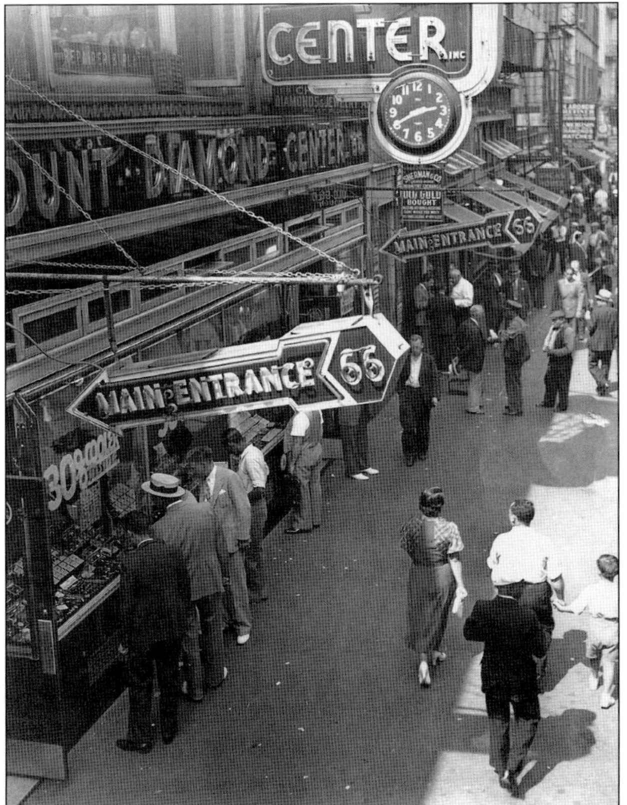

Since the late 1800s, there has been an important jewelry district on the Bowery, especially on the block between Canal and Hester Streets. Many of these businesses offer discounts and are unafraid of bargaining. This 1930s photograph shows the Paramount Diamond Center at 66 Bowery. Today, there are dozens of jewelry makers and retailers in this same area. (Eric Ng Collection, Museum of the Chinese in America.)

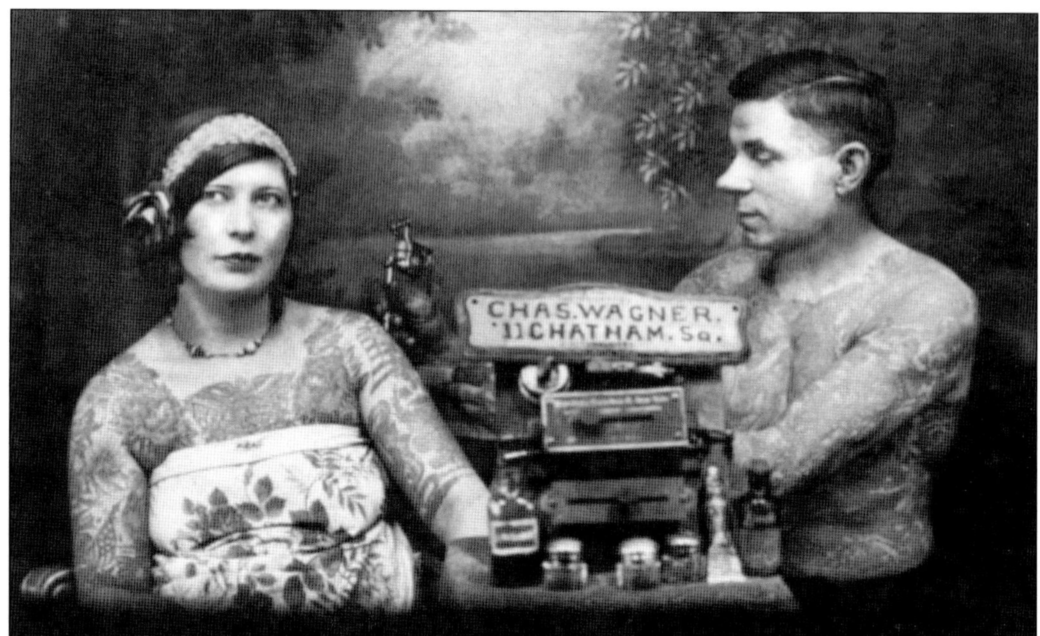

A walk on the Bowery wild side was not complete without gawking through the window of a tattoo parlor. Getting a tattoo in the early days was considered daring; something sailors and roughnecks did. Modern tattooing traces its roots here through the patented instruments of Samuel O'Reilly and his protégé Charlie Wagner, "the Michelangelo of tattoo." Their legendary studio at 11 Chatham Square, near Bowery, lasted from the 1890s until Wagner's death in 1953. Wagner also had parlors at 208 and 223 Bowery, and mentored former circus dancer Mildred Hull, whose 16 Bowery studio billed her as "New York's only woman tattooist." Because these tattooers cosmetically treated black eyes, they were sometimes called "Bowery beauticians." The above 1910s photograph shows Charlie Wagner, and the 1930s image below shows Mildred Hull's studio. (Above, Daredevil Tattoo; below, Ross Morgan Collection.)

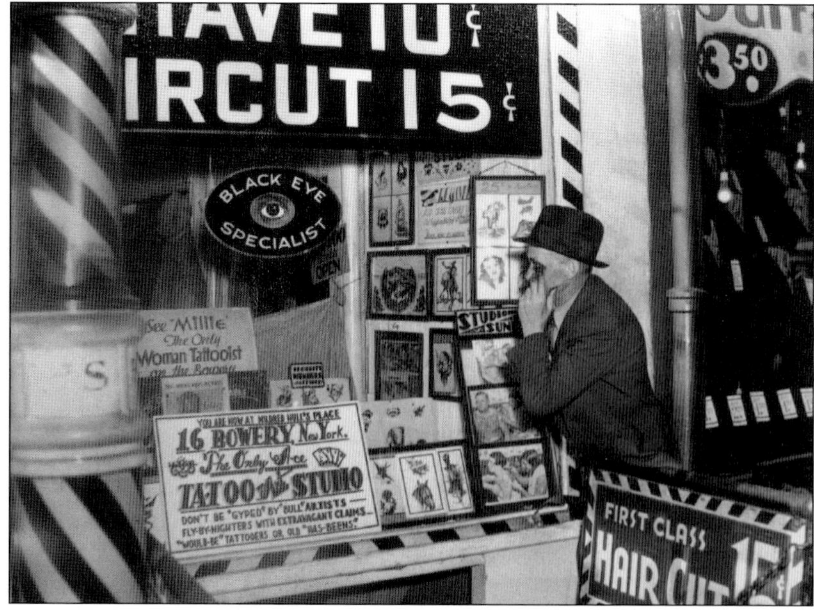

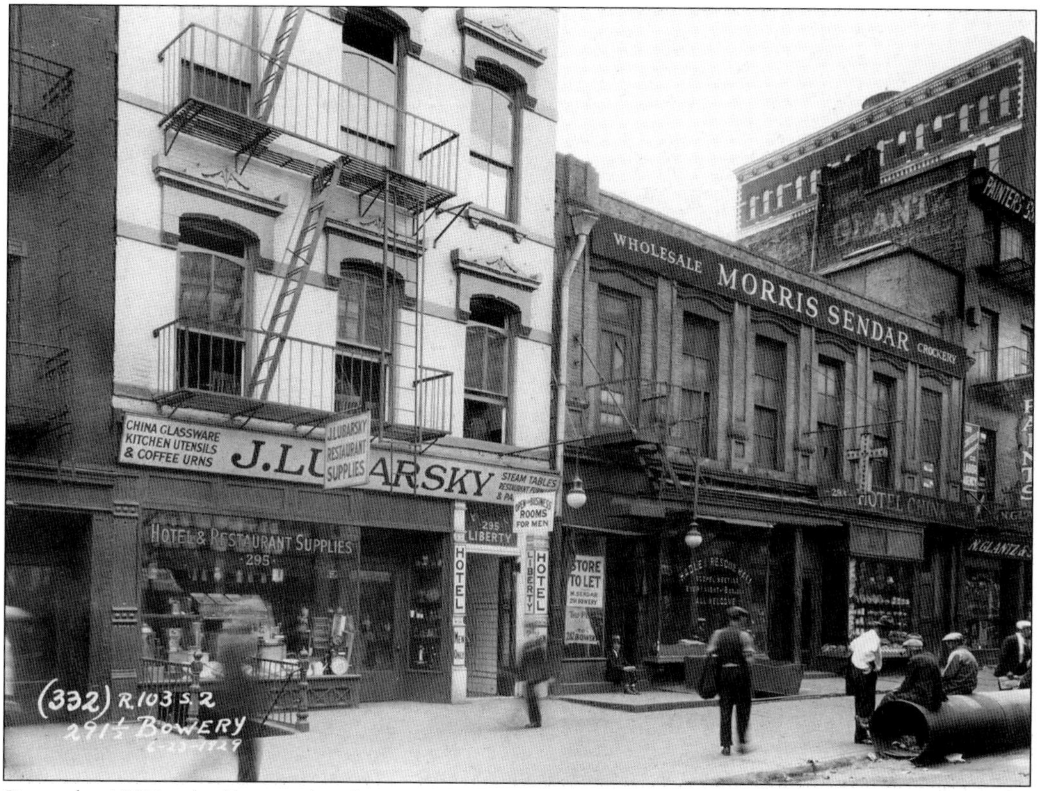

Since the 1920s, the Bowery has been a restaurant supply and lighting store district, as seen in this 1929 photograph of 291-295 Bowery, which also shows a paint store, Liberty lodging house, and Hadley Rescue Mission. 291-293 once housed a German beer garden, and in the 1890s, the property at 295 was the infamous McGurk's Suicide Hall, the scene of a dozen suicides by young female prostitutes. This 1929 photograph is from the New York Board of Transportation. (NYHS.)

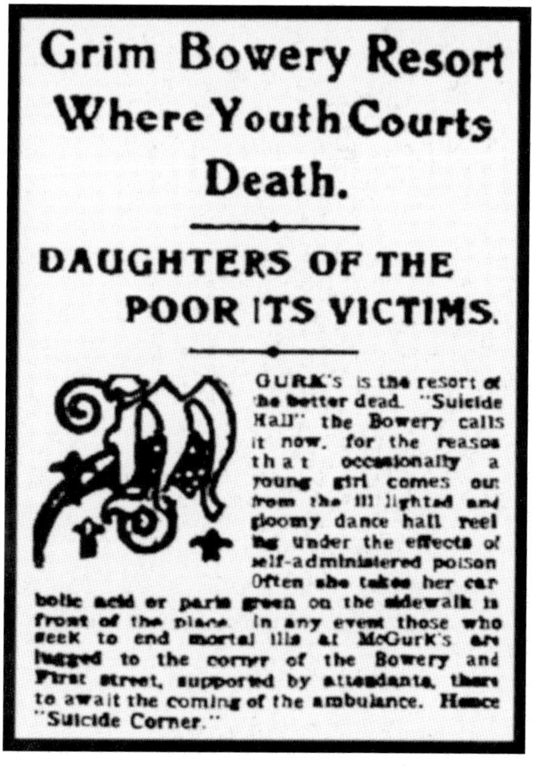

In 1897, two despairing young prostitutes ingested whiskey and carbolic acid. One died, the story went viral, and McGurk's Saloon became a slumming tour sensation. The incident inspired copycat suicides before the city closed the place. Years later, feminist writer Kate Millet, a resident at 295 Bowery, tried to landmark the building and establish a museum commemorating the hard lives of the women who died there. The building was demolished in 2005. This *New York Herald* article is from March 12, 1899. (AWC.)

Grim Bowery Resort Where Youth Courts Death.

DAUGHTERS OF THE POOR ITS VICTIMS.

GURK'S is the resort of the better dead. "Suicide Hall" the Bowery calls it now, for the reason that occasionally a young girl comes out from the ill lighted and gloomy dance hall reeling under the effects of self-administered poison. Often she takes her carbolic acid or paris green on the sidewalk in front of the place. In any event those who seek to end mortal ills at McGurk's are lugged to the corner of the Bowery and First street, supported by attendants, there to await the coming of the ambulance. Hence "Suicide Corner."

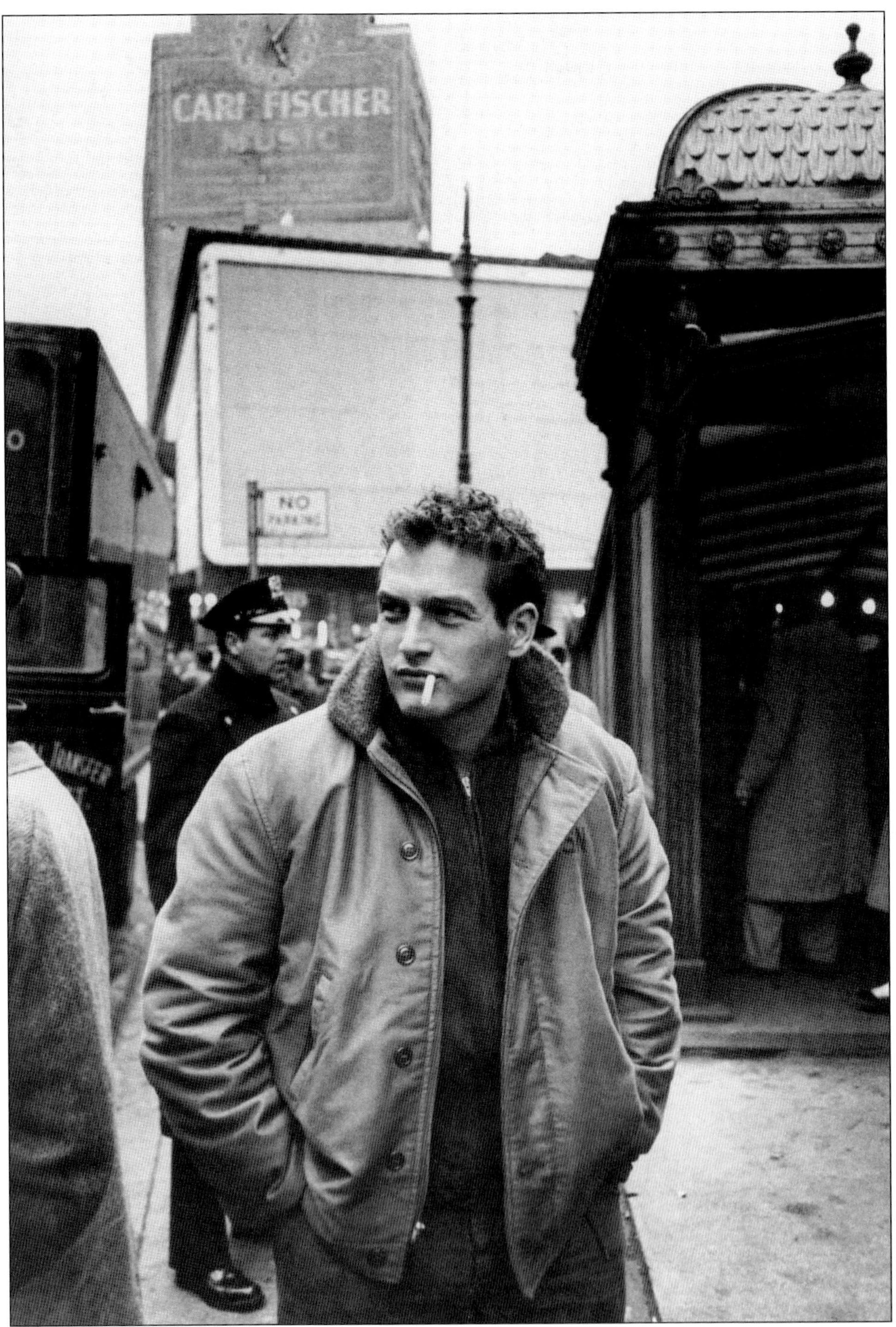

Paul Newman visited Astor Place during the 1956 filming of the boxing film *Somebody Up There Likes Me*. The Astor Place subway station's cast-iron entrance kiosk was designed by Heins & LaFarge and cast by Brooklyn's Hecla Iron Works. The station opened in 1904. The Carl Fischer Music building is also seen in this Sanford Roth photograph. (MPTV Images.)

The Astor Place Subway station contains a series of glazed bas-relief architectural tiles depicting a beaver, which evokes the original fur trading source of John Jacob Astor's immense wealth. This image is from 2023. (DM.)

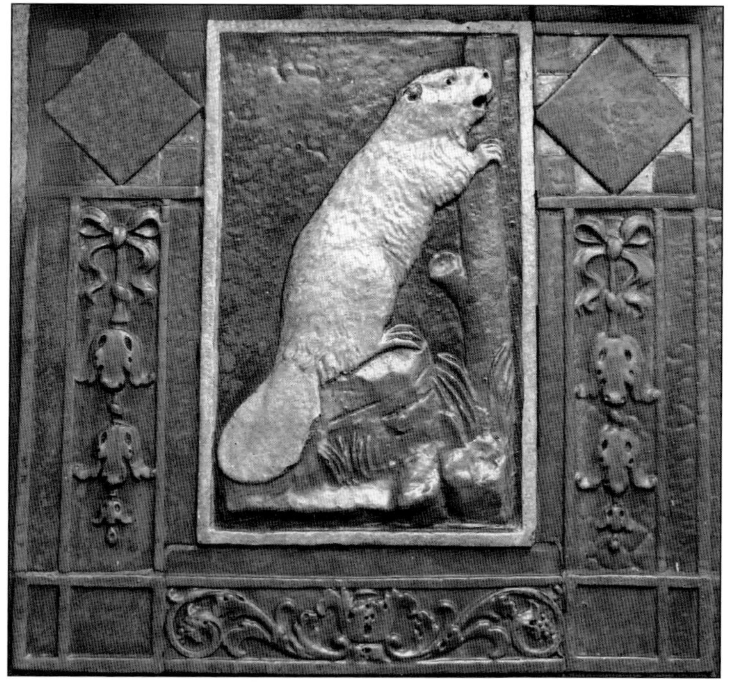

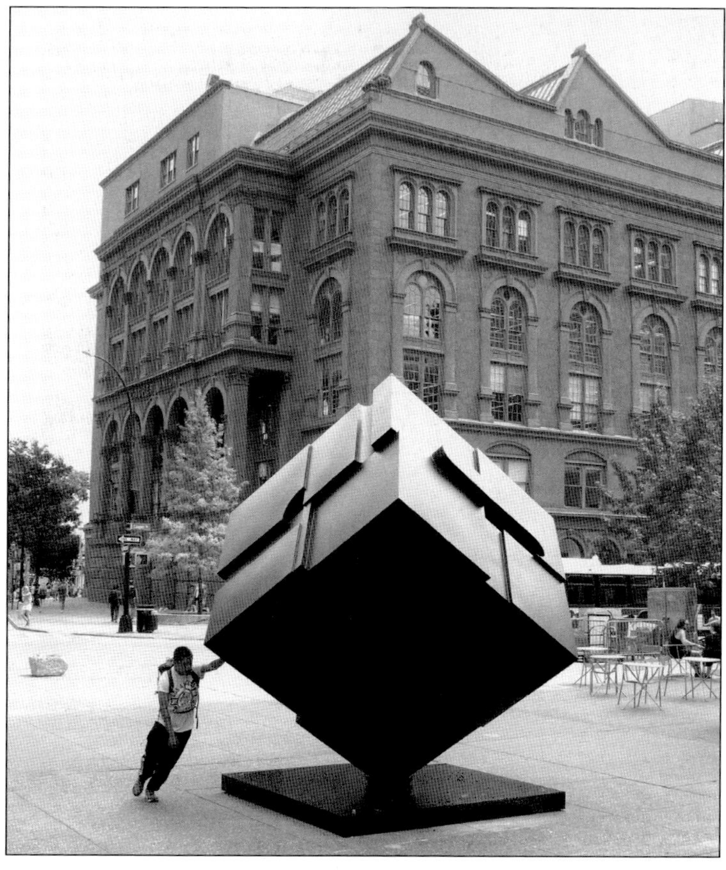

Since 1967, sculptor Tony Rosenthal's beloved *The Cube*, also known as *Alamo*, has been the centerpiece of Astor Place. Made of Cor-Ten steel, this 15-foot tall, 1,800-pound sculpture rests on a hidden interior pole which allows it to rotate. For decades, spinning it has been a rite of passage for thousands of young people. Its Astor Place location was originally a trade and meeting place of the Lenape people. This photograph is from 2023. (DM.)

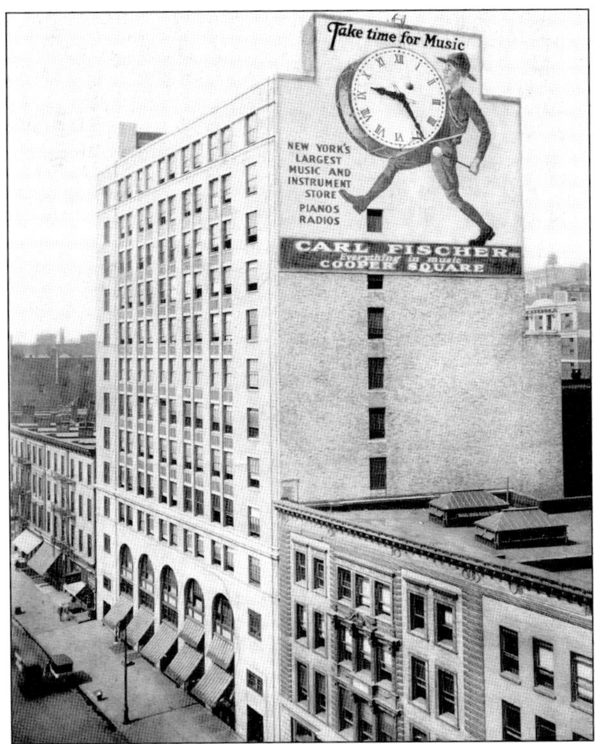

The Carl Fischer Music company printed and sold sheet music, and musical instruments on Cooper Square for 120 years; first at 46-54 Cooper Square (1880–1922), and then at 56-62 Cooper Square (1922–1999), a 12-story Neoclassical structure, designed by W.K. Benedict. Though the music company moved, the Carl Fischer Music Building, seen here in about 1930, remains part of the NoHo Historic District. (Carl Fischer Music.)

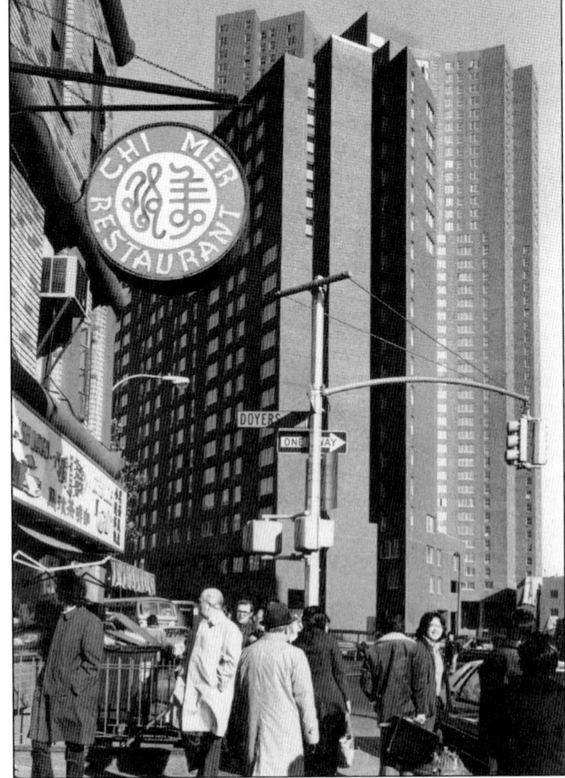

The passage of the Immigration and Nationality Act of 1965 prompted a surge in Chinatown's population and geographic size. In response, the city approved the construction of Confucius Plaza (1975) at 1 Bowery, a 44-story public housing project containing 762 apartments, a school, and street-level businesses. The construction crew's lack of diversity caused protests, with one sign reading, "Asians built the railroads; why not Confucius Plaza?" This photograph is from 1975. (Carin Drechsler-Marx.)

At the south end of Confucius Plaza, near the corner of Bowery and Division Street, is this statue of philosopher Confucius by sculptor Liu Shih. A popular meeting place, it was presented to the City of New York by the Chinese Consolidated Benevolent Association and dedicated in 1976. This image is from 2016. (DM.)

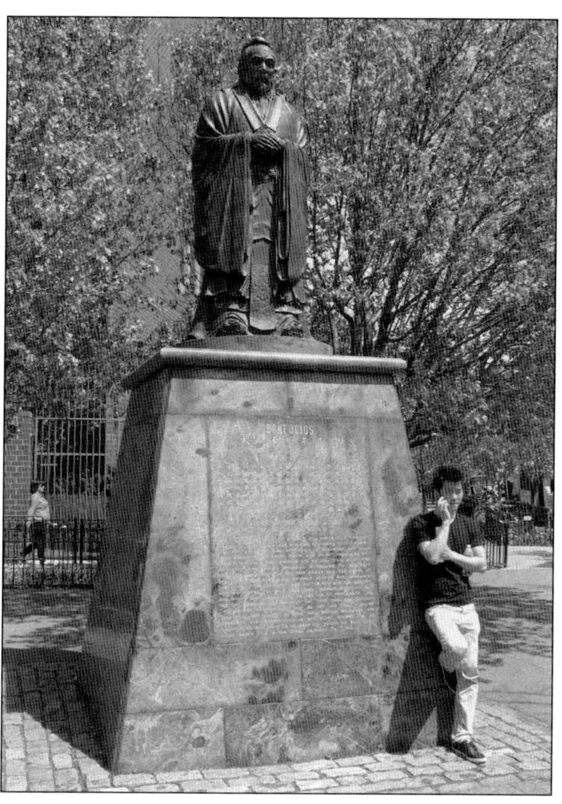

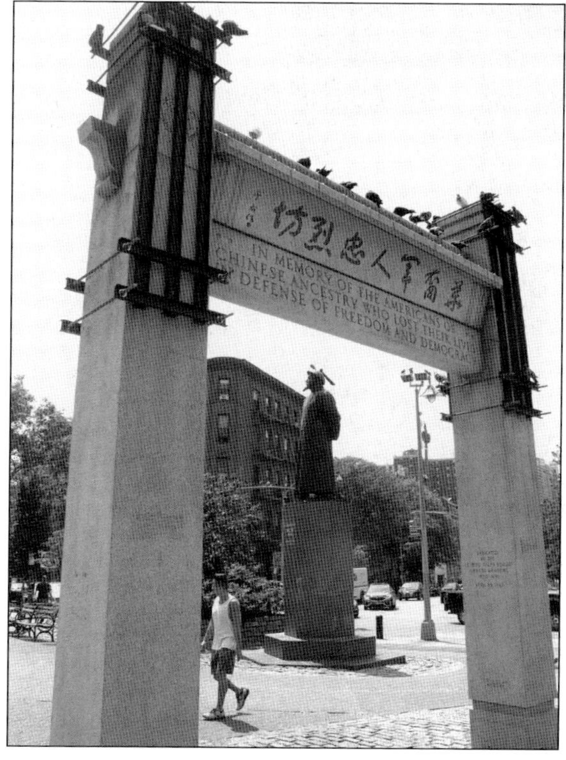

Just south of Bowery is the Kimlau Memorial (1962) honoring fighter pilot Lt. Benjamin Kimlau (1918–1944) and "Americans of Chinese ancestry who lost their lives in defense of Freedom and Democracy." Designed by Poy Gum Lee, it is the first NYC Landmark recognizing Chinese American history. The 1999 sculpture by Li Wei-Si is of Qing dynasty-era scholar-warrior Lin Ze Xu, central to fighting the British in the Opium Wars. This photograph is from 2023. (DM.)

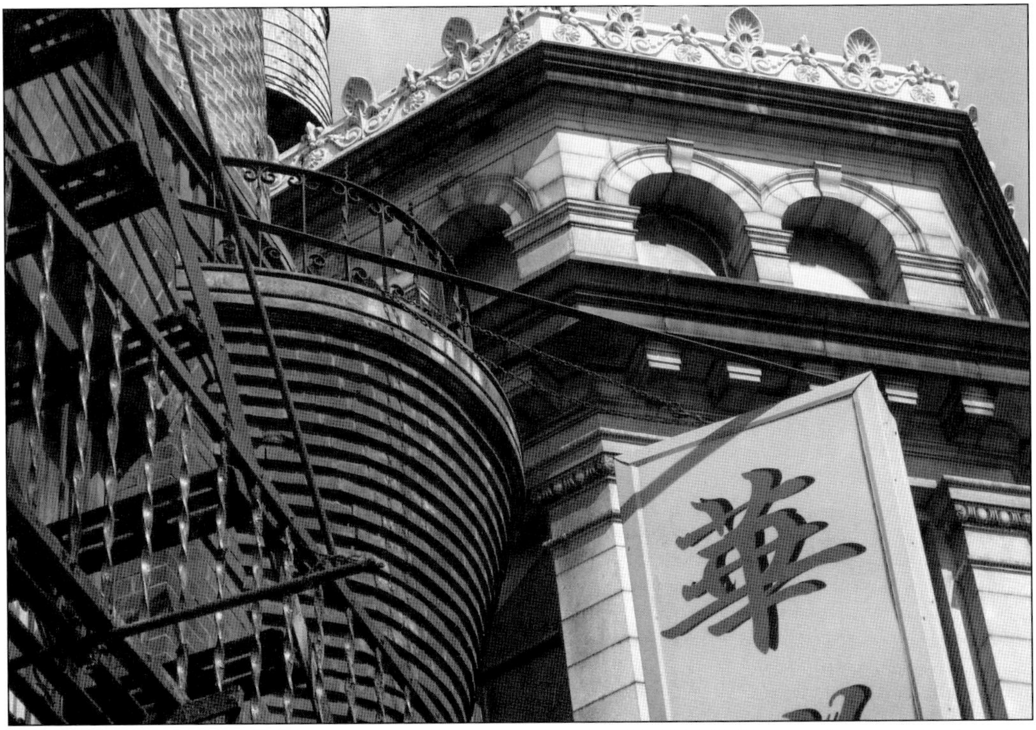

The Bowery's architectural diversity is well expressed in this 2010 Sally Young photograph, showing the Romanesque Revival elements of 188 Bowery juxtaposed beside the Beaux Arts elements of the Germania Bank Building at 190 Bowery. This Spring Street corner is today a destination for tattoos and skateboards. (Sally Young.)

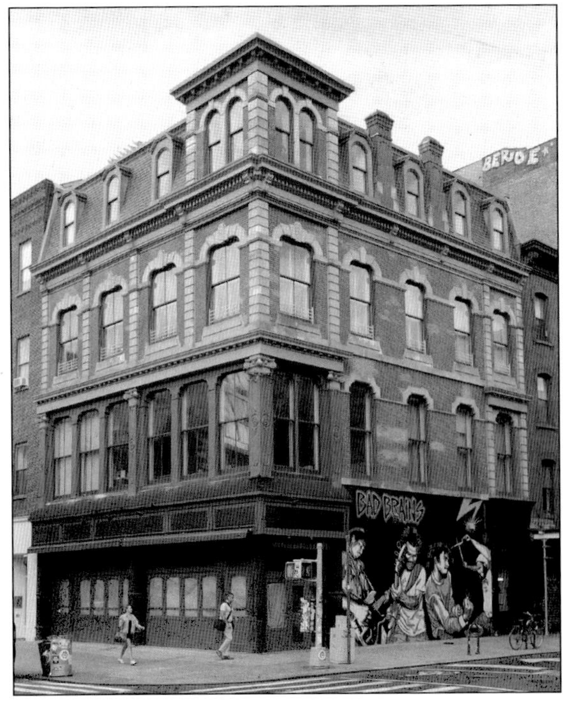

This three-and-a-half-story Italianate building with slate-clad mansard roof and arched dormer windows is located at 316-318 Bowery in the NoHo Historic District. Designed by Nicholas Whyte, the 1868 structure has housed a hotel, hat shops, restaurants, the Bleecker Street Theatre Workshop, and a hardware store famously photographed by Berenice Abbott in 1938. Seen here in 2024, its periodically changing murals celebrate musicians who played CBGB. This one depicts the band Bad Brains. (DM.)

Two

New York City's First Entertainment District

In the 1700s, when the Bowery was a country road, horse races, and bull and bear baiting were popular diversions. In the early 1800s, its Vauxhall Garden was fashionable for music, plays, and fireworks. Later, the Bowery became renowned as NYC's first popular entertainment district, but unlike Broadway, which came later, it was affordable; the place the working class went to eat, drink, be entertained, and express themselves. It boasted 3,000-seat theaters, zoos, circuses, dime museums, tattoo parlors, photography studios, concert saloons, boxing saloons, Mozart in beer gardens, opera, dance halls, billiard halls, skating rinks, oyster bars, shooting galleries, and gambling dens. Later, there were risqué drag shows, burlesque and vaudeville. Like Coney Island, with its own Bowery named for the Manhattan original, the street itself was a theatrical attraction, with singers, clowns, violinists, German oompah bands, Italian organ grinders, hot corn girls, magicians and a passing parade of gangs, gays, pickpockets, sailors, shopgirls, sporting men, painted ladies, slumming parties, and a cacophony of barkers, salesmen, and voices that spanned the globe. America's first shocked glimpse of ballet was on the Bowery, as were the first productions of the anti-slavery play *Uncle Tom's Cabin.* An incubator for tap dance, minstrelsy, vaudeville, Yiddish theater, and American song, the Bowery witnessed the early ascent of entertainment greats including Al Jolson, W.C. Fields, Irving Berlin, and Harry Houdini.

During its 19th-century heyday, journalist George G. Foster wrote that the Bowery was "a perpetual kaleidoscope from morning till night; something rare and strange constantly starting up." But by the early 1900s, its entertainment district was in steep decline. The theatrical center had moved uptown, vaudeville was fading, and a new subway system gave the masses other options, as did the movies, and later radio. The final blows were Prohibition (1920–1933), which shuttered saloons, and the Great Depression (1929–1939), which surged the numbers in Bowery lodging houses and breadlines. Because of the street's notoriety, Bowery/Chinatown tours, first popularized in the 1880s, continued to attract thrill-seekers, as did Sammy's Bowery Follies, which thrived for decades with its spirited mix of high and low life. Beginning in the 1950s, the Bowery got a second creative wind, which will be explored in Chapter Five.

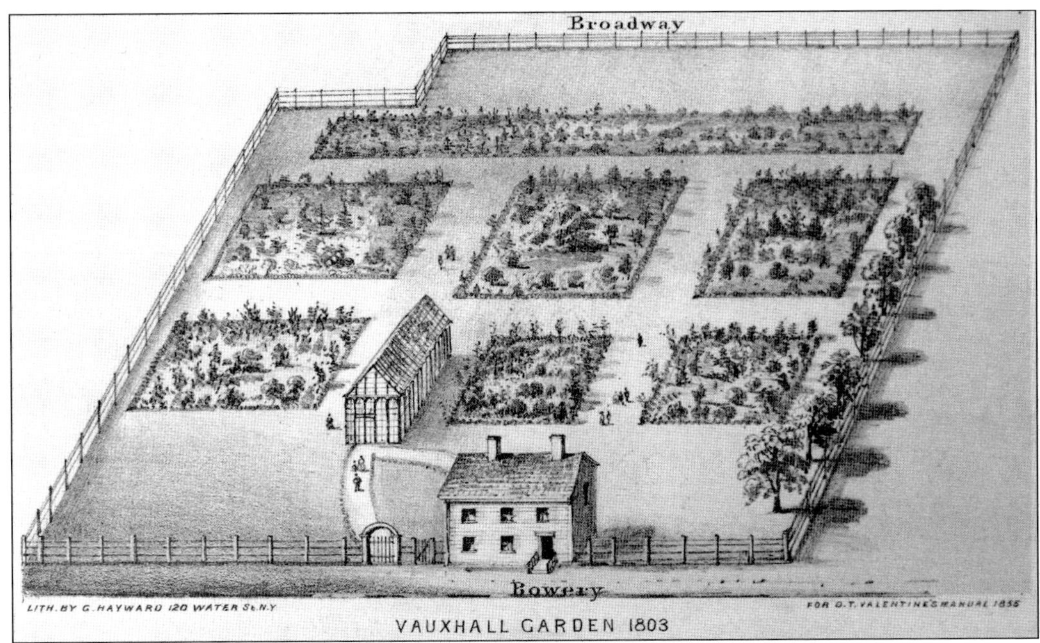

From 1803 to 1859, the land between Bowery, Broadway, Fourth Street, and Astor Place was the fashionable Vauxhall Garden. Established by Joseph Delacroix on land owned by John Jacob Astor, it featured gravel walks among trees and flowers. It offered ice cream, juleps, and an open-air theater for concerts, plays, fireworks, and hot-air balloon launches, making it "as gay a place of recreation as was to be found . . . anywhere in the civilized world." (AWC.)

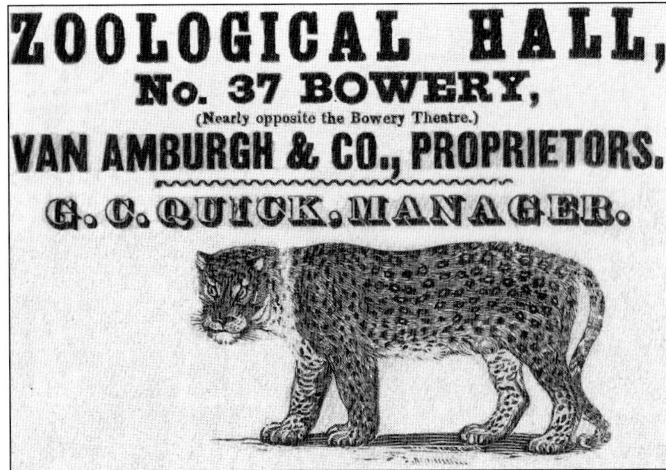

Zoological Hall opened here in 1833 as one of America's first zoos. Exotic animals were displayed in a grand exhibition hall lit by chandeliers, accompanied by an orchestra. Its biggest attraction became the legendary Isaac Van Amburgh (1808–1865), "the Great Lion Tamer," who dressed as a gladiator and was the first to stick his head into the mouth of a lion. A favorite of Queen Victoria, his brutal methods, were criticized. (AWC.)

The 3,000-seat Bowery Theatre opened at 46-48 Bowery in 1826 as America's largest theatre. Built to attract the elite, it instead became the favorite of the working class who loved its equestrian battle scenes, "blood and thunder" melodrama, and Shakespeare. Walt Whitman admired the democratic seating of tradesmen next to presidents. It burned five times but survived 103 years—until 1929—rebuilding and reinventing itself, staging shows for Italians, Irish, Germans, Jews, and Chinese. This image is from 1867. (NYPL-PC.)

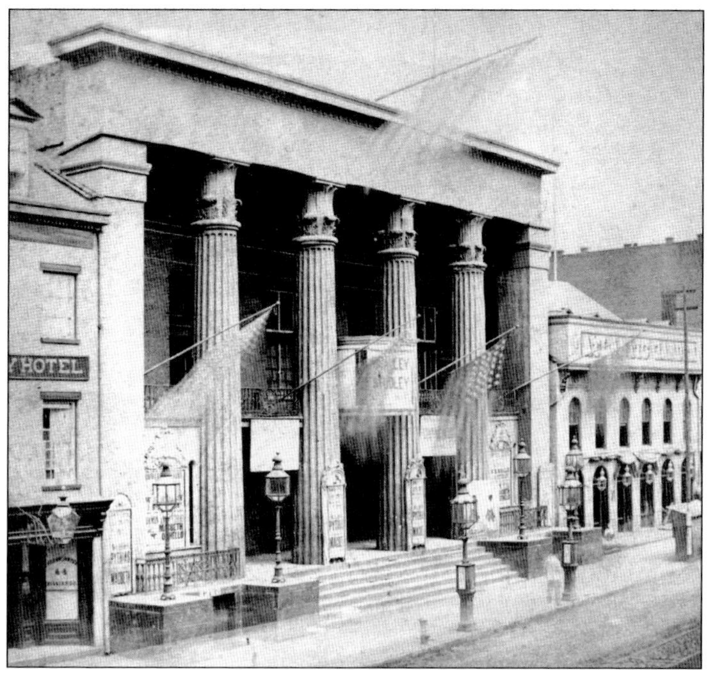

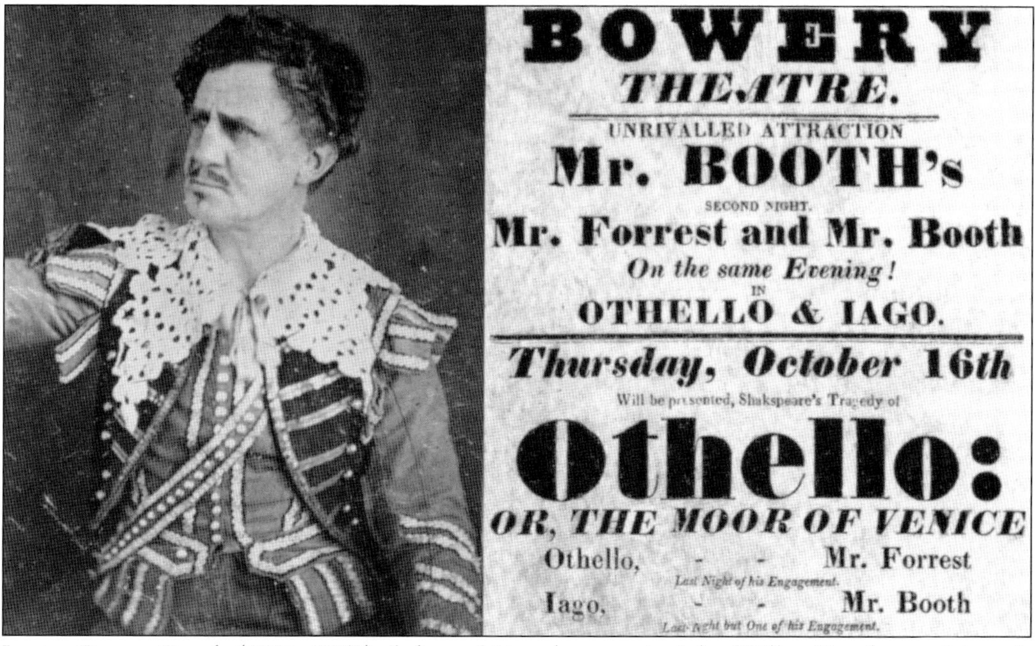

Junius Brutus Booth (1796–1852), father of Lincoln assassin John Wilkes Booth, was his era's greatest Shakespearean actor. Walt Whitman considered him a genius, but alcohol and mental health issues made him an erratic, sometimes violent performer, with actors terrified to perform dueling scenes with him. Father of 12, another son, Edwin Booth, became an equally great tragedian. The c. 1850s photograph at left is by Matthew Brady; the poster is from 1828. (Left, LOC; right, Harvard Theatre Collection.)

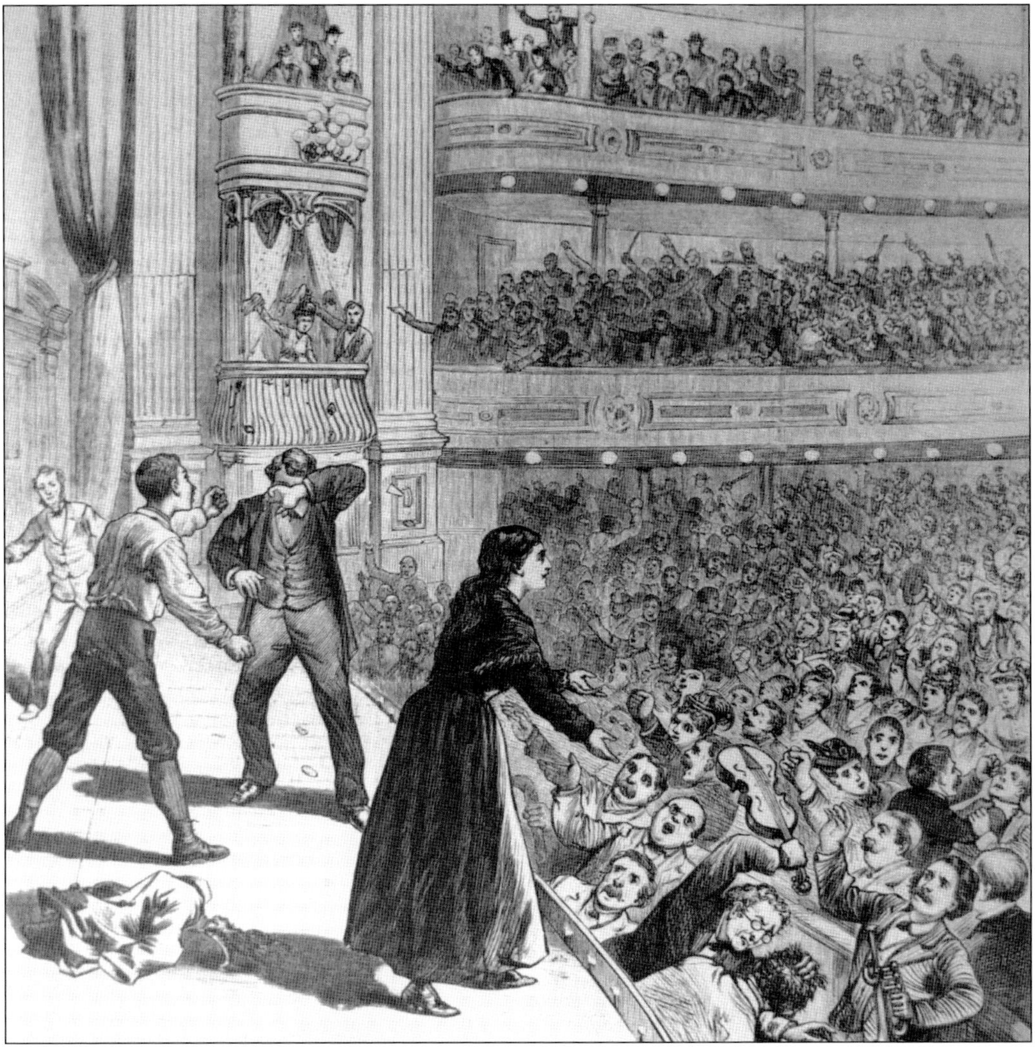

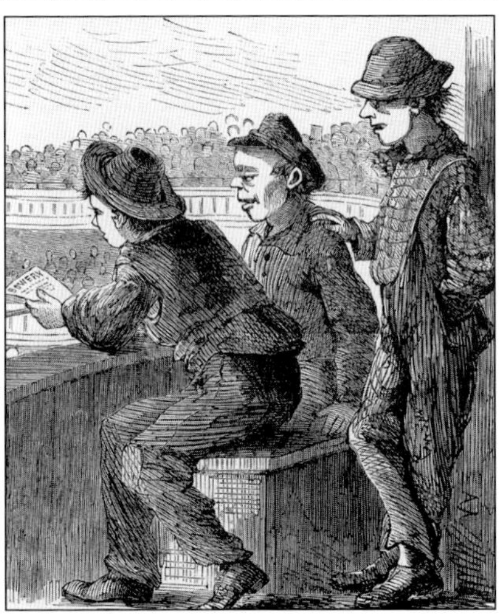

Known as the "Bowery Slaughterhouse," the raucous audience of the Bowery Theatre rivaled those of Shakespeare's time. Though audiences jeered or made catcalls if they disliked a performer, Whitman recalled that favorites received "long kept-up tempests of handclapping peculiar to the Bowery—no dainty kid-glove business, but electric force and muscle." The priciest seats were in the second level Dress Circle, and the cheapest—affordable even to newsboys—were the wooden benches in "the pit" (in front of the stage), and up high in the gallery's "nose bleed section." Prostitutes were known to ply their trade on the third tier, and one actor recalled seeing kids munching on apples and mothers breastfeeding in the pit. English writer Frances Trollope was appalled to see feet hanging over the banisters. The image at left is from the May 18, 1867, issue of *Harper's Weekly.* (Above, HTC; left, NYPL-Pic.)

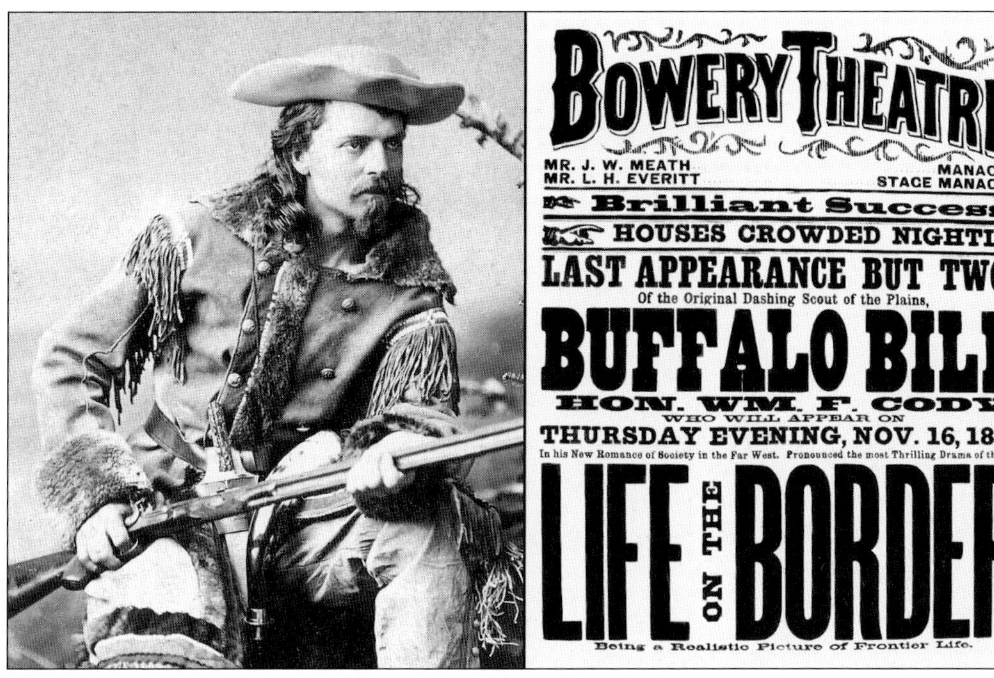

The personification of the Wild West, Buffalo Bill Cody (1846-1917) was a good fit for the Bowery, the personification of the Wild East. His first ever stage appearance was in 1872 at the Bowery Theatre, where he was attending a show about his life. Pulled on stage to speak, he was terrified and made a hasty retreat, though he would return to the Bowery many times. This c. 1880 photograph is by Napoleon Sarony. (Left, LOC; right, RMC.)

Appearances at the Bowery Theatre included actors Edwin Forrest, Charlotte Cushman, Adah Isaacs Menken, Fanny Herring, Thomas Hamblin, James O'Neill, and Bertha Kalich. Others included magician J.H. Anderson; anarchist Emma Goldman; and bare-knuckle boxers Tom Hyer, Jem Ward, and Joe Coburn. In 1827, when Madame Francisque Hutin introduced America to ballet while wearing tights, some shocked spectators stormed out. This 1856 illustration shows Irishman John Brougham's play *Pocahontas*. (HTC.)

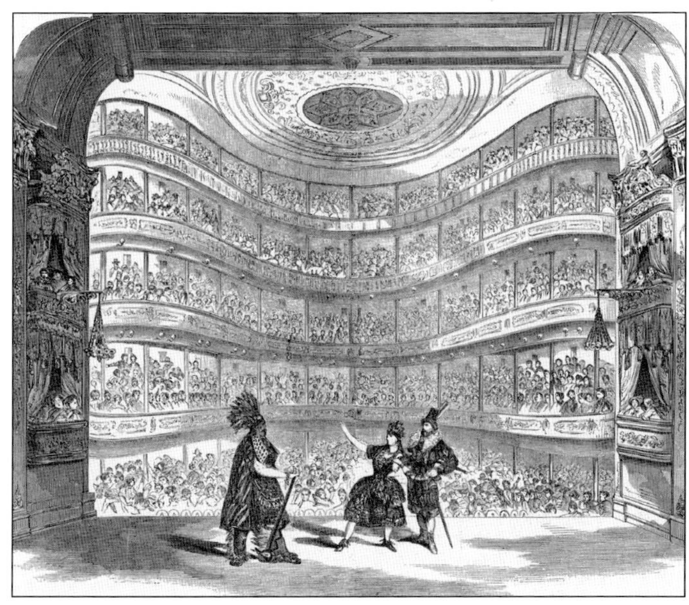

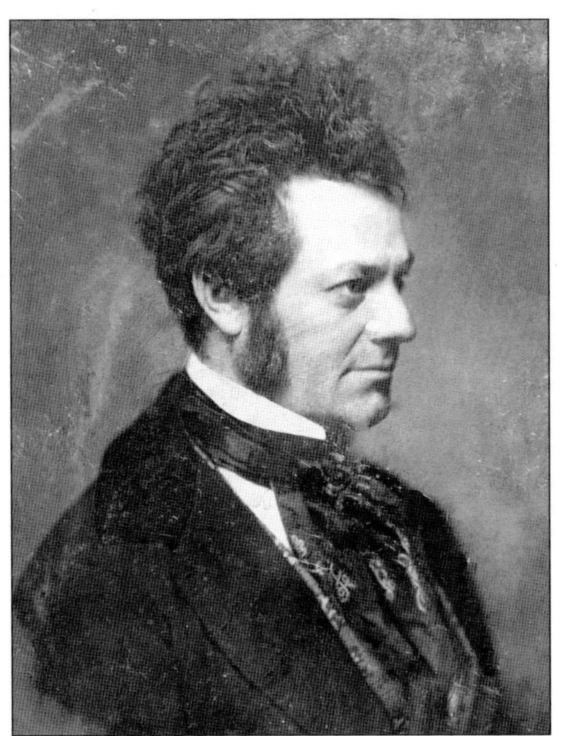

Before Philadelphia-born Edwin Forrest (1806–1872) burst on the scene at the Bowery Theatre in 1826, American theater was dominated by the actors and style of the British. His booming voice and muscular build, well used playing Othello and Spartacus, brought a physicality to the profession that audiences embraced as uniquely American. Forrest's feud with British actor Charles Macready led to the Astor Place Riot. This c. 1850 photograph is by Matthew Brady. (LOC.)

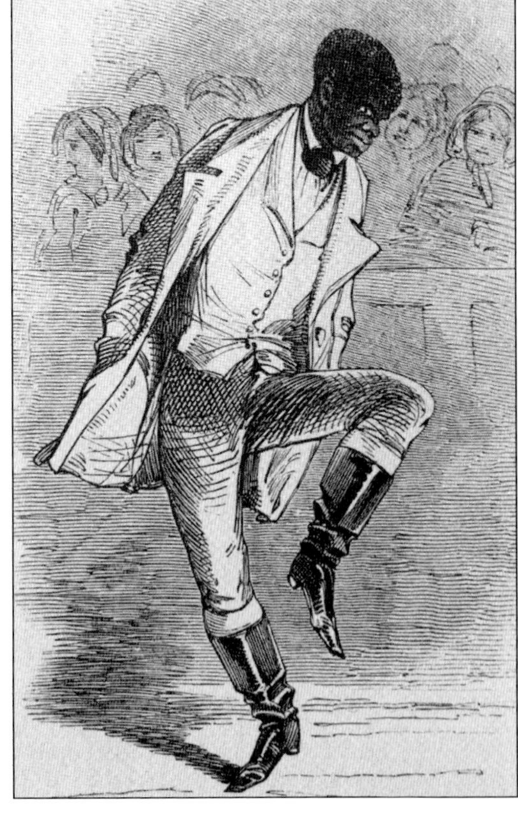

Hailed by Charles Dickens as "the greatest dancer known," William Henry Lane (1825-1853) also known as "Master Juba: King of All Dancers," is the father of tap dance. An African American native of the racially mixed Five Points ghetto, his dancing fused African and Irish dance traditions, which evolved from the neighborhood's competitive challenge dances. He electrified thousands at the Bowery Theatre and became a sensation in England. This lithograph is from 1848. (HTC.)

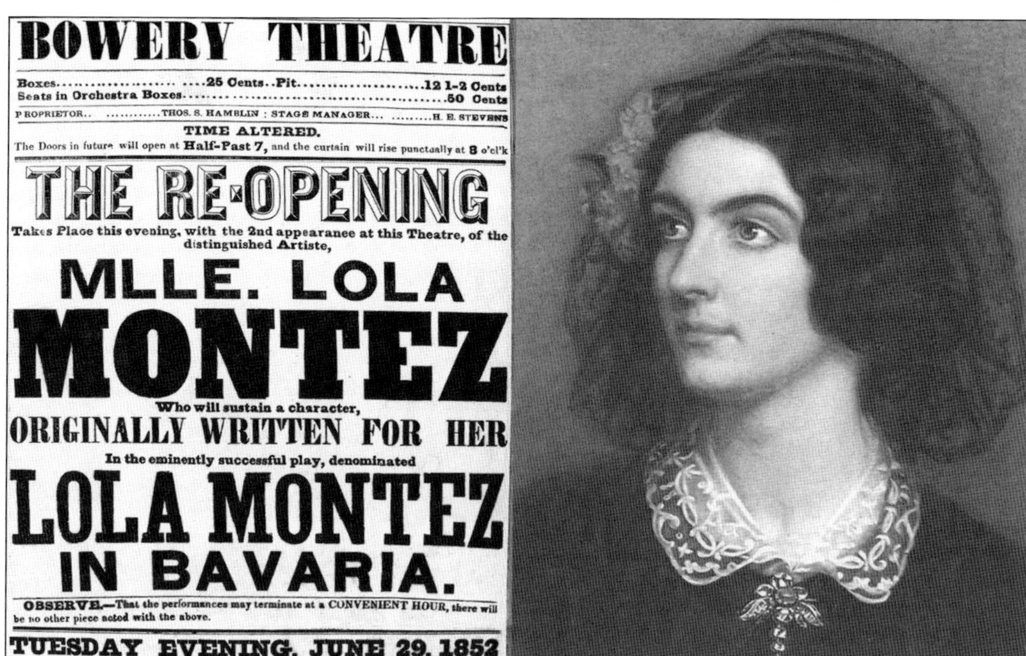

In 1852, scandalous Lola Montez (1821–1861) appeared as herself for $1,000-a-week at the Bowery Theatre. An Irish-born "Spanish dancer," she married thrice, had a duel fought over her and affairs with Franz Liszt and Bavaria's King Ludwig, who made her a countess. In 1848, revolutionary upheaval and Ludwig's abdication prompted Lola to flee Bavaria. In 1858 she lectured on marriage and free love at 37 Bowery's Stadt Theatre. The portrait is by Joseph Karl Stieler. (Left, HTC; right, PD.)

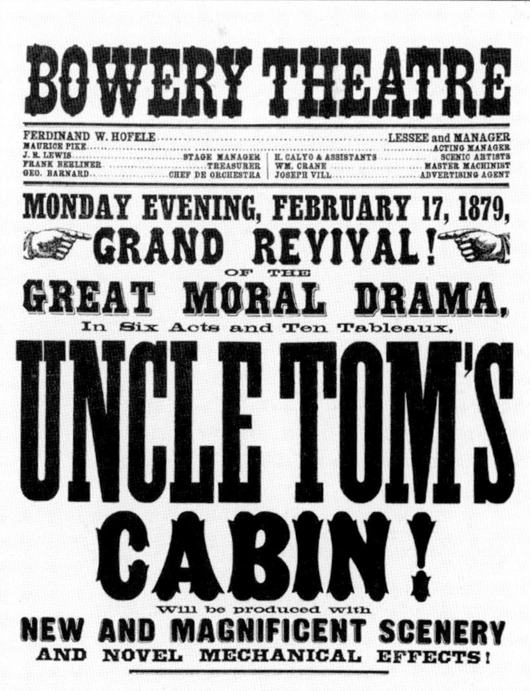

When the era's best-selling novel—Harriet Beecher Stowe's *Uncle Tom's Cabin*—was turned into the era's hottest theatrical property, the first production premiered on August 23, 1852, at the National Theatre on Chatham Street, the Bowery's original lower stretch. Because of weak copyright laws, multiple versions were circulated, none approved by Stowe. Though some productions stressed the anti-slavery message, others used comic stereotypes from minstrelsy, which made the proceedings ludicrous. (NYHS.)

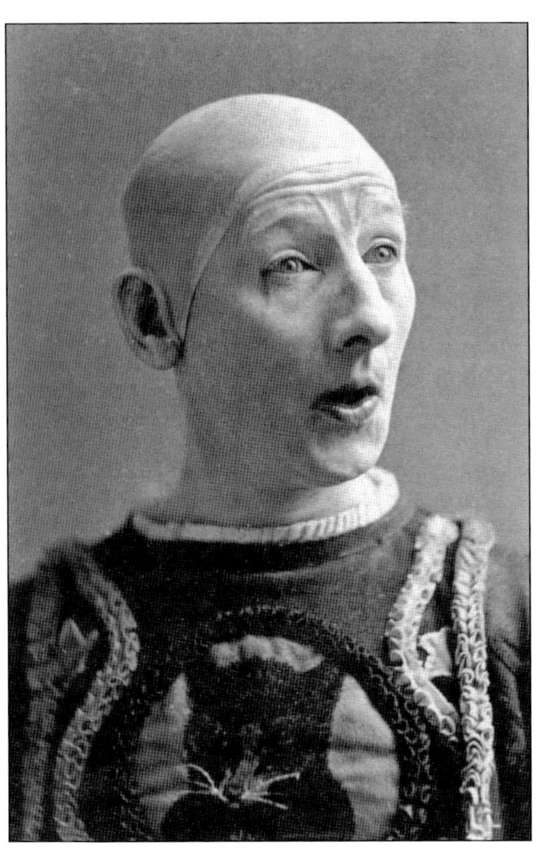

George L. Fox (1825–1877) was 19th-century America's most famous clown. When he leased the Bowery Theatre, it was renamed Fox's Old Bowery Theatre. Among the first entertainers mass-marketed in toys, he influenced the violent tradition of American comedy, anticipating the Keystone Cops, Three Stooges, cartoons, and the Krazy Kat comic strip. This photograph is by Napoleon Sarony. (PD.)

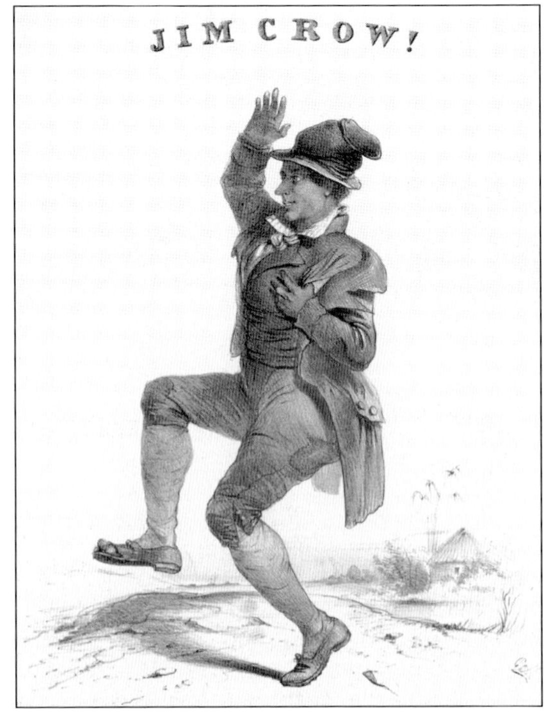

Minstrelsy was a theatrical genre established by Northern white men in blackface make-up that mimicked the supposed singing, dancing, and speaking manner of African Americans. It codified demeaning Black stereotypes that pervaded American culture for over 120 years. It hit the big time in 1832 when T.D. Rice performed his "Jump Jim Crow" act before thousands at the Bowery Theatre. (Jim Crow became the namesake for post–Civil War segregation laws). Minstrelsy expanded to full-evening group performances with the Virginia Minstrels 1943 appearance at the Bowery Amphitheatre (37 Bowery). One member, Dan Emmett, penned "Turkey in the Straw" and "Dixie," which he regretted became the anthem of the Confederacy. This sheet music Illustration of Rice is from 1836. (AWC.)

As minstrelsy became a huge, lucrative theatrical phenomenon, some African Americans recognized an opportunity for Black talent. While white minstrels represented cultural theft and fraud, Black minstrels were billed as genuine, though they, too, were locked into the genre's stereotyping. Black troupes like Callender's Minstrels performed on the Bowery, as did singer-dancer-acrobat-comedian-entrepreneur Billy Kersands. Decades before Bert Williams broke Broadway's color barrier, Kersands appeared on mainstream stages all over the country. The poster is from about the 1870s. (Cincinnati Historical Society.)

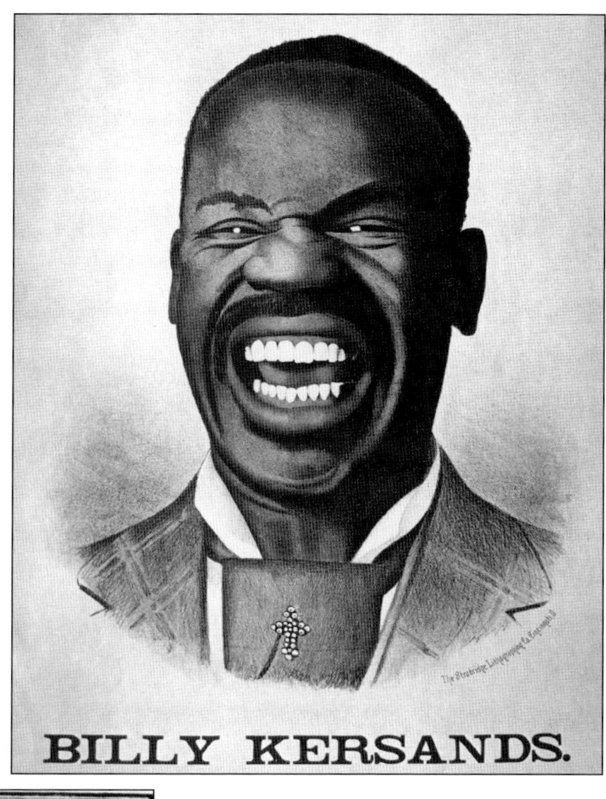

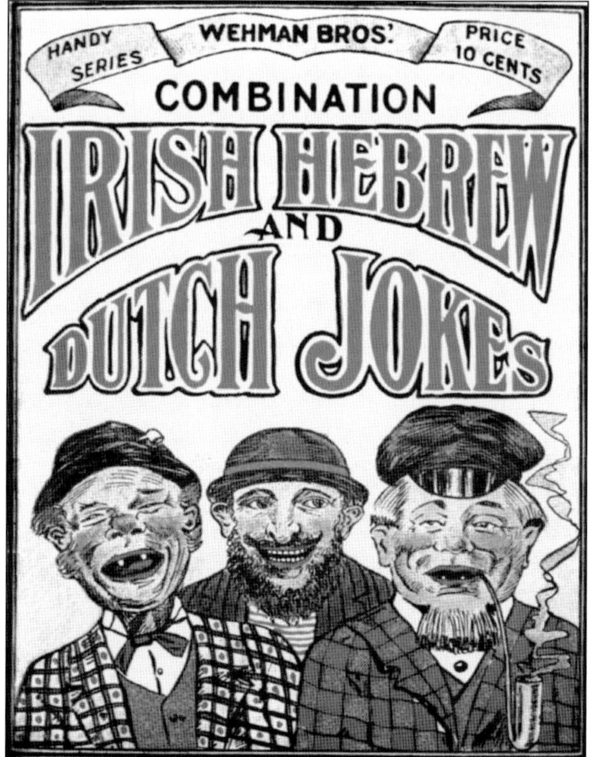

Though African Americans were subjected to the most unrelenting, virulent stereotyping, American stages were a cornucopia of racial, ethnic, and national stereotyping, especially in variety theater where performers could build careers burlesquing particular stereotypes. This 1916 joke book caricatures Jews, Irish, and Germans, referred to here as "Dutch," a bastardization of Deutsch. (Tamiment Library, NYU.)

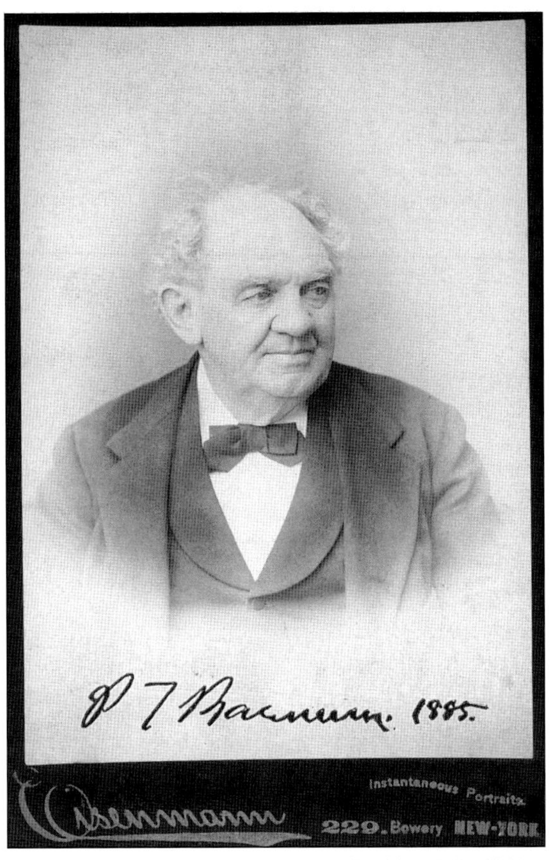

Whether or not showman P.T. Barnum ever said, "There's a sucker born every minute," he proved the point in 1836 when throngs lined up at Bowery and Division Street to see Joice Heth, the supposed 46-pound, 161-year-old former slave nurse to George Washington, father of our country. Popular with audiences, Heth smoked a pipe, sang hymns, and reminisced about baby George. The grueling 10-hour shifts and multi-state touring schedule almost certainly hastened her death. Barnum's other Bowery involvements include writing advertising hype for the Bowery Amphitheatre at 37 Bowery, presenting song and dance acts at the Vauxhall Garden, and marketing bear's grease hair-loss ointment at 101 Bowery. He later spoke at Cooper Union and had this 1885 portrait taken at Charles Eisenmann's studio at 229 Bowery. (Left, estate of Michael Mitchell; below, Somers Historical Society.)

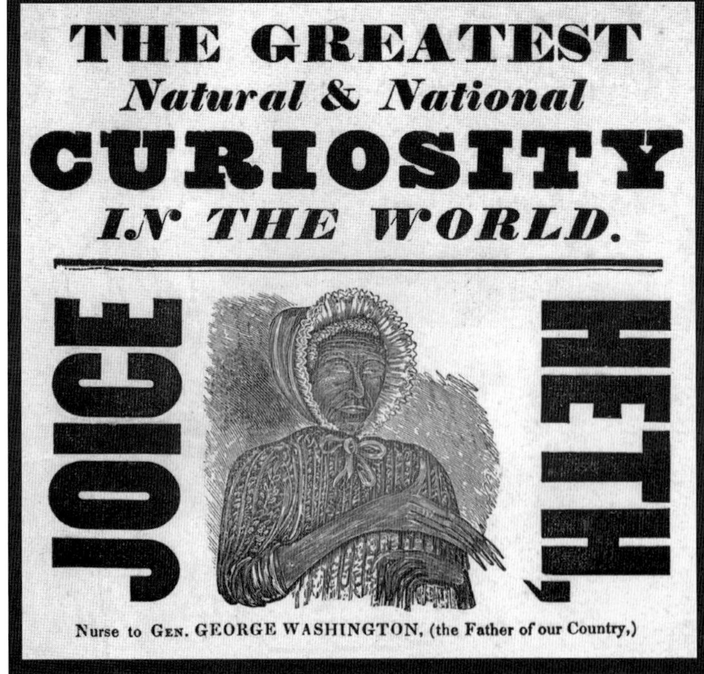

Beautiful and audacious, a sensation in Europe and America, actress-poetess Adah Isaacs Menken (1835–1868), a Bowery favorite, appeared at the Stadt, Bowery, and New Bowery theaters. A semi-nude horseback scene as Ukrainian freedom fighter *Mazeppa* raised eyebrows and brought her fame, as did four marriages (including to boxer John C. Heenan), an affair with elderly writer Alexandre Dumas, and her penchant for androgyny. This photograph was taken by Napoleon Sarony in about 1860. (Huntington Library.)

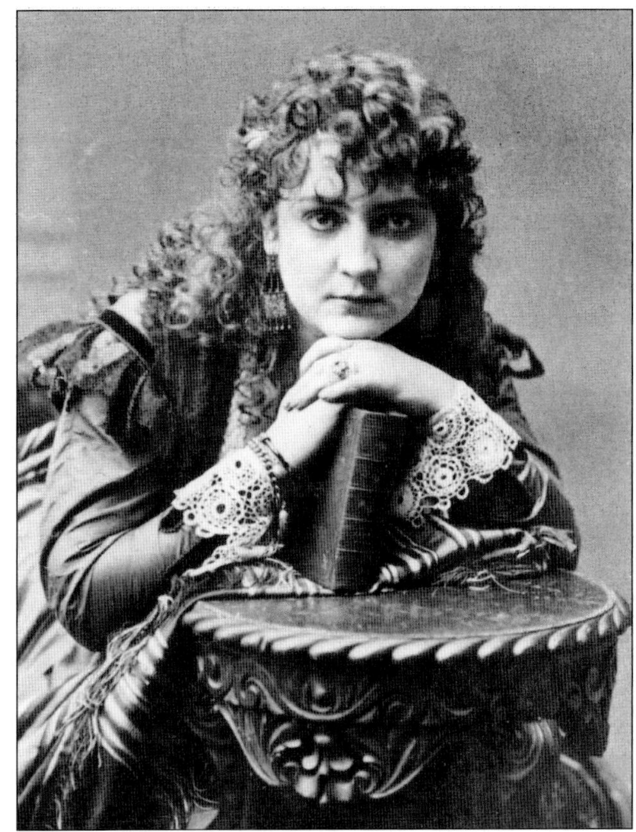

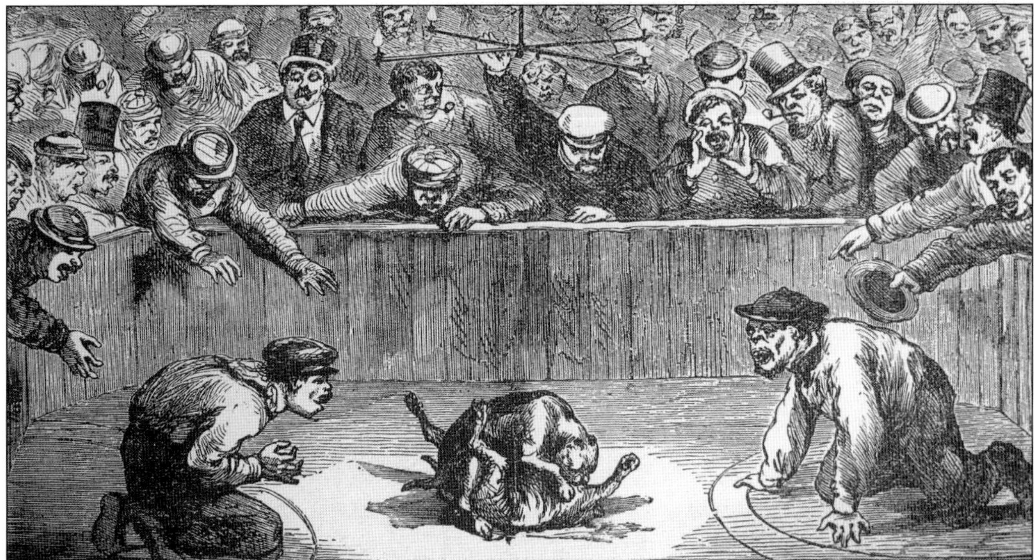

The area's most grim attractions, held in basements, were the vicious dog, cock, and rat pits where men gambled on the fate of warring animals. Writer Lucy Sante says the 1800s' biggest betting blood sport was rat-baiting. This involved dropping dogs into rat-filled pits, with spectators betting on how long it took the dog to kill them. The ASPCA helped outlaw these spectacles. The illustration is from *Lights & Shadows of NY Life*, published in 1872. (DM.)

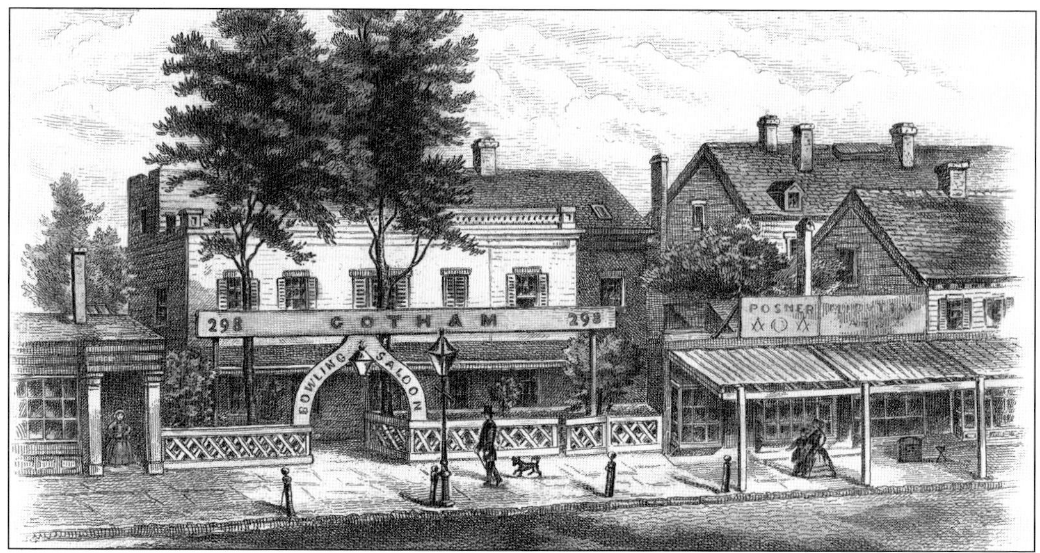

This 1862 lithograph shows the Gotham Inn (also known as Gotham Cottage) at 298 Bowery, a farmhouse-turned-tavern that in 1837 became headquarters for the Gothams, America's first baseball club and the first to write down the game's rules. The National Association of Base Ball Players held its first convention here in 1857. Over the years, bowling, billiards, variety theater, and even a grisly murder happened here. In 1878, it was replaced by a five-story dime museum. (AWC.)

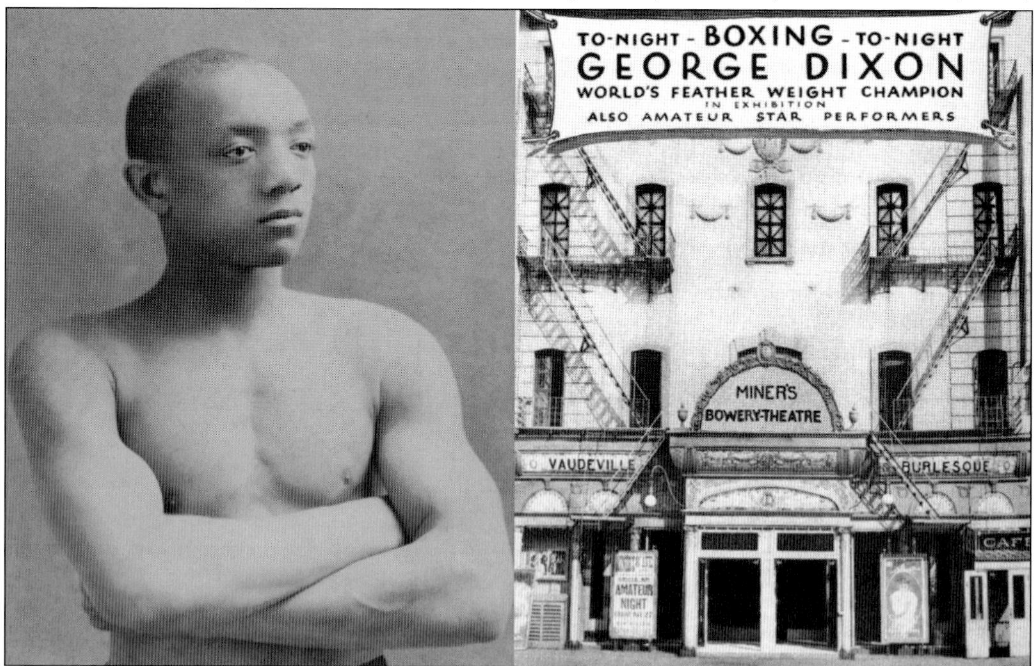

The Bowery nurtured the culture of boxing, both in its 19th-century bare-knuckle days and during its more respectable gloved sport era. In addition to boxing saloons like Owney Geoghegan's, Bowery theatres featured boxing exhibitions. This one, c. 1893, featured Canadian-born George Dixon (1870–1909), the first Black athlete to win a world championship in any sport. The photograph of Dixon is by Elmer Chickering, c. 1890. (Left, Fine Arts Library Harvard; right, Hesburgh Library Notre Dame.)

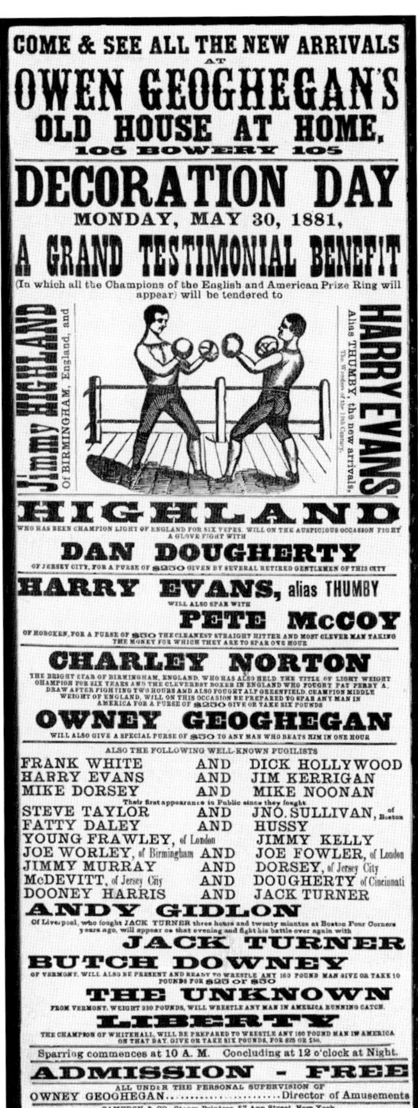

While boxing greats John L. Sullivan, Tom Allen, Joe Coburn, and John Morrissey fought bouts or gave exhibitions on the Bowery, others hung out in its saloons. "Gentleman Jim" Corbett acted in a play on the Bowery, as did Tom Hyer, who also owned a Bowery bar. Former pugilist Owney Geoghegan's boxing saloon advertised America's largest sparring hall, fistic rings on two floors, with semiprofessional bouts in the main hall, and amateur bouts—including women—in the other. One reporter called the mix of liquor and violence "a carnival of debauchery," and in 1883 when children were discovered hanging out there, it was forced to close. To Geoghegan's credit, he paid the passage to America for a lot of English and Irish up-and-coming boxing talent. The c. 1880 photograph of Sullivan is by Jose Maria Mora. (Right, AWC; below, FALH.)

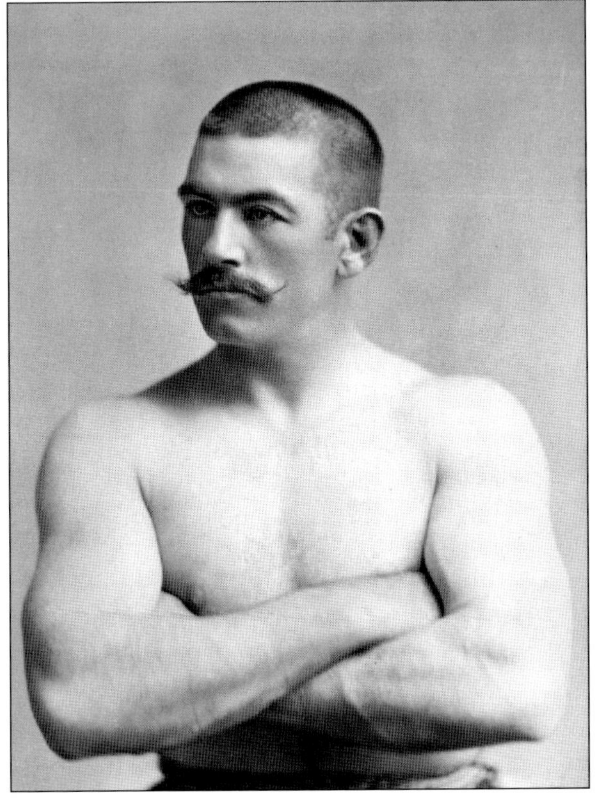

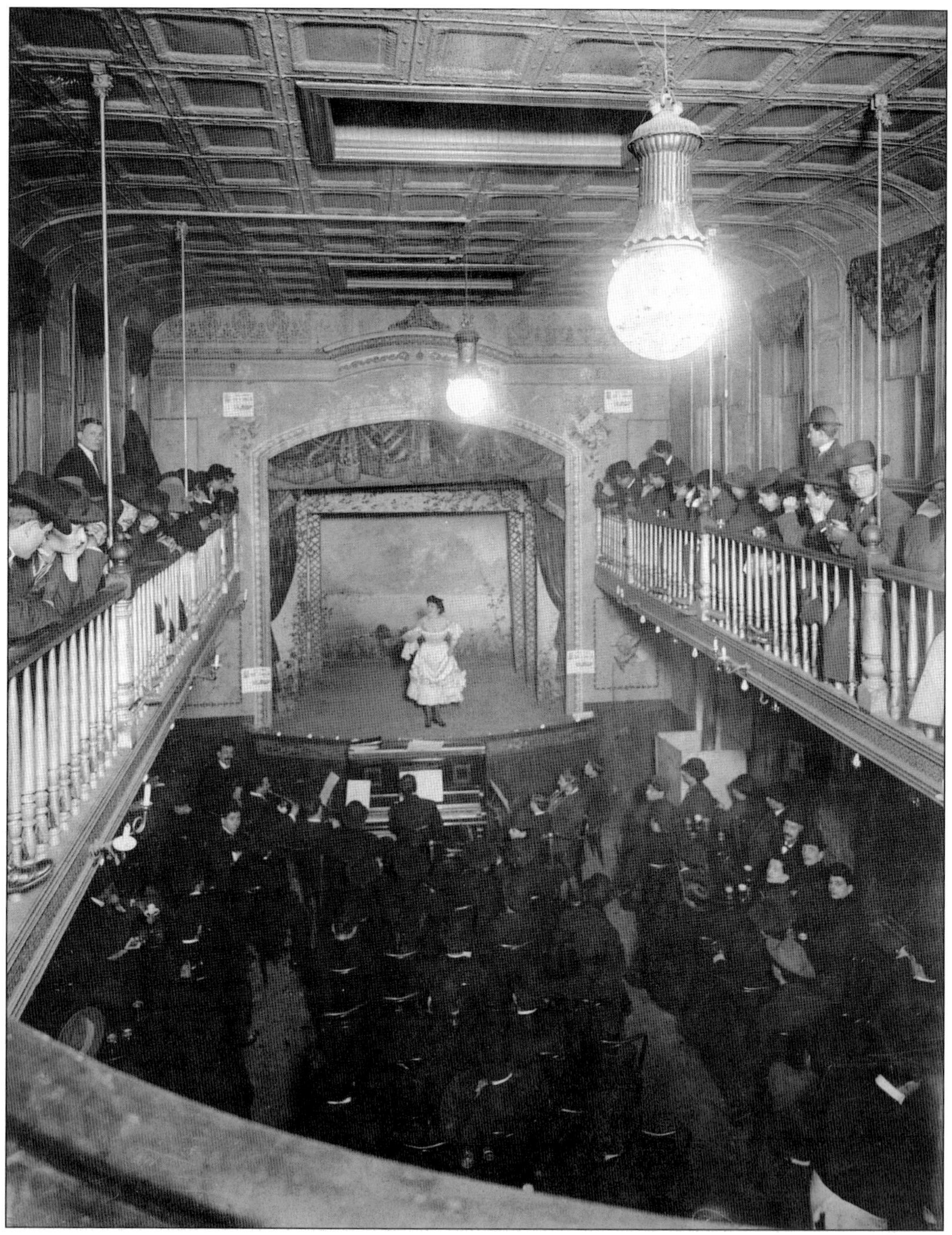

The Bowery concert saloon in this 1890 photograph featured an all-male audience. Because of the drinking and rowdiness, women avoided such places. In Stephen Crane's *Maggie: A Girl of the Streets* (1893), Maggie is taken to a concert saloon by a man who causes her ruin. While boozy, mostly male concert saloons and variety theaters made money, a more profitable, cleaned-up family-friendly approach—called vaudeville—would come to predominate. (NYHS.)

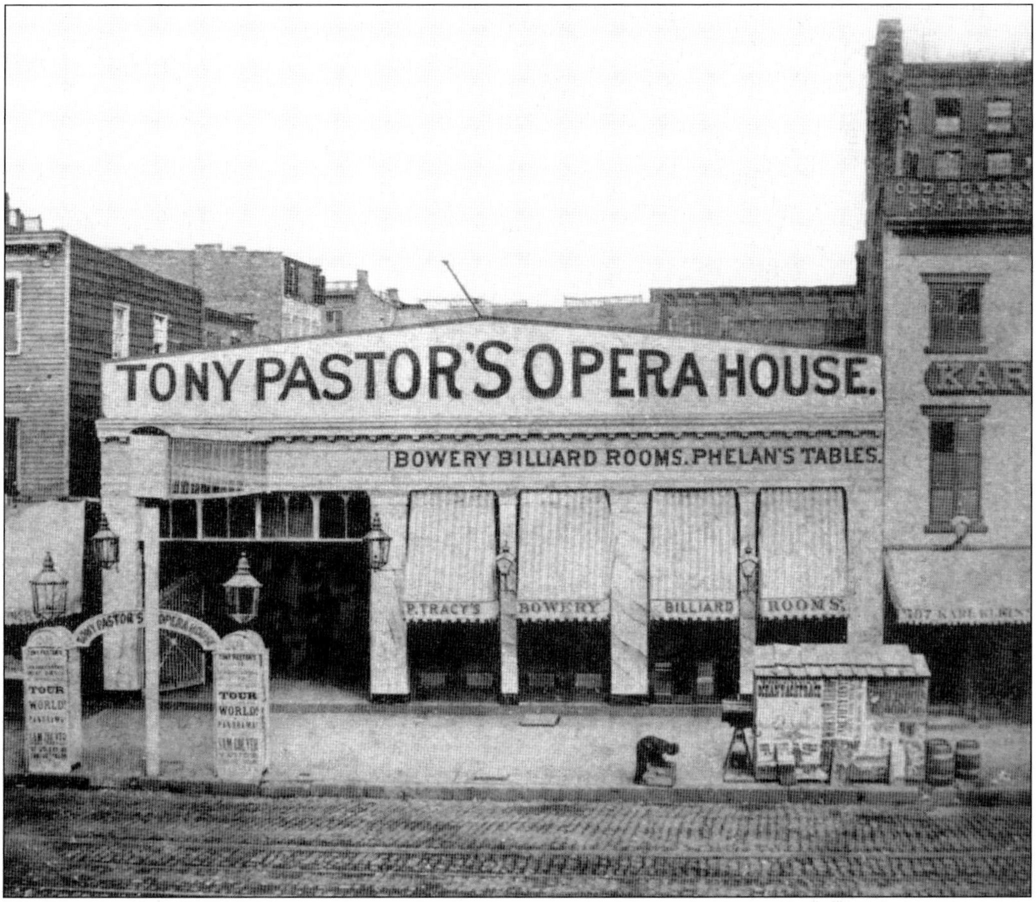

Tony Pastor's Opera House (199-201 Bowery), shown here in about 1870, was the birthplace of vaudeville. It was here, from 1865 to 1875, that Pastor began cleaning up variety theater—removing the liquor, profanity, and bawdiness—and promoting his "Great Family Resort." Shows opened with "The Star-Spangled Banner," and acts included Harrigan & Hart, the "fathers of American musical comedy." Performer-impresario Tony Pastor (1837–1908) was also a songwriter. (AWC.)

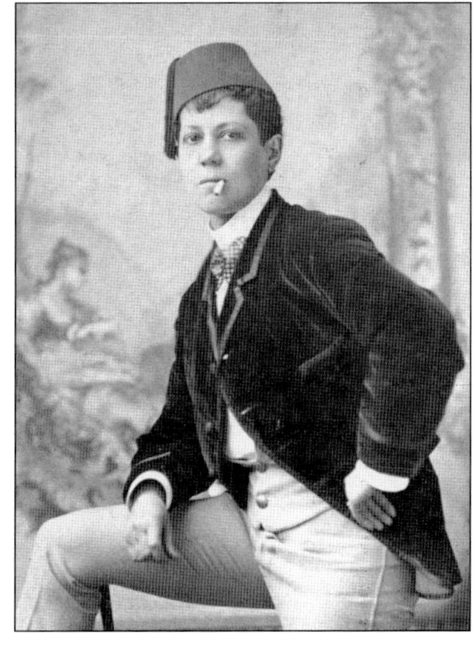

Jersey-born Ella Wesner, seen in this c. 1880 photograph by Napoleon Sarony, was a pioneer male impersonator who started out at Tony Pastor's Opera House on the Bowery and achieved success on two continents. A fine singer-dancer, her lightning-quick costume changes and spot-on caricatures of male types—from street toughs to uptown swells—brought the house down. Wesner also played the Bowery Theatre, People's Theatre, and Miner's Bowery Theatre. (HTC.)

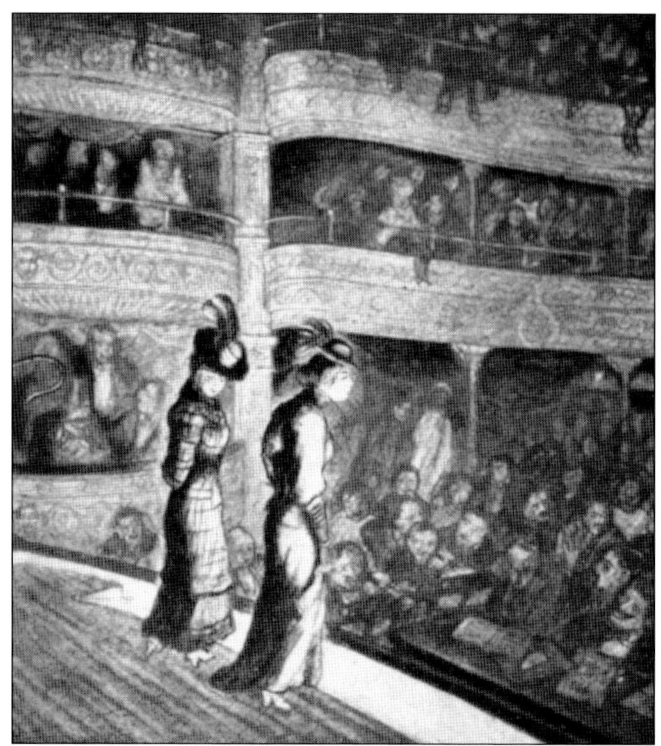

Opened in 1878, Miner's Bowery Theatre at 165-167 Bowery was famous for its Amateur Night and the innovation of the "vaudeville hook," a long shepherd's crook that pulled lousy performers off stage, prompted by spectators shouting, "Get the hook!" Famous performers at Miner's included W.C. Fields, Al Jolson, Weber & Fields, Kitty O'Neil, Saharet, and the magician Houdini Brothers. This illustration, "Amateur Night at Miner's," is by Glenn O. Coleman. (DM.)

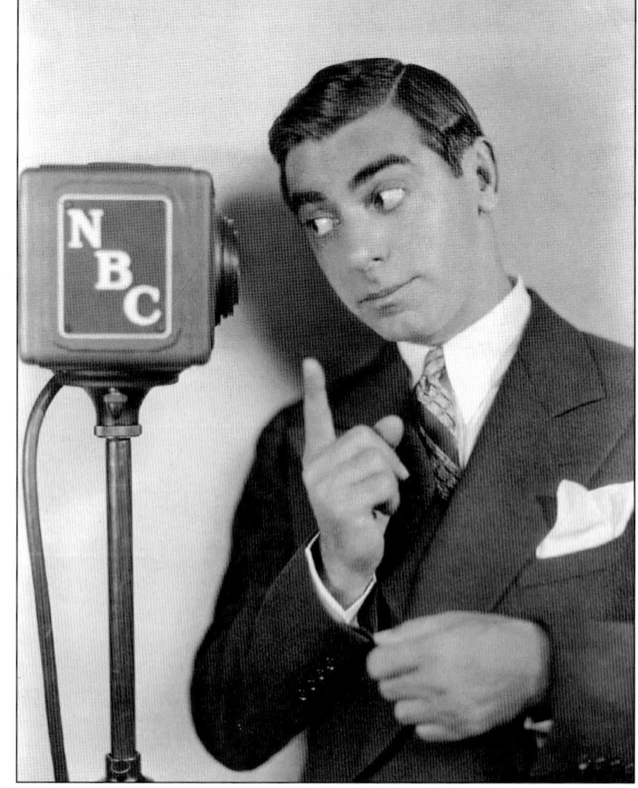

One Amateur Night success story at Miner's was Isidore Itzkowitz, who won the prize in 1908. Son of Russian Jewish immigrants, as actor-comedian-singer-songwriter-dancer Eddie Cantor (1892–1964) he became a major stage, screen, radio, and recording star. Though his performance history included blackface, which mars our memory of him, Cantor was a huge figure. His philanthropic work included creating the name "March of Dimes" for the fight against polio. (Margaret Herrick Library.)

A star of stage, screen, and radio, Ukrainian-born actress-comedian-singer Sophie Tucker (1886–1966), shown here c. 1930, was known as "the Last of the Red-Hot Mamas." She credited her early work in Bowery cafes with teaching her how to put a song "over." (NYPL-BRC.)

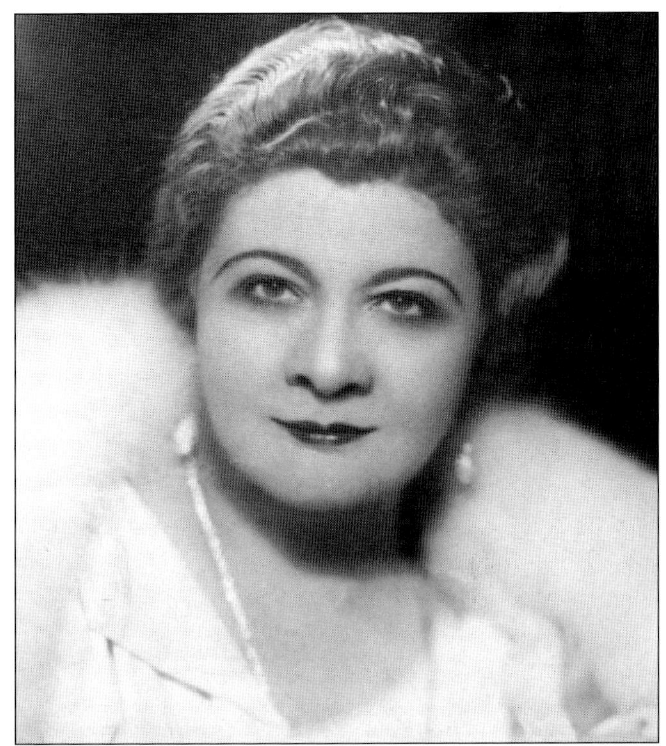

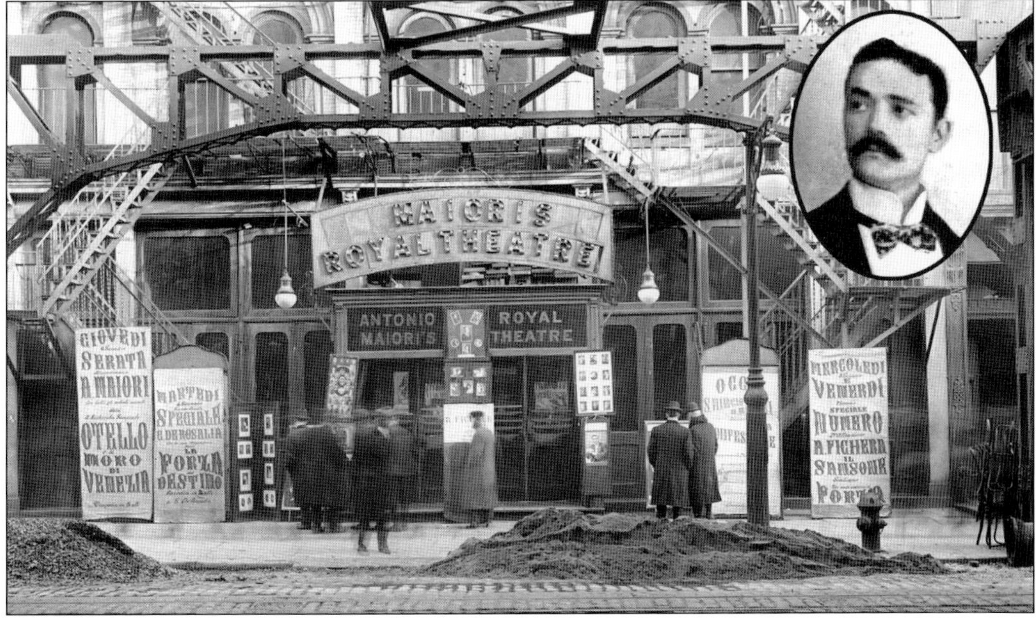

Italian Theater gained a foothold on the Bowery through the handsome, charismatic figure of Antonio Maiori. His 1902 appearance as Cellini at Bowery's 3,500-seat Windsor Theatre had the city's elite 400 swooning. After socialite Louisine Havemeyer pronounced him "the greatest tragedian in the world," they descended on the Bowery in slumming parties. Italian-born actor-producer Maiori later established Italian theaters at 138, 235, and 165 Bowery, seen here in 1916. (Theatre photograph, AWC; inset of Maiori, NYPL-BRC.)

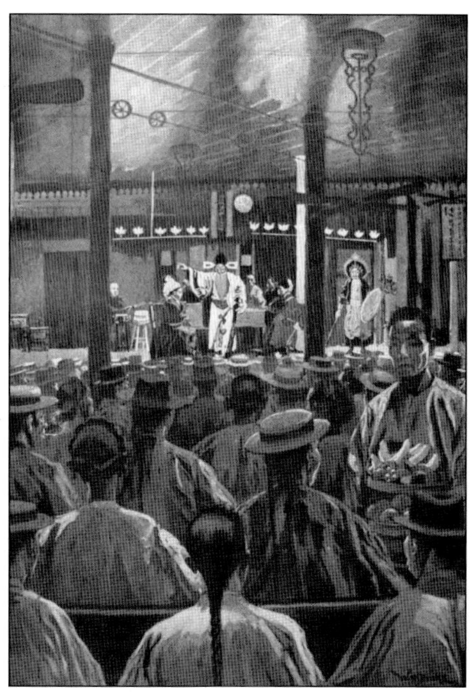

In 1893, a Chinese Opera House opened at 5-7 Doyers Street, near Bowery, and became a sensation with tourists who found the language, music, colorful costumes, and aesthetics fascinating. For the Chinatown community, separated from families and forced into a bachelor society by the long-standing Chinese Exclusion Act, it was an exciting social scene and a respite from hard work. The illustration by W.H. Drake is from *Century Magazine* Vol. 31, 1897. (NYPL-MD.)

From 1858 to 1945, the aptly named People's Theatre at 199-201 Bowery witnessed an astonishing multi-cultural procession that reflects both neighborhood changes and changes in popular culture: German concert hall, minstrel theatre, vaudeville, Yiddish theater, Italian opera, plays by Ireland's Dion Boucicault, appearances by boxer John L. Sullivan, juggler W.C. Fields, French magician Alexander "Herrmann the Great," and a racy final 10 years as a neon-lit burlesque house. This 1902 photograph by George F. Arata shows 193-203 Bowery. (MCNY.)

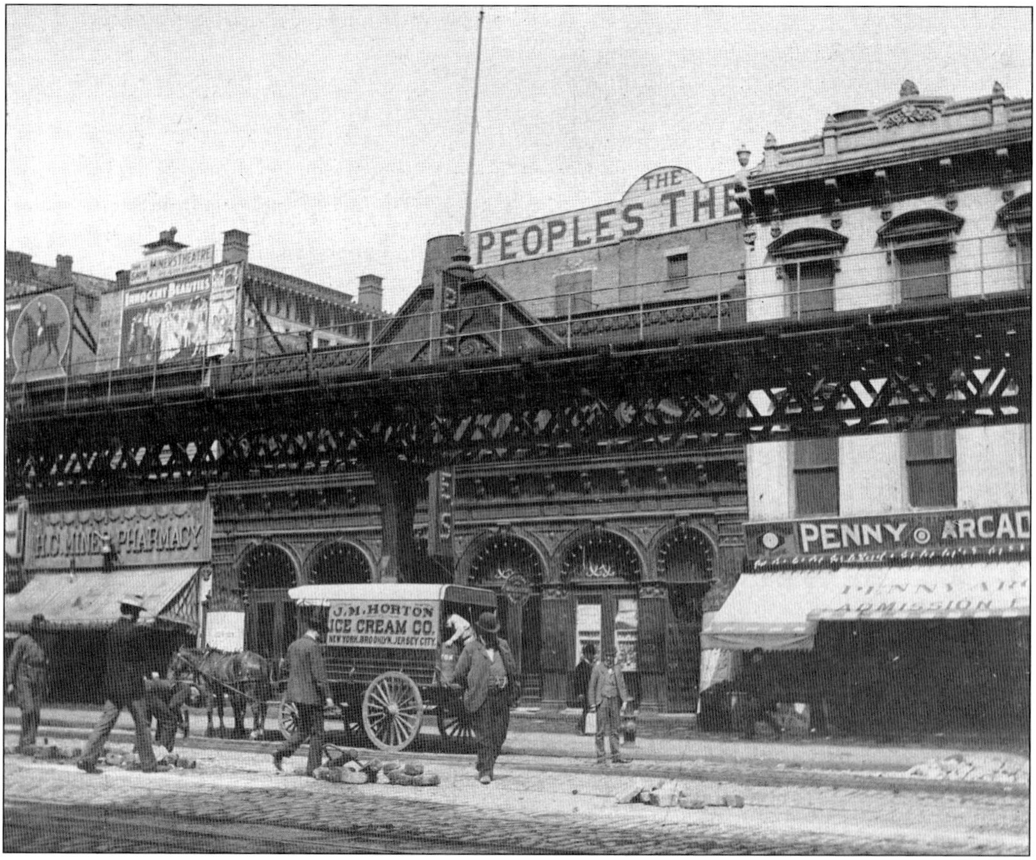

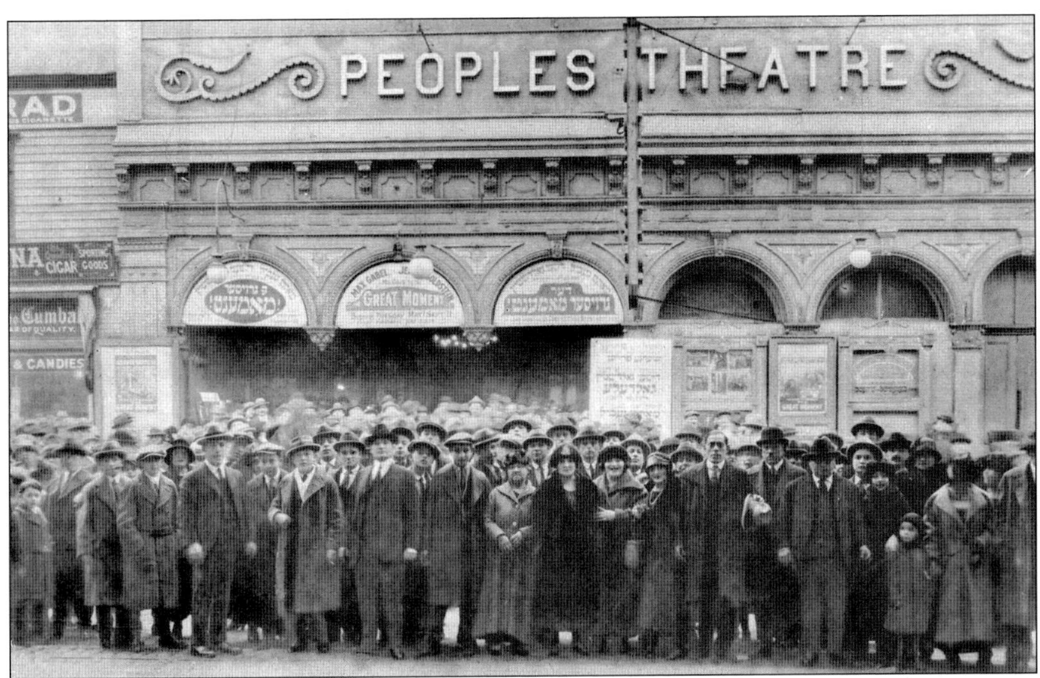

In the 1880s, the Bowery became Yiddish theater's first American home, including four theaters with thousands of seats: the Windsor, London, Thalia, and People's Theatre, seen here in 1925. According to Joyce Mendelsohn, "Jewish immigrants came here to escape poverty, tedium and despair and immerse themselves in the comedy, tragedy and spectacle unfolding onstage." Key figures included Russian playwright Joseph Gordin, and Ukrainian-born actors Jacob Adler, Bertha Kalich, and Boris Thomashefsky. (Forward Association.)

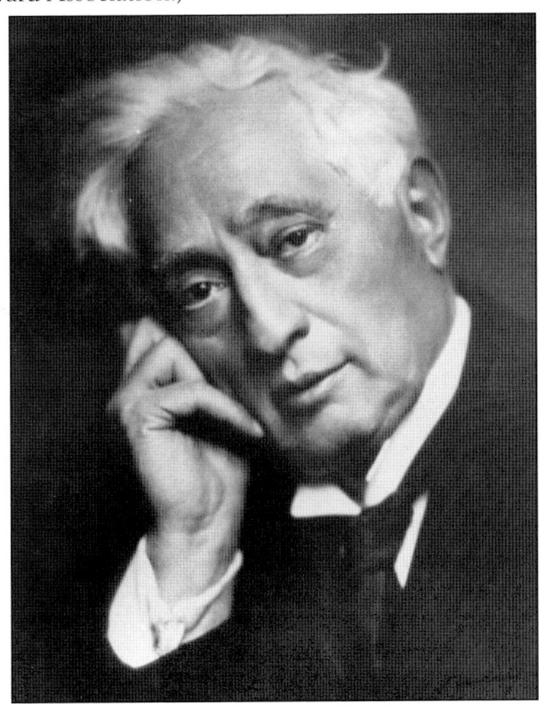

Actor Jacob Adler (1855–1926) became a Yiddish theater legend on the Bowery. Roles included the title characters in Shakespeare's *King Lear* and *The Merchant of Venice.* In 1903, Adler's enormous Grand Theatre opened on Grand near Bowery as America's first purpose-built Yiddish theatre. Adler also established an acting dynasty, most enduringly through daughter Stella Adler, the teacher of Marlon Brando, who popularized the Stanislavski acting technique. The photograph is from about 1920. (NYPL-BRC.)

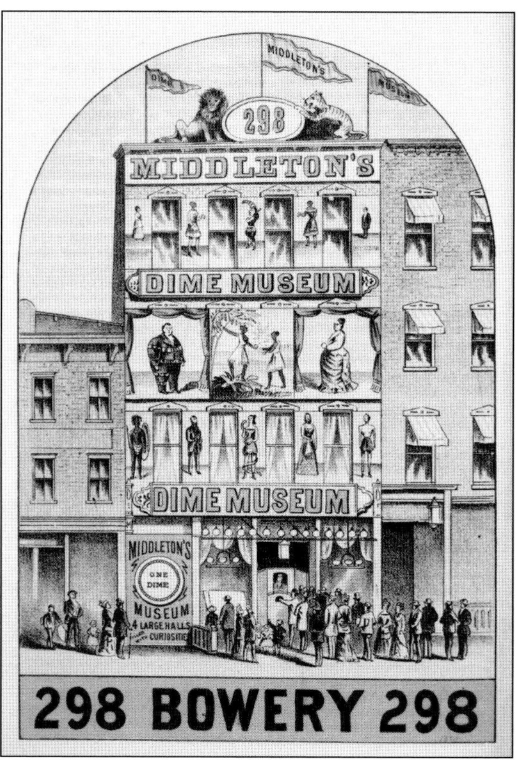

One long-forgotten 19th-century entertainment phenomenon, popularized on the Bowery, was the dime museum. A pint-sized version of Barnum's American Museum on Broadway, dime museums featured sensationalistic, sometimes fraudulent exhibitions, and an auditorium for lectures and stage shows. Exhibits included menageries, dioramas, waxworks, and people with physical abnormalities. Though exploited, these so-called "freaks" often had greater salaries and job security. Some museums were fronts for gambling or prostitution. This lithograph is from 1885. (HTC.)

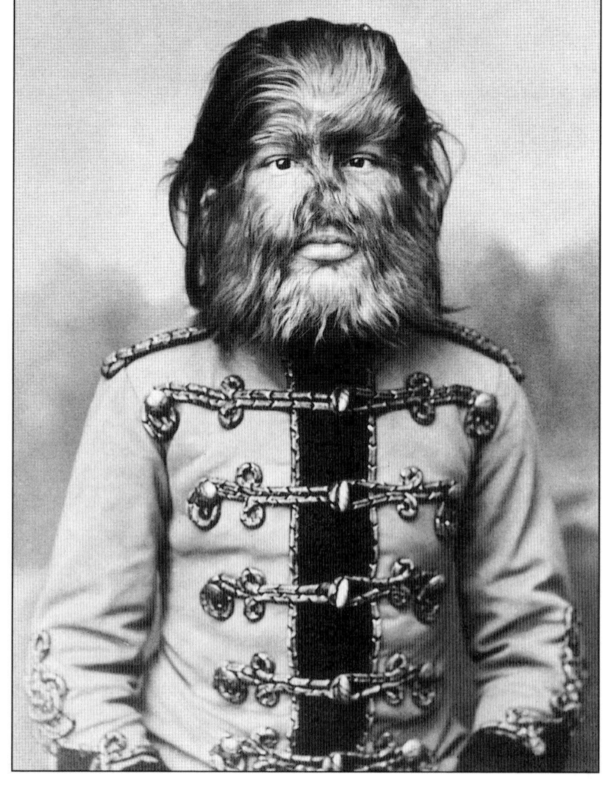

Jo-Jo "the Dog-faced Boy" was the dime museum circuit's most enduringly popular attraction. Born in Russia with hypertrichosis, Fedor Jeftichew (1868–1904) was brought to America by P.T. Barnum. An elaborate wild-man narrative was concocted, but in reality, Fedor spoke three languages, commanded a high salary, and was nobody's fool. Appearances included the Gaiety Museum (138 Bowery) and Alexander's Musee (317 Bowery). This c. 1884 photograph was taken by Charles Eisenmann at 229 Bowery. (Estate of Michael Mitchell.)

From 1879 to 1893, German immigrant Charles Eisenmann, the premier photographer of sideshow exotics, lived and worked at 229 Bowery, the c. 1830 Federal-era house now part of the Bowery Mission. Headliners like J.D. Avery ("the Living Skeleton") and John Hanson Craig ("the World's Heaviest Man") went there to get mass quantities of cabinet card portraits, which sold well after shows. This 1879 photograph shows Eisenmann with the giants, Captain Martin Van Buren Bates ("the Kentucky Giant") and his wife, Anna Swan Bates. (AWC.)

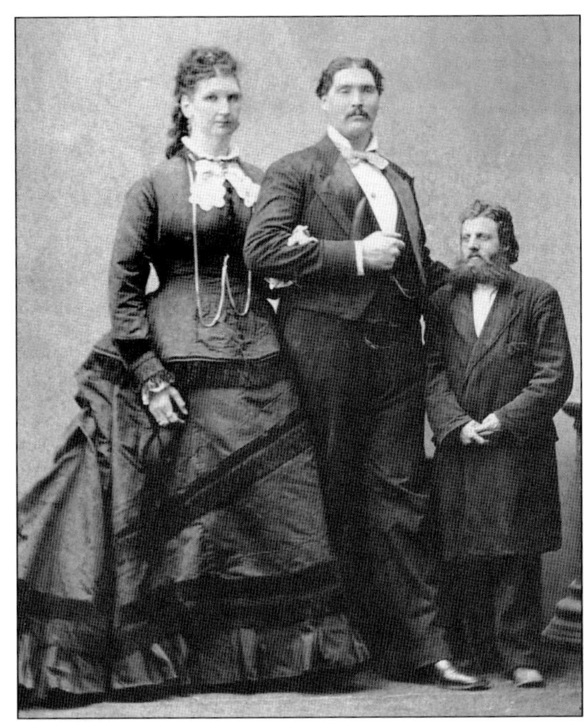

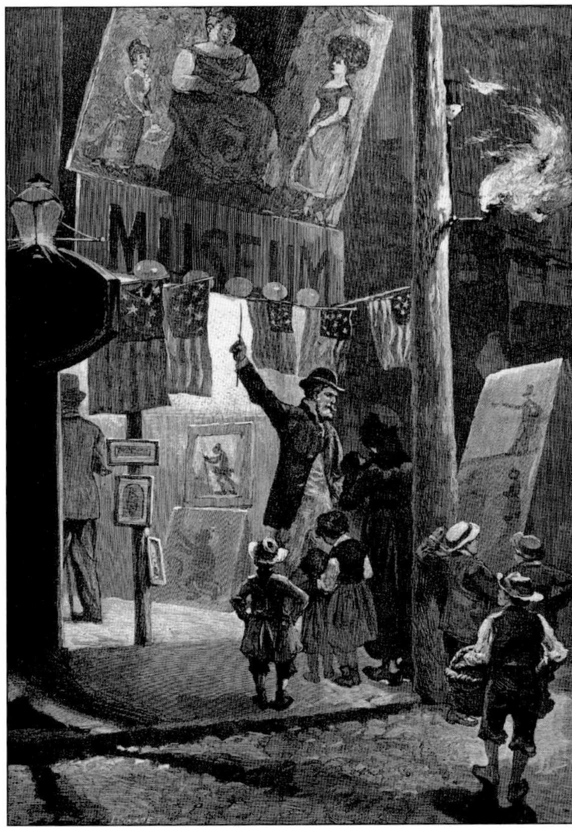

Heavily reliant on hype, hyperbole, and titillation, no dime museum was complete without a persuasive barker out front to catch the ears and eyes of passersby. How else could one market Chinese mermaids, a three-headed songstress, a petrified man, or Flossie La Blanche, "the female Hercules." With multiple exhibits on multiple floors and separate charges for stage shows, there was a lot to sell. This illustration is from *Harper's Weekly*, February 26, 1881. (LOC.)

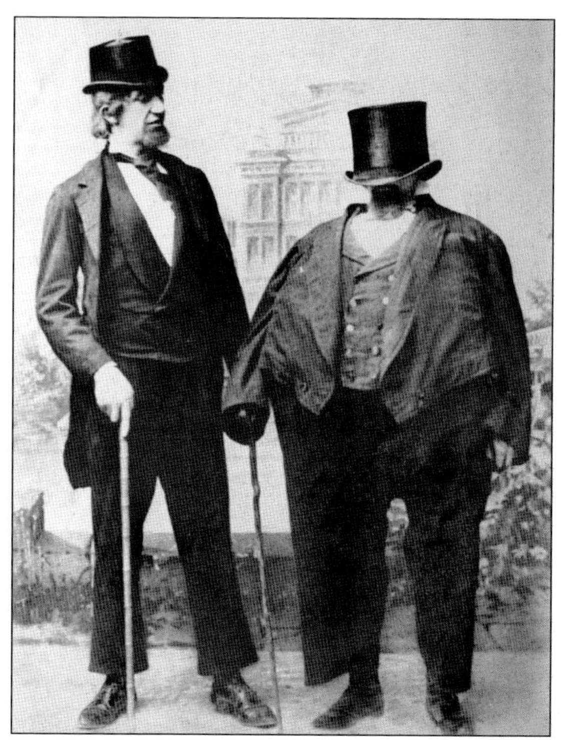

Weber & Fields were vaudeville's greatest comic duo. Sons of Jewish Polish immigrants, Lew Fields (1867–1941) and Joe Weber (1867–1942) had performed in Bowery dime museums by age 10 and, before age 30, owned a Broadway theatre. Dialect comedians, their violent knockabout "Dutch Act," which burlesqued German immigrants, premiered at the Globe Dime Museum (298 Bowery) and made them famous. Their dumb-and-dumber antics anticipated Laurel & Hardy, Gleason & Carney, and other comedic duos. (Marc Fields Collection.)

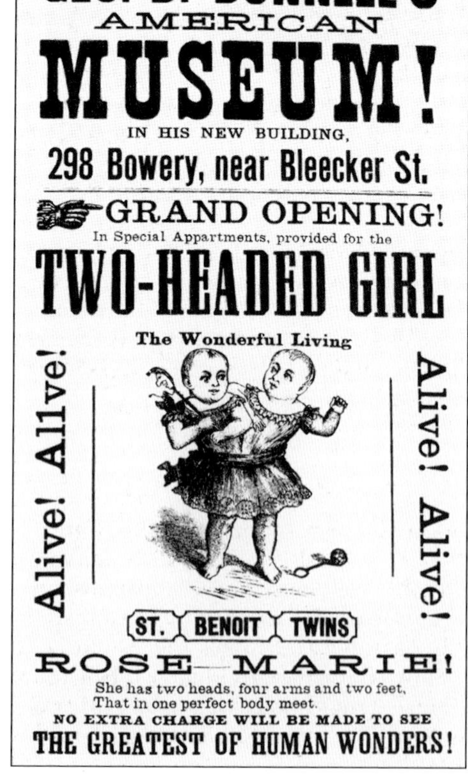

Exhibiting an actual set of conjoined twins should have been sensation enough, but note how Barnum protégé George Bunnell promotes these girls as one girl with two heads (i.e., a two-headed monster). Bunnell had also operated a museum at 103-105 Bowery, where, in 1876, he originated the idea of lowering admission from a quarter to a dime, thus the term "dime museum." This poster is from February 22, 1879. (HTC.)

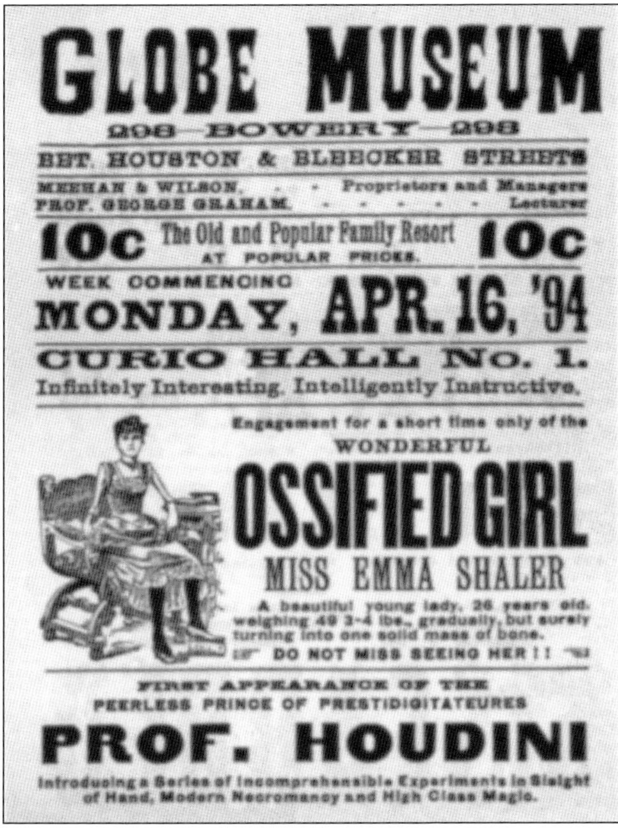

GLOBE MUSEUM
298—BOWERY—298
BET. HOUSTON & BLEECKER STREETS
MEEHAN & WILSON, - - Proprietors and Managers
PROF. GEORGE GRAHAM, - - - - - - Lecturer
10c The Old and Popular Family Resort AT POPULAR PRICES. 10c
WEEK COMMENCING
MONDAY, APR. 16, '94
CURIO HALL No. 1.
Infinitely Interesting, Intelligently Instructive.
Engagement for a short time only of the
WONDERFUL
OSSIFIED GIRL
MISS EMMA SHALER
A beautiful young lady, 26 years old, weighing 49 3-4 lbs., gradually, but surely turning into one solid mass of bone.
DO NOT MISS SEEING HER ! !
FIRST APPEARANCE OF THE
PEERLESS PRINCE OF PRESTIDIGITATEURES
PROF. HOUDINI
Introducing a Series of Incomprehensible Experiments in Sleight of Hand, Modern Necromancy and High Class Magic.

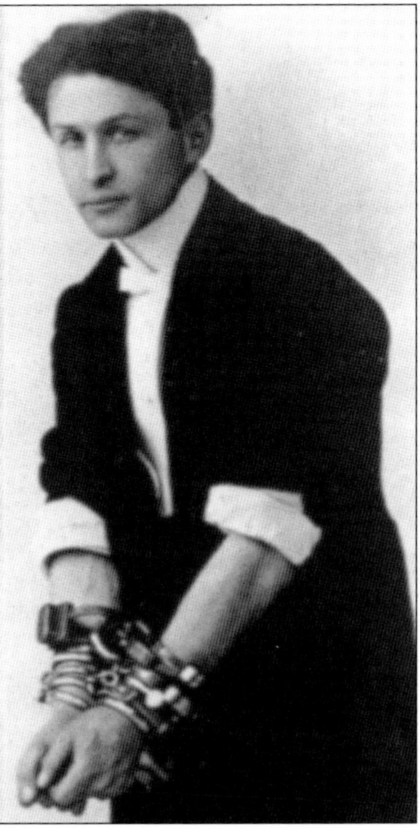

Legendary magician and escape artist Harry Houdini was 20 and already a Bowery veteran when he appeared at this dime museum in 1894, having previously appeared at Miner's Bowery Theatre as one half of the Houdini Brothers. A Hungarian rabbi's son, Erich Weisz's stage name referenced French magician Robert-Houdin and American magician Harry Keller. Magicians J.H. Anderson and Alexander "Herrmann the Great" were also popular at Bowery theatres. This photograph is from around 1905. (Left, Harry Ransom Collection; right, LOC.)

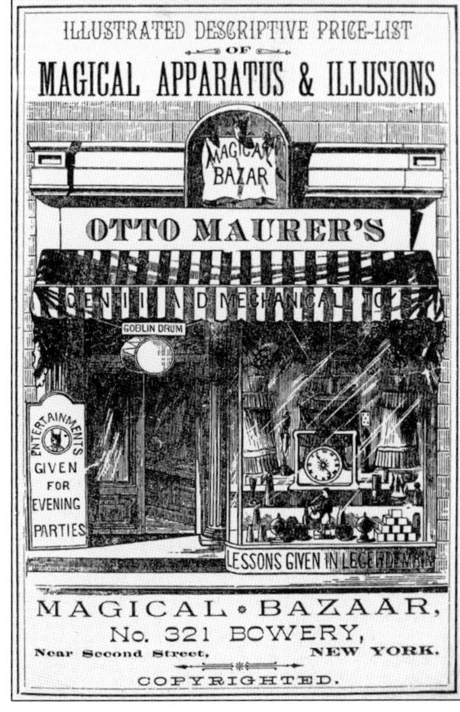

For over 20 years in the late 1800s, Otto Maurer's Magical Bazaar at 321 Bowery made and sold magic and juggling apparatus, offered magic classes, and was an unofficial magicians' clubhouse. It was here that the "Wizard of the Bowery," German-born Maurer is believed to have originated the famous back palm card trick, which he picked up from a Mexican magician who passed through his shop. (Tom Klem.)

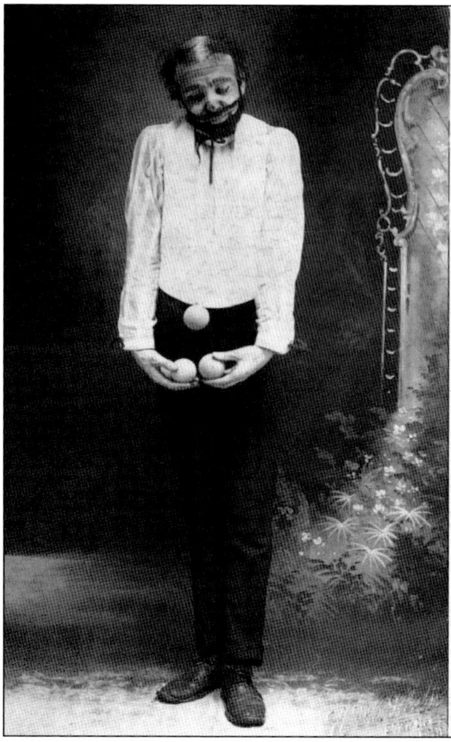

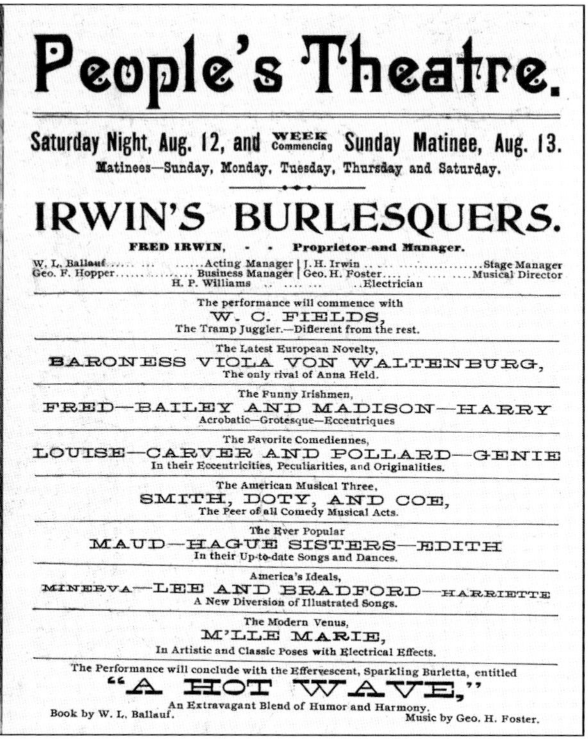

People's Theatre.

Saturday Night, Aug. 12, and WEEK Commencing Sunday Matinee, Aug. 13.

Matinees—Sunday, Monday, Tuesday, Thursday and Saturday.

IRWIN'S BURLESQUERS.

FRED IRWIN, - - Proprietor and Manager.

W. L. Ballauf .... Acting Manager | J. H. Irwin .... Stage Manager
Geo. F. Hopper .... Business Manager | Geo. H. Foster .... Musical Director
H. P. Williams .... Electrician

The performance will commence with
W. C. FIELDS,
The Tramp Juggler.—Different from the rest.

The Latest European Novelty,
BARONESS VIOLA VON WALTENBURG,
The only rival of Anna Held.

The Funny Irishmen,
FRED—BAILEY AND MADISON—HARRY
Acrobatic—Grotesque—Eccentriques

The Favorite Comediennes,
LOUISE—CARVER AND POLLARD—GENIE
In their Eccentricities, Peculiarities, and Originalities.

The American Musical Three,
SMITH, DOTY, AND COE,
The Peer of all Comedy Musical Acts.

The Ever Popular
MAUD—HAGUE SISTERS—EDITH
In their Up-to-date Songs and Dances.

America's Ideals,
MINERVA—LEE AND BRADFORD—HARRIETTE
A New Diversion of Illustrated Songs.

The Modern Venus,
M'LLE MARIE,
In Artistic and Classic Poses with Electrical Effects.

The Performance will conclude with the Effervescent, Sparkling Burletta, entitled
"A HOT WAVE,"
An Extravagant Blend of Humor and Harmony.
Book by W. L. Ballauf. Music by Geo. H. Foster.

Legendary film comedian W.C. Fields (1880–1946) rose to fame through his juggling, performing while 18 and 19 at the Bowery's Gaiety and Globe dime museums and the London, People's, and Miner's Bowery theaters. Fields said, "It seemed that I did my act every 5 minutes, all through the day and half the night . . . gaining plenty of practice." The photograph is from about 1900, and the poster is from 1899. (Left, MHL; right, AWC.)

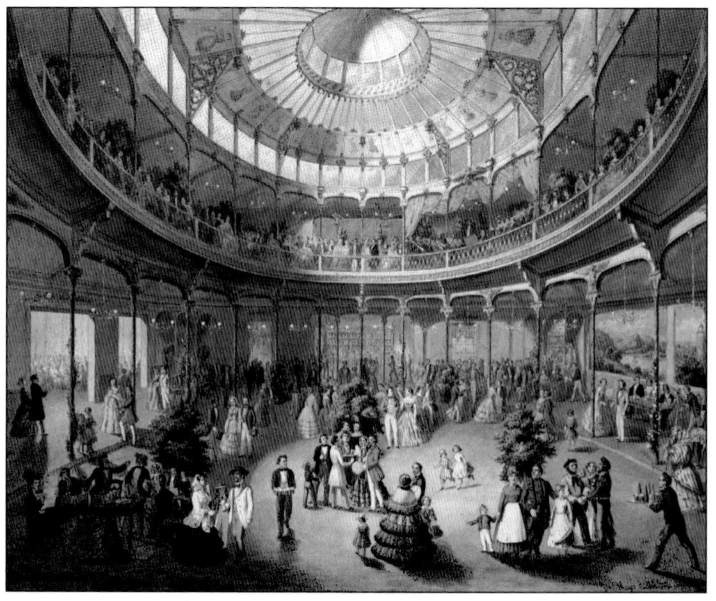

The German Winter Garden (Volks Garten) at 45 Bowery, seen in this 1856 Fritz Meyer painting, was designed by Henry Hoffmann when Bowery was the social hub of the city's Kleindeutschland (Little Germany), then the third largest concentration of Germans in the world. It was one of many stately German theaters, banks, and biergartens on the Bowery. Several works by Mozart and Wagner had their American premieres in those theaters. (Metropolitan Museum of Art.)

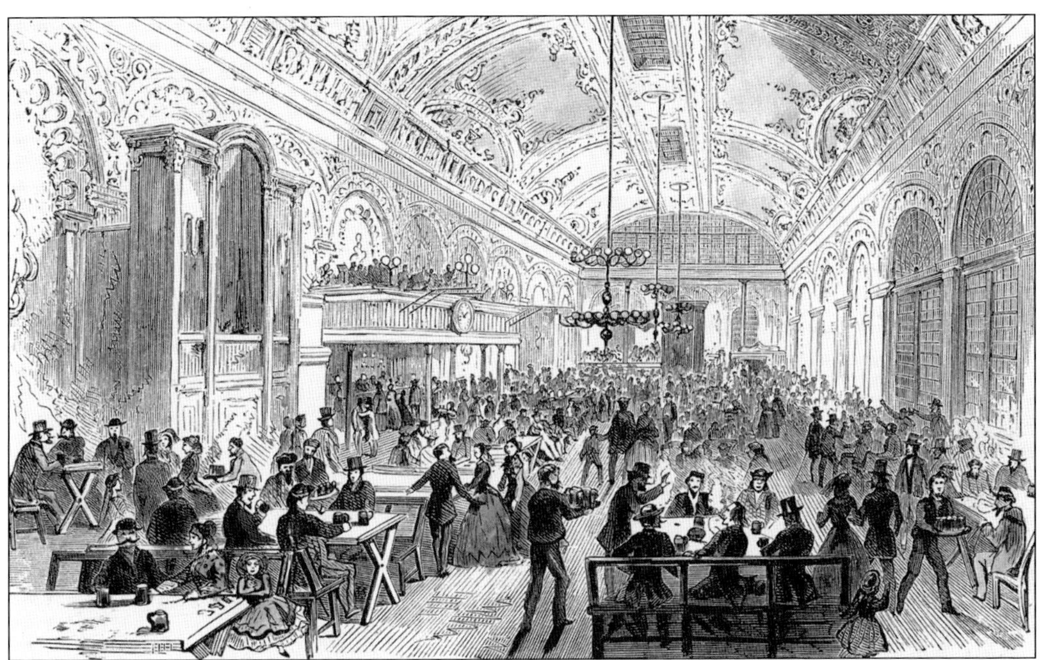

Built in 1858, the skylit Atlantic Garden, seen here in 1870, was the city's most popular German beer garden. A gathering place for Bohemians, it was one of the Bowery's few family-friendly night spots, with a restaurant, bowling alley, billiard tables, an endless flow of lager, and a famous all-ladies orchestra. Another big attraction was its *orchestrion*, an 18-foot-tall mechanical music box. A popular after-theater spot, customers included Shakespearean actor Edwin Booth. According to David Freeland, the Atlantic Garden "was largely free of the prejudice and class stratification that typified costlier establishments on Broadway." Its patrons included nationalities from all over the world. The Atlantic Garden survived for over 50 years, though it switched to Yiddish vaudeville and a 1,200-seat boxing arena before converting to a movie theater in 1915. The orchestra illustration is from 1886. (Above, AWC; below, NYPL-MD.)

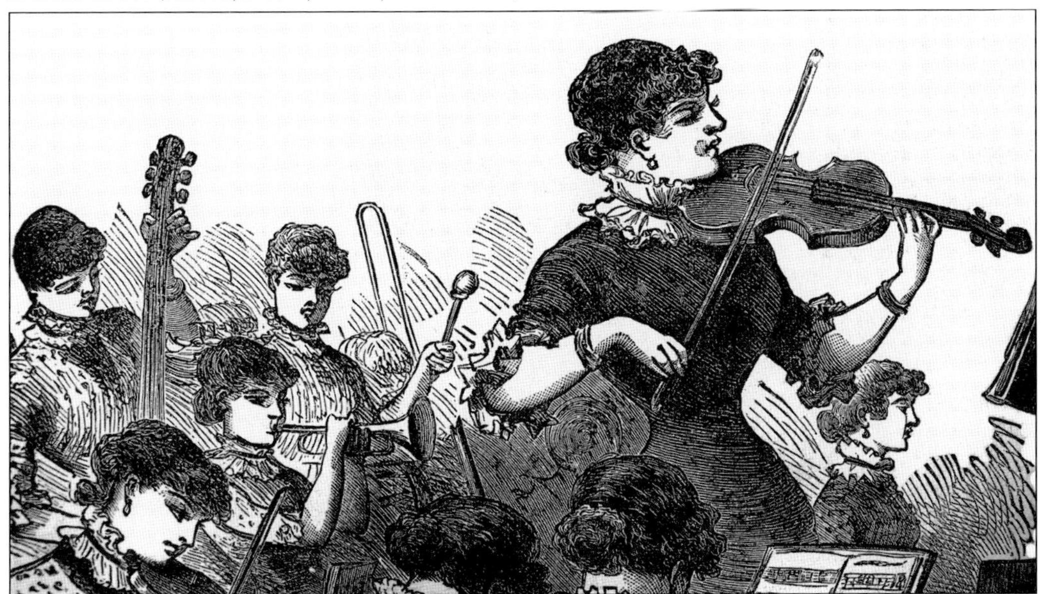

SEE

"CHINATOWN'S"

ORIENTAL RESTAURANTS
JOSS HOUSES
GAMBLING DENS
OPIUM JOINTS
THEATRES

"LITTLE ITALY"

PUSH CARTS
FRUIT STANDS
STREET PIANOS

THIS FEATURE ATTRACTION IN ADDITION TO THE REGBULAR PROGRAM.

"TOMBS PRISON"

ARCADE

DECEMBER 15TH, ONE DAY ONLY.

"New York's Chinatown AND THE Bowery"

A COMPLETE WORK ON THE FAMOUS EAST SIDE, WITH ALL ITS PECULIAR AND INTERESTING TYPES, ITS NARROW STREETS, BUSTLING THRONGS, CROWDED TENEMENTS, SQUALID LODGING HOUSES, TIRESOME SWEAT SHOPS AND ALL ITS LIGHTS AND SHADOWS.

"I am the White Mayor of Chinatown"
--'Chuck' Connors

SEE

"THE BOWERY'S"

ATLANTIC GARDEN
KELLEY'S DANCE HALL
BARNEY FLYN'S CAFE
STEVE BRODY'S PLACE
FLEISCHMAN'S BREAD LINE

"THE GETTO'S"

NARROW STREETS
CROWDED TENEMENTS
PAWN SHOPS

THESE PICTURES ARE FULLY EXPLAINED BY A COMPETENT LECTURER

"FIVE POINTS"

Though the Arcade's location is unknown, this ad for its Bowery/Chinatown slide show is likely from the 1890s. The stirring, colorful assortment of sites gives a good indication of why this district was such a wildly popular and fascinating destination. (AWC.)

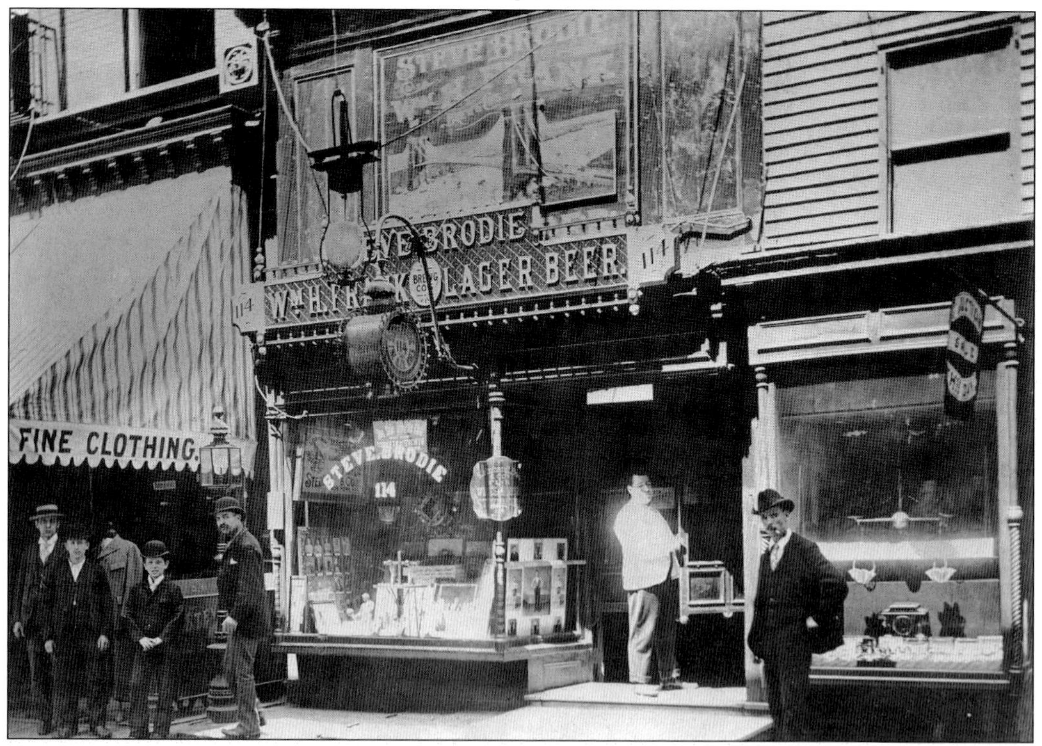

One popular attraction was the saloon of daredevil folk hero Steve Brodie (1861–1901), allegedly the first to survive a jump off the Brooklyn Bridge. Undertaken on a bet, the stunt brought the former newsboy and bootblack instant fame, paid off gambling debts, and got him his own saloon and a performing career. Brodie's 114 Bowery saloon, seen here in 1890, was popular with boxers including Terry McGovern and Tom Sharkey. (NYHS.)

The strutting embodiment of the Bowery itself, Chuck Connors's staged-to-shock Bowery-Chinatown "slumming tours" included roughneck bars and opium dens. The self-described "Mayor of Chinatown," his annual Chinatown Ball attracted society swells and dance couplings that sometimes crossed racial barriers. Connors (right) is pictured c. 1900 outside Barney Flynn's Saloon, his headquarters at 20 Bowery. Connors gave an early career boost to songwriter Irving Berlin. (AWC.)

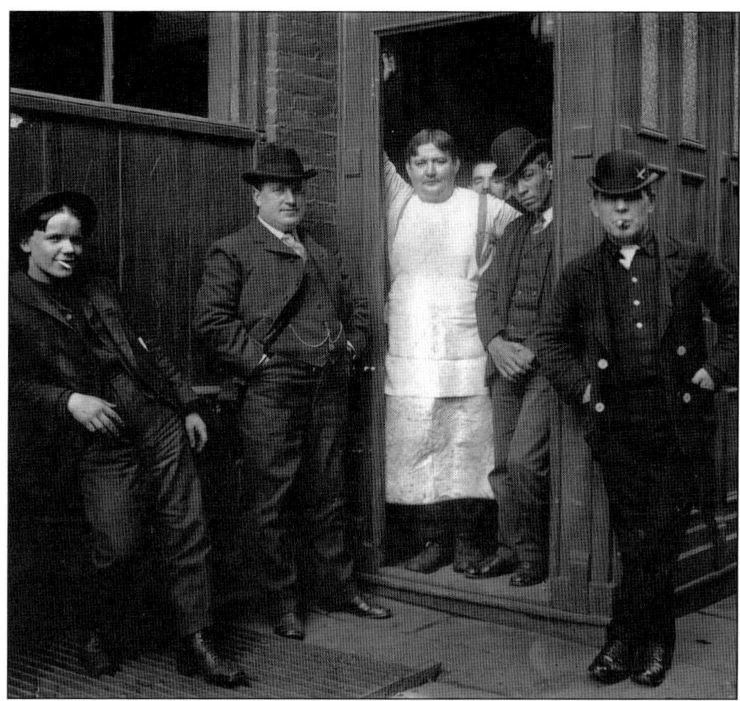

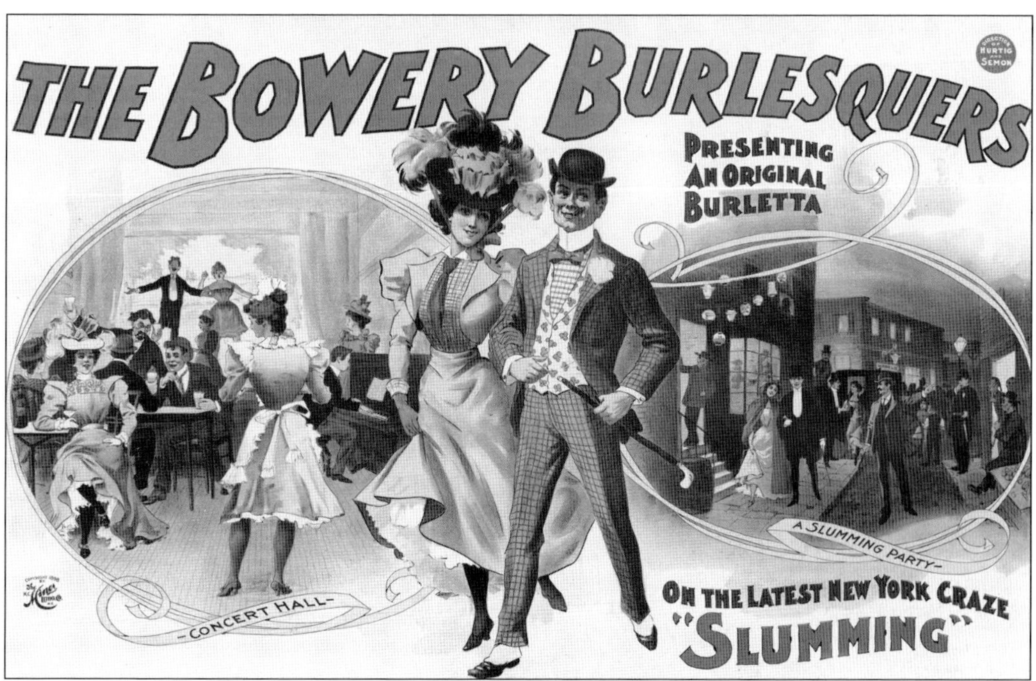

In the 1890s, slumming tours, in which well-heeled uptowners and tourists visited the tenements and social scene of the laboring class, became a phenomenon both here and in Britain. This 1898 theater poster shows an elegant slumming party on the right, a flamboyantly dressed Bowery couple in the center, and a racy concert saloon on the left. (LOC.)

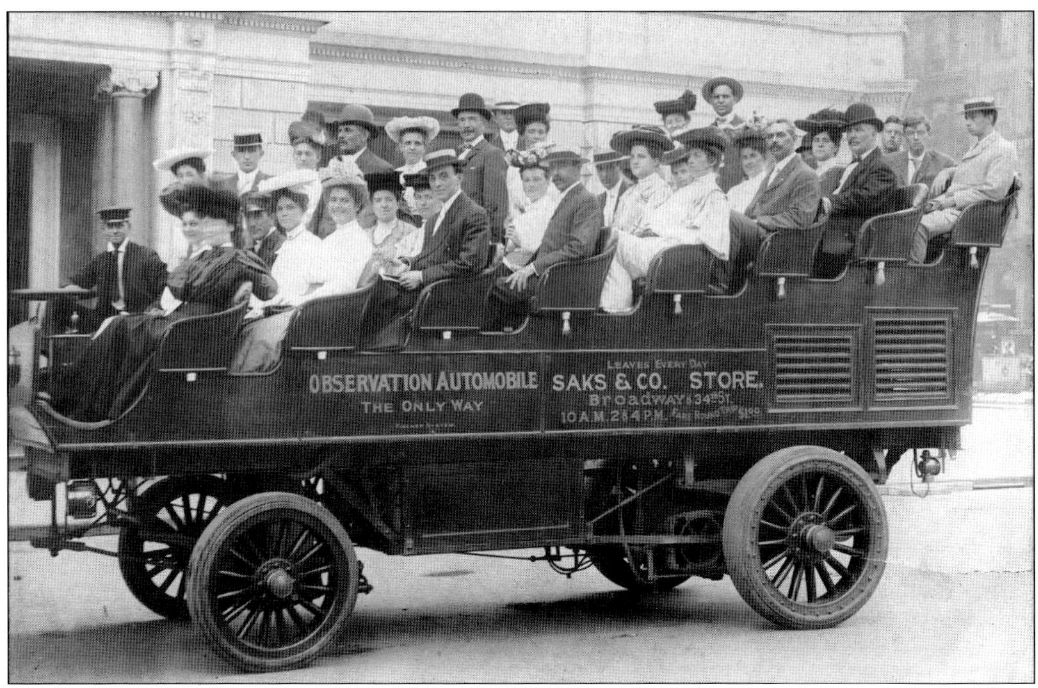

Open-air touring cars were the easiest way to experience the Chinatown-Bowery tours, which, for obvious reasons, were ideally conducted at night. Stops included the Chinese Opera House, a Chinese joss house (temple), Steve Brodie's Saloon, a Bowery dance hall, and the Atlantic Garden. Some included Little Italy, the Jewish quarter, the Tombs Prison, the Five Points ghetto, and a walk through a supposed opium den. (AWC.)

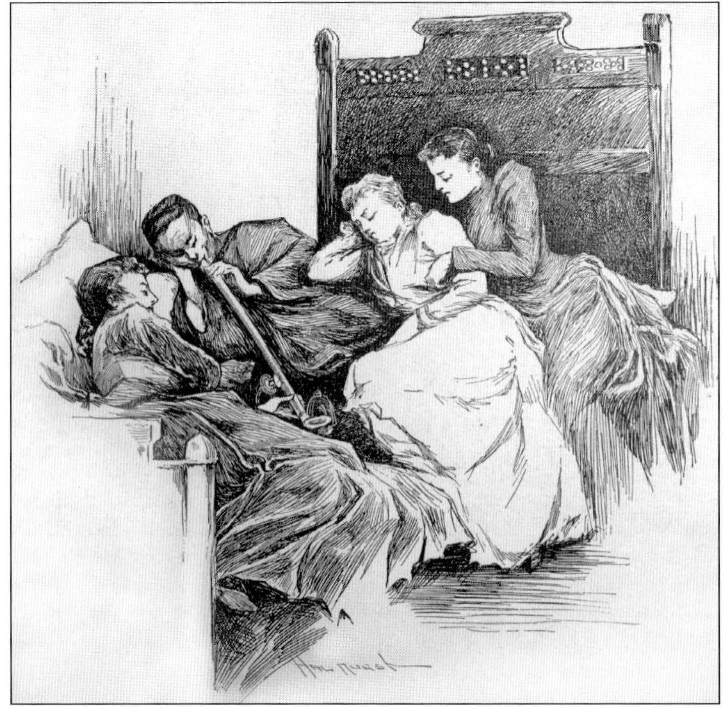

This Hal Hurst illustration of a Chinatown opium den appeared in a November 29, 1890, *Illustrated American* article entitled "The Opium Curse." (DM.)

In 1894, at the London Theatre, 235 Bowery, Lottie Gilson introduced the iconic song "Sidewalks of New York," a paean to the city and the people. Swiss-born Gilson was called "the Little Magnet" because she drew large audiences and boosted sheet music sales. At various points a German, Chinese, Yiddish, and Italian theater, performers at the London included W.C. Fields, Al Jolson, Eddie Cantor, Weber & Fields, and Antonio Maiori. (MCNY.)

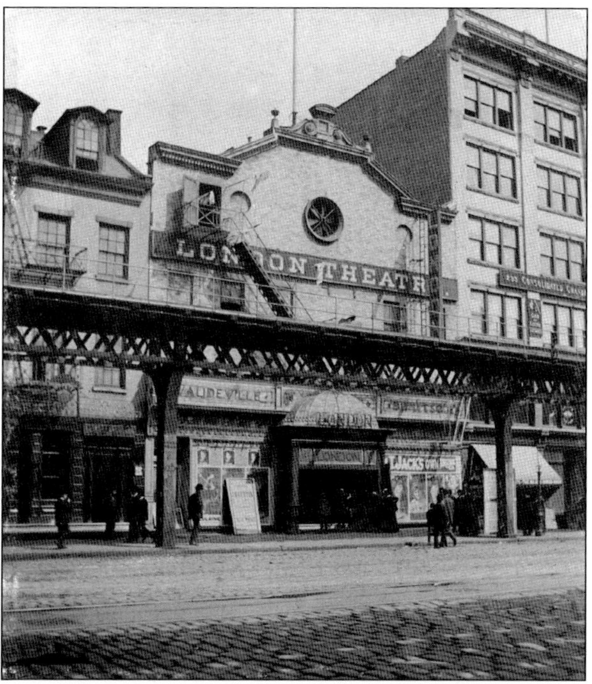

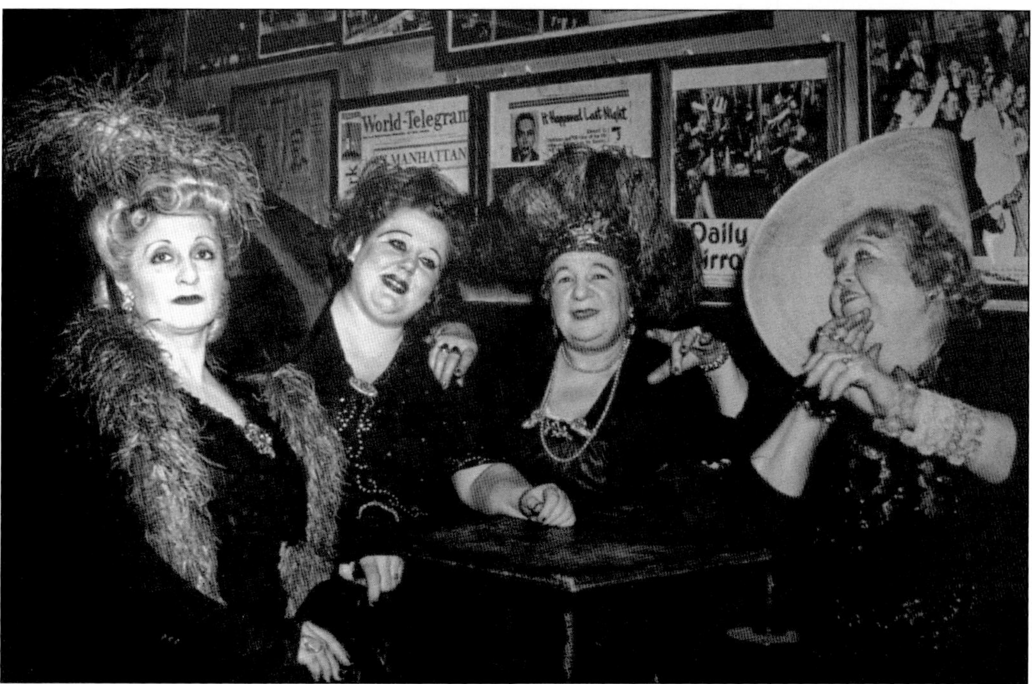

Sammy's Bowery Follies, 265-267 Bowery, was a celebrated mid-20th-century nightspot where "the high life meets the low life." Owner Sammy Fuchs hired old vaudeville talent and welcomed the Bowery inebriates to keep the scene lively and authentic. Visiting celebs included Albert Camus, Jean-Paul Sartre, Simone de Beauvoir, Rosalind Russell, and Jimmy Durante. Photographers Eisenstadt, Weegee, Lisette Model, and Erika Stone captured the theatricality, as in Stone's 1942 "Bowery Beauties." Sammy's closed in 1970. (Erika Stone.)

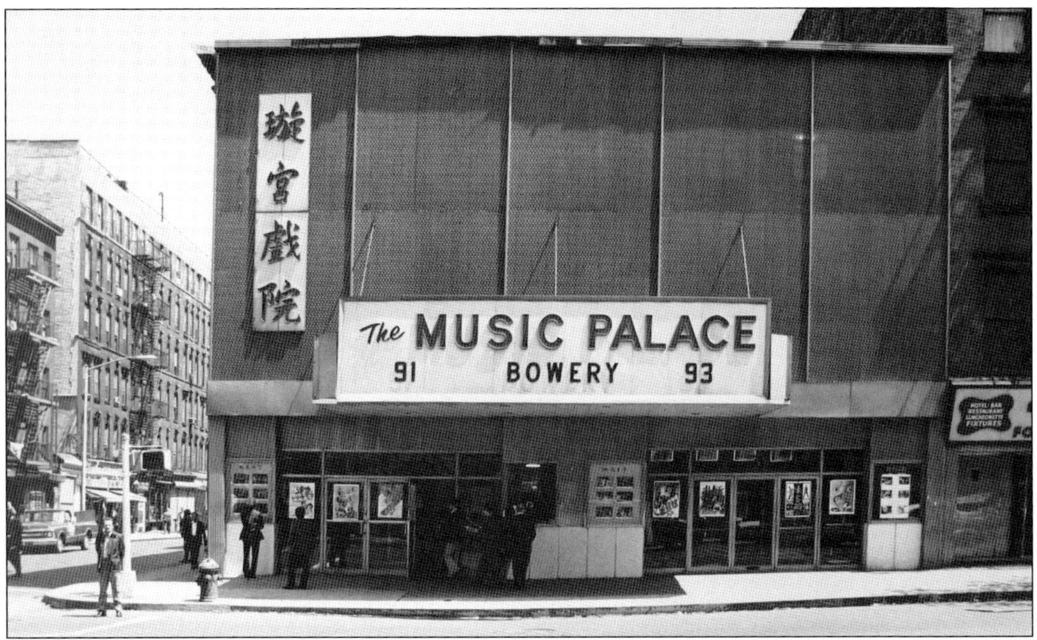

A movie theater since 1914, when it opened as the Universal Photoplay, from the early 1970s until 2000, the Music Palace was a popular Chinese language cinema, the last in Chinatown. It was replaced by a high-rise hotel in 2011. This 1974 photograph is by Carin Drechsler-Marx. (CDM.)

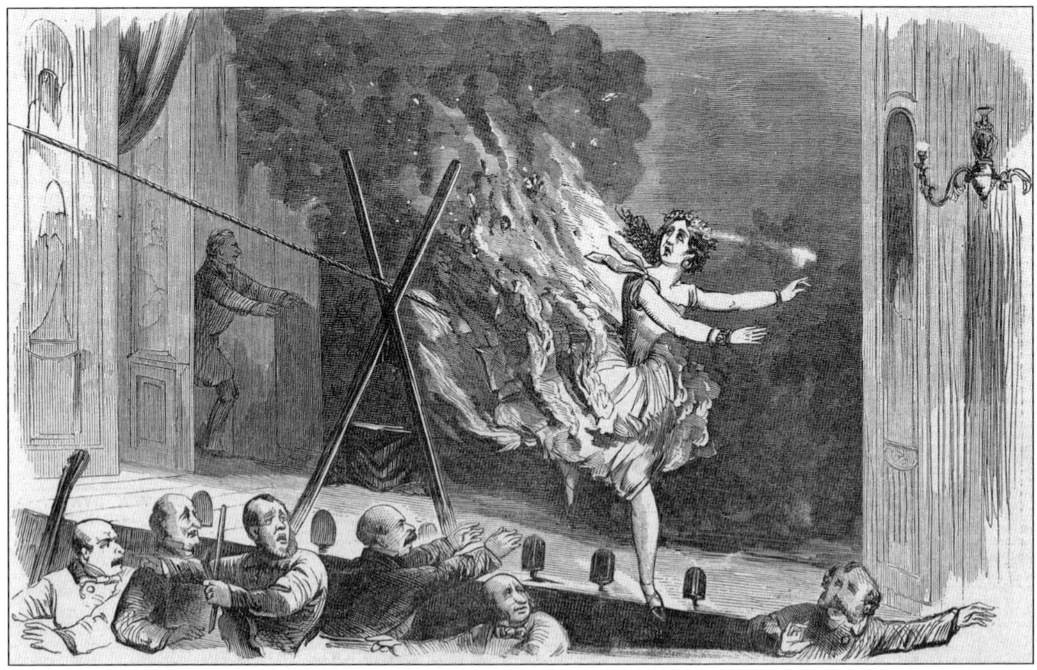

In Memoriam: On February 4, 1860, the Volks Garten Theatre at 199-201 Bowery witnessed a freakish, real-life tragedy when popular tightrope dancer Josephine Farren's dress touched a footlight, which quickly engulfed her in flames in full view of the audience. Musicians rushed over to put out the flames, but Farren—the sole support of her mother and young sisters—died the next day. This drawing is from *Frank Leslie's Illustrated Newspaper*, February 18, 1860. (NYPL-DC.)

Three

The Street of Forgotten Men

During its early 1900s decline, the Bowery was called "Satan's Highway," "Street of No Return," and the "Street of Forgotten Men." A skid row hell that reckless teens were warned they might end up on, it was synonymous with dive bars, flophouses, and breadlines. But broad-brushing Bowery hotels and lodging houses as "flops" and their occupants as "bums" obscures the origin and range of functions these places served, and the diverse push-pull factors that landed men here, dating back to the mid-1800s.

Starting in the 1820s, as the Bowery emerged as a working-class entertainment mecca, boardinghouses and hotels lined the street, housing the men arriving in town for work or pleasure. Later, as their numbers surged, a new type of transient hotel appeared: the lodging house. Ranging from the decorous to disreputable, lodging options included a small room, a cubicle, a hammock, a bed in a barracks-like hall, or a spot on the bare floor—the literal flop. Many such places were overcrowded and poorly ventilated; some were located in basements. Some catered to sweatshop workers and immigrants, and others to shoeshines and newsboys, while the majority catered to unmoored men. Some lodging house men were there because of job loss, family tragedy, economic depression, or mental illness; many were disabled veterans, and many were alcoholics.-

Notorious as a place of vice and debasement, the Bowery became a focus for religious, humanitarian, and reform organizations. While axe-wielding temperance radicals like Carrie Nation wanted to outlaw liquor, and Anthony Comstock's anti-vice crusaders fought to suppress gambling, prostitution, contraception, and anything un-Christian, others, like the Bowery Mission and Salvation Army concentrated on rescue work, saving lost souls by offering food, clothing, shelter, jobs and a chance at rehabilitation. Though the flophouse era has passed, the Bowery Mission soldiers on, as do social services organizations like Project Renewal and Bowery Residents Association, each helping men find jobs, housing, healthcare, and sobriety.

Providing shelter and a safety net for the city's down and out—thousands during the Depression—it is amazing, even heroic, that one street could bear such a magnitude of suffering and desolation. As is said in Alcoholics Anonymous, "There but for the grace of God go I."

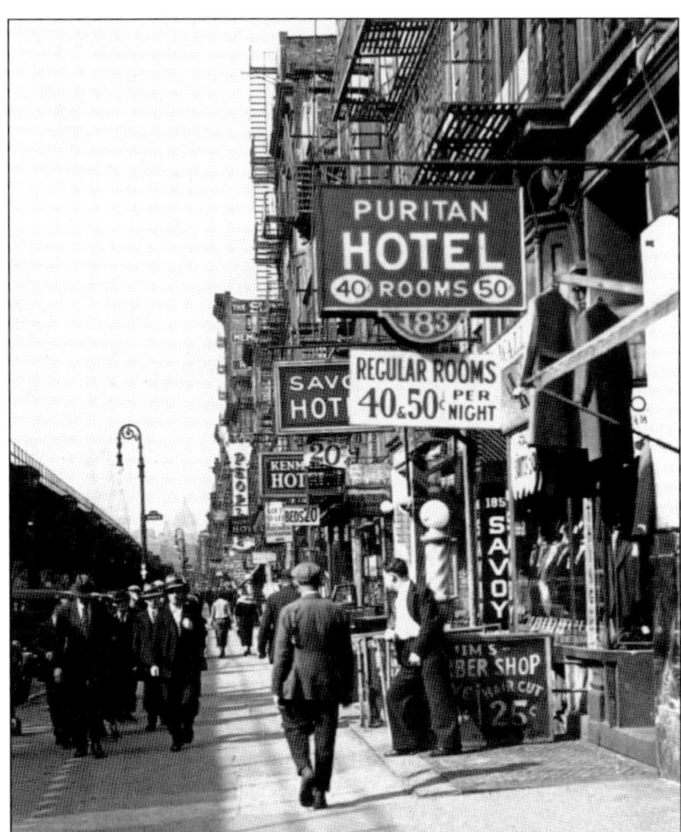

Looking up Bowery from the corner of Delancey Street, this 1934 Depression-era photograph shows a dense line of lodging houses—the Puritan, Savoy, Kenmare, and Montauk—with signs advertising beds for 20¢ and rooms for 40¢ and 50¢. (NYPL.)

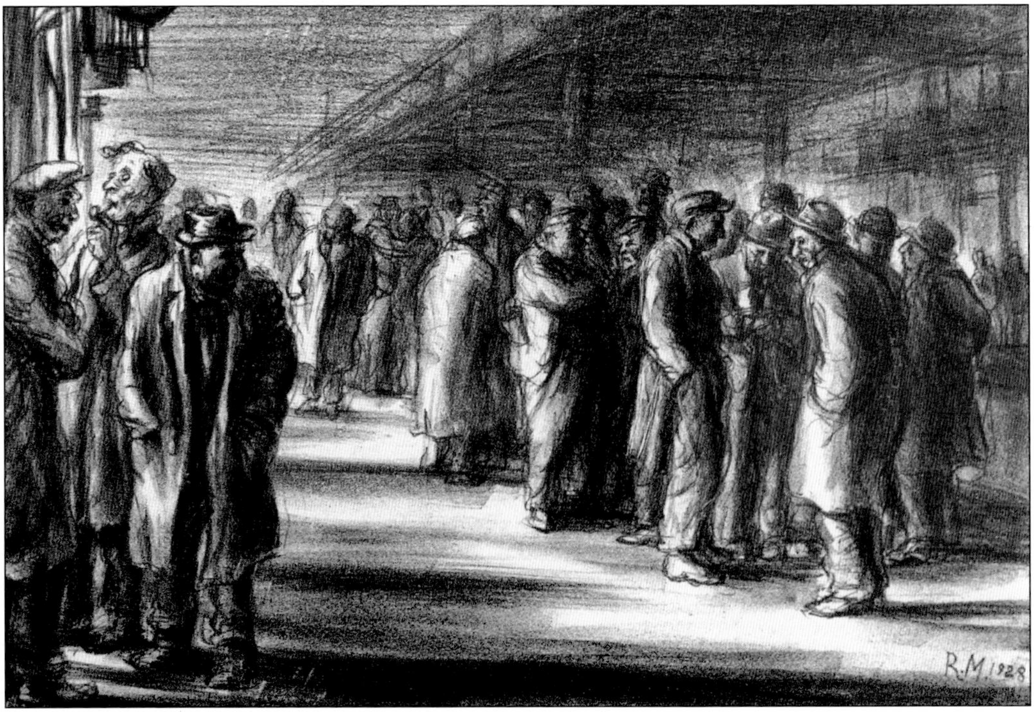

This Reginald Marsh (1898–1954) etching entitled "The Bowery" (1928) shows groups of men gathered near the elevated train. Born in France and raised in New Jersey, Marsh is one of the artists most closely associated with the street, especially its down-and-out. (Art Students League of New York.)

This 1921 Bain News Service photograph shows the Lanier Hotel and Fuerst Restaurant at 15 Bowery. Alex and Sigmund Fuerst, shown here with their dog, also owned restaurants at 109 and 221 Bowery. A moderately priced lodging house, the Lanier was just north of Chatham Square. Its second-floor lobby would have accommodated smoking, reading, card playing, and a great view of the Edward Mooney House and Pell Street's gateway to Chinatown. (LOC.)

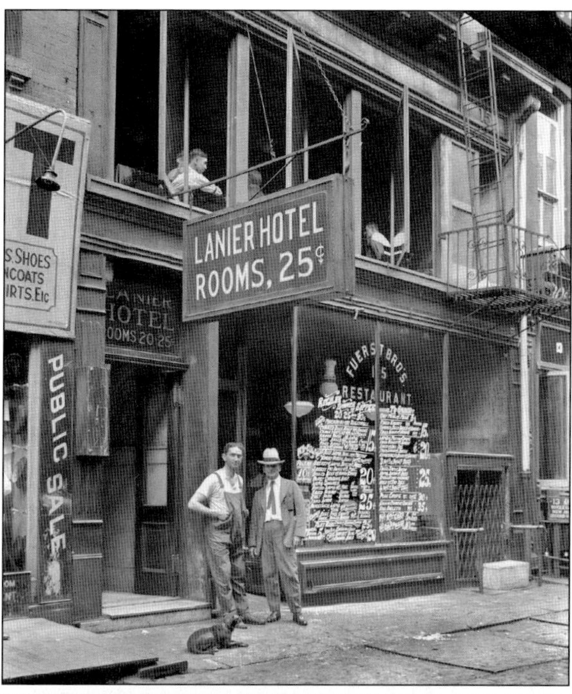

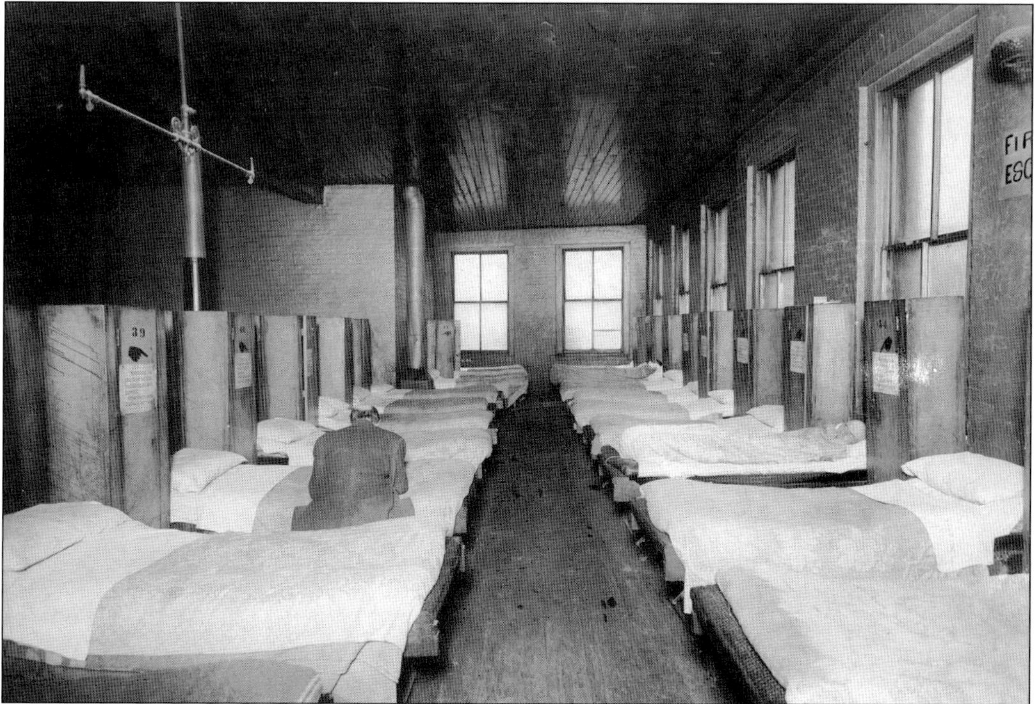

Though quarters are tight in this barracks-style hall, the clean sheets, lockers, heater, and omnipresent signs—"Spitting on the floor of this building is unlawful. Offenders are liable to arrested"—indicates this was a well-run establishment. Beginning in 1867, laws were established and revised periodically to address heat, air, water, hygiene, and building safety issues. This Bowery lodging house photograph was taken around the 1910s. (AWC.)

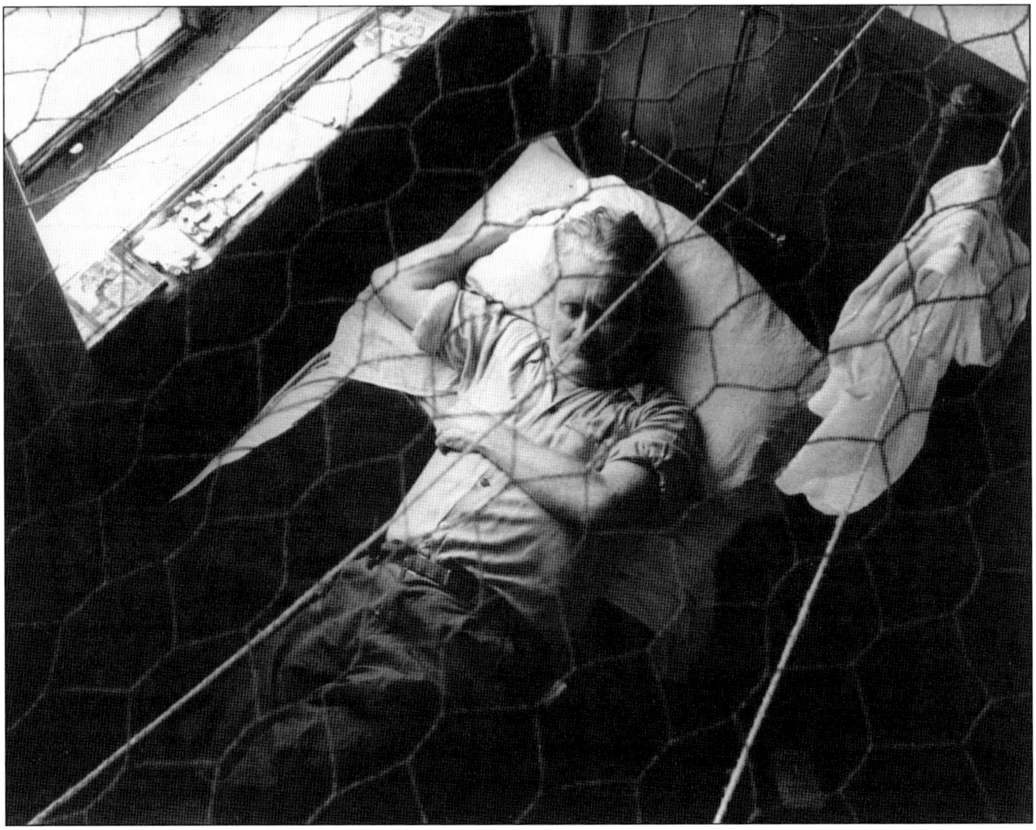

While rescue missions housed men dormitory style, with multiple cots in open rooms, the lodging houses typically offered tiny four-by-six-foot cubicles, each about seven feet high, with a chicken wire covering overhead for air circulation and to prevent theft. Cubicles contained a bed, a locker, and an overhanging light bulb. This is from Lionel Rogosin's semi-documentary film *On the Bowery*, 1956. (Rogosin Heritage Inc.)

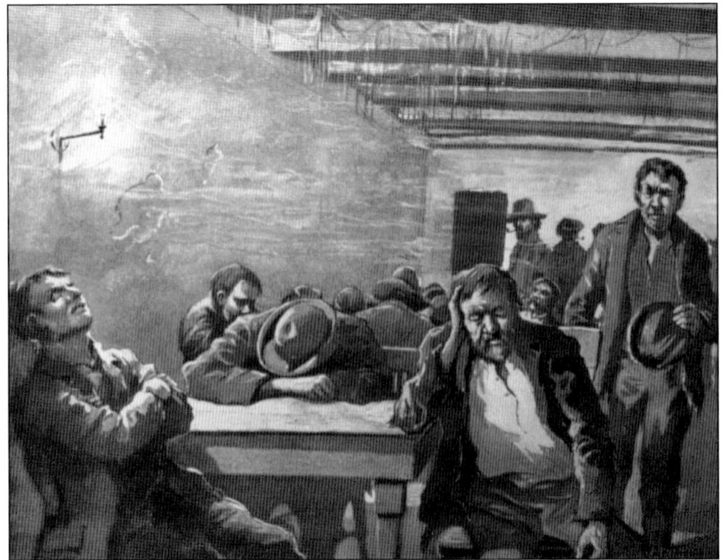

This illustration of "homeless men in a 2-cent cellar lodging house" is from *New Metropolis: Memorable Events of Three Centuries* (1898). Spaces even more squalid than this were photographed by Jacob Riis during the 1890s. Such scenes are fine examples of what Mark Twain and others felt was the underbelly of the Gilded Age. (NYPL-MD.)

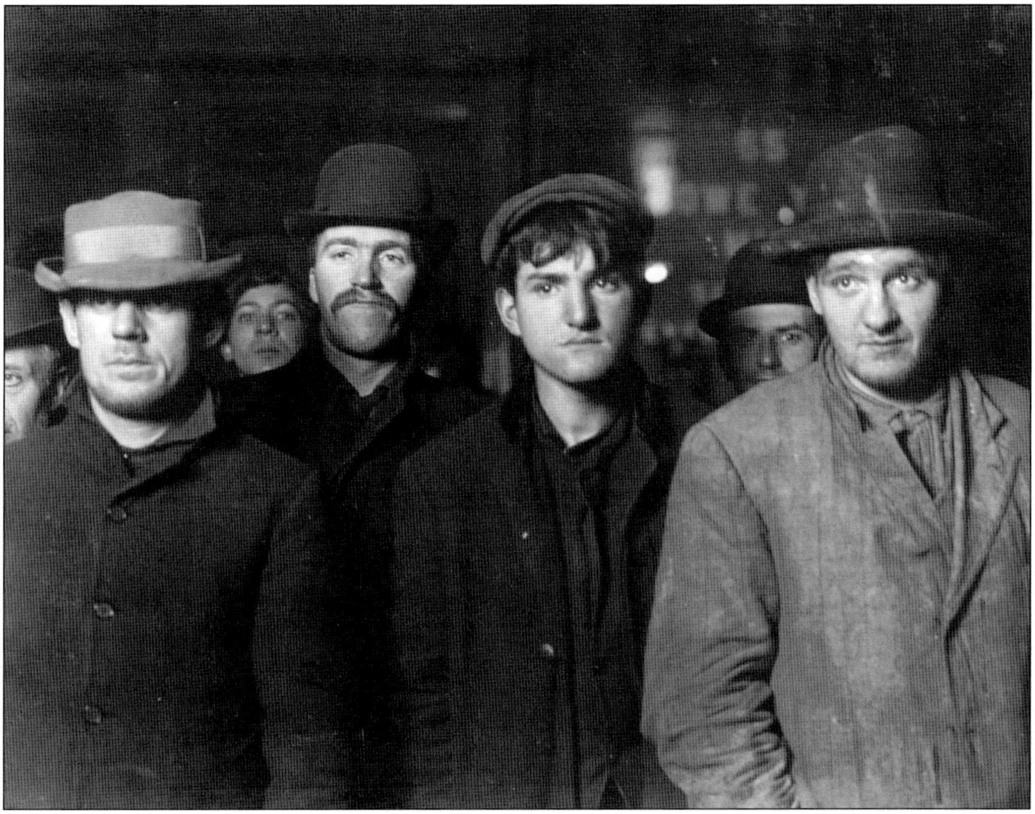

This Lewis Hine photograph shows the Bowery Mission breadline, 55 Bowery, on a cold night in 1909. Established in 1879, the mission was located at 14, 36, 55, and 105 Bowery before moving to its present location at 227 Bowery, in 1909. (It added 229 Bowery in 1980). For almost 150 years, the Bowery Mission has provided food, clothing, shelter, medical assistance, and employment help to millions. (NYPL-PC.)

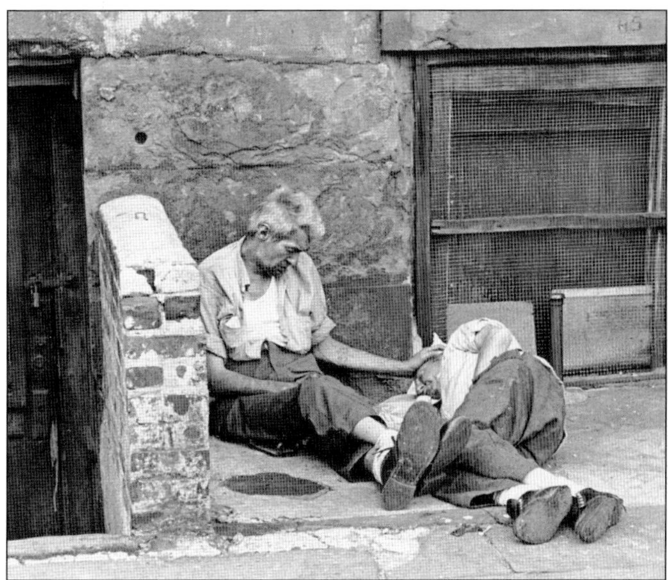

Though some men without means pass out on the street, many choose to sleep there since they consider it safer than shelters. This powerful c. 1970 Joseph C.A. Mercurio photograph is from a little-known series he took of the Bowery men in the late 1960s and early 1970s. (© Joseph C.A. Mercurio.)

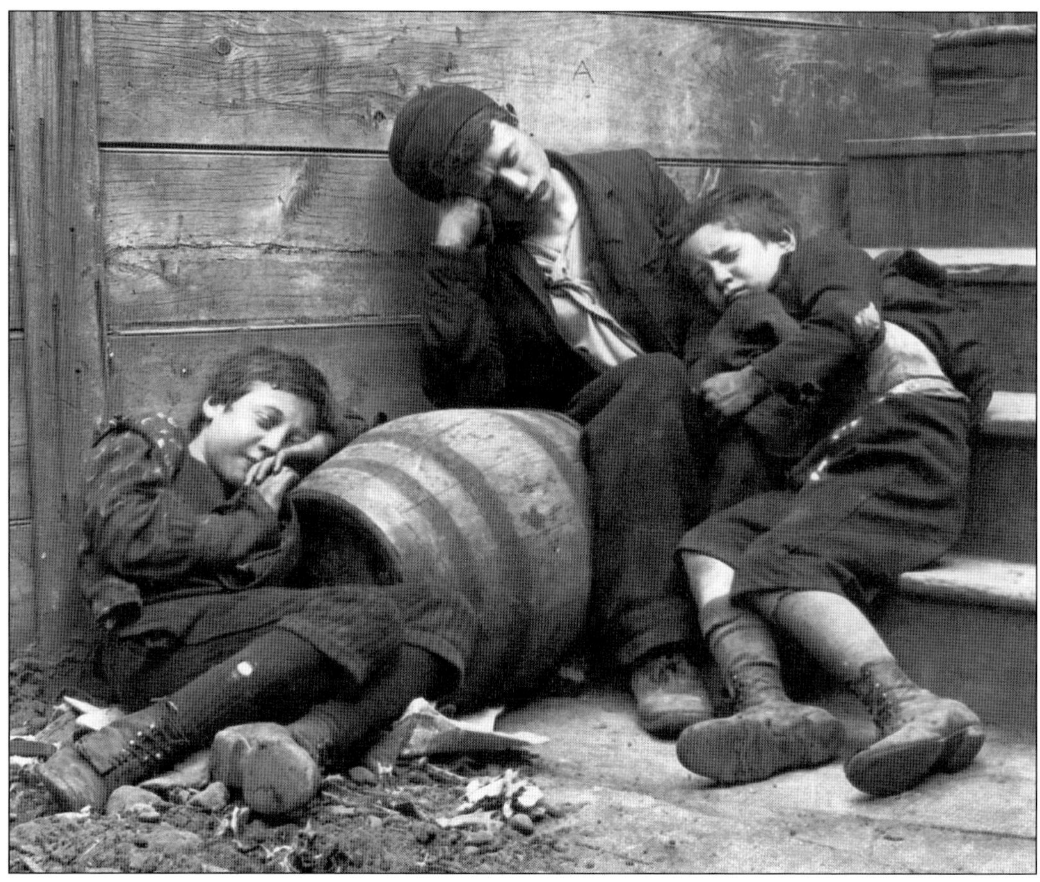

Jacob Riis' photograph of homeless boys sleeping on the street is from his epochal *How the Other Half Lives: Studies Among the Tenements of New York* (1890), which strongly influenced the reform movement. Though the book's early editions had to use illustrated renderings of his photographs, thousands saw them projected as glass slides on Riis' lecture tours. The Children's Aid Society operated several shelters for homeless children. (LOC.)

LOST FIDDLE—DIES

Old Street Musician Becomes Disconsolate and Commits Suicide.

(By Associated Press.)

New York, May 26.—Frederick Luer, an old street musician, killed himself in his Bowery lodging shortly before midnight by inhaling gas through an old rubber boot. He bored a hole in the boot's sole, inserted a gas tube in the hole, turned on the gas, then placed the top of the boot over his face. He was dead when found. Luer had been disconsolate since a truck on the Bowery smashed his cherished violin a few days ago.

Street musicians were everywhere on the Bowery, but it was a hard life. The working poor lived on the edge, and their means of livelihood was everything. Frederick Luer, like Hurstwood in Dreiser's *Sister Carrie* (1900), used gas in a Bowery lodging house to end his life. This 1910 news clipping is one of hundreds in Bowery archivist Adam Woodward's sad but revealing collection, *295 Bowery Suicides*. (AWC.)

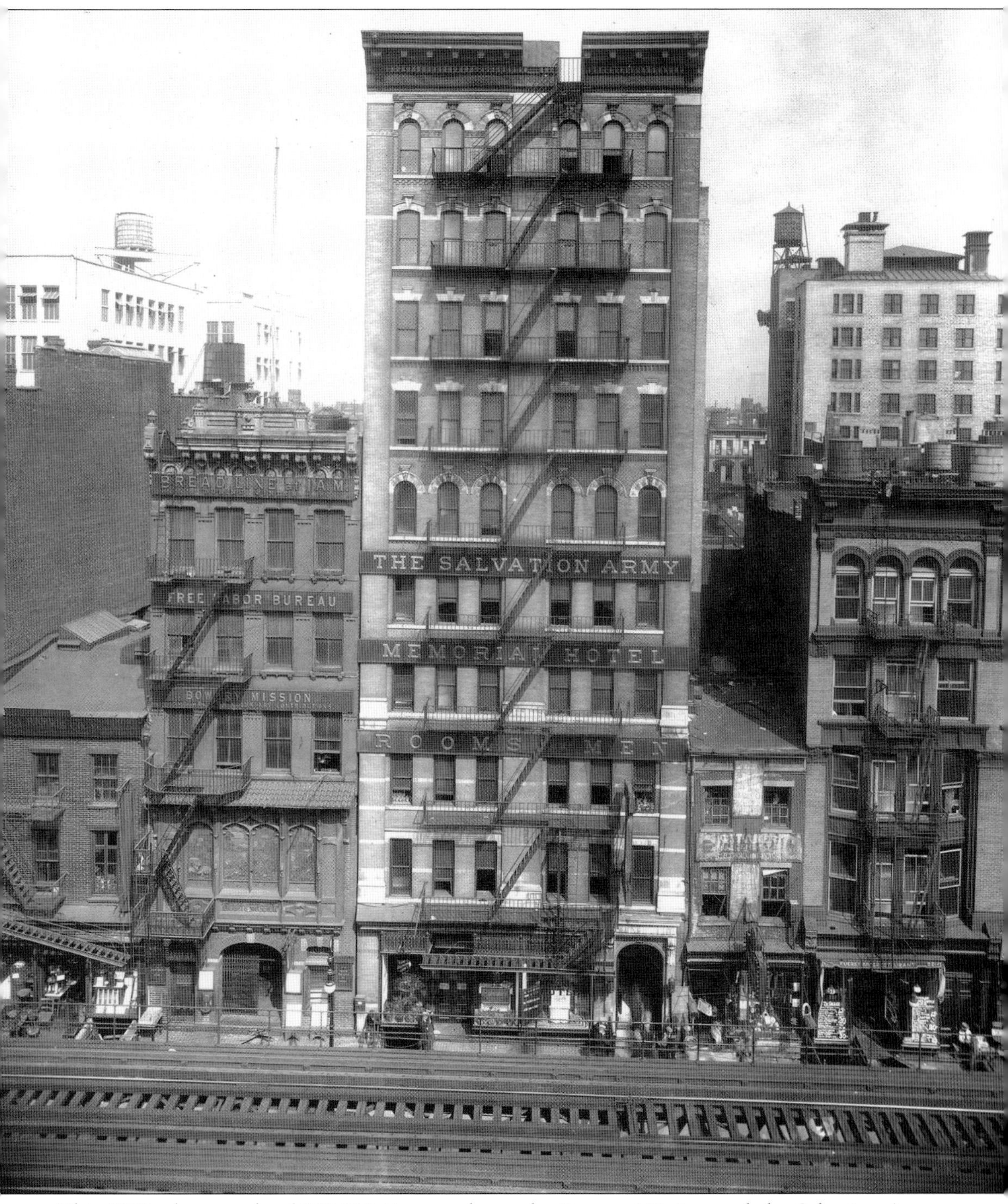

This 1928 photograph of 219-229 Bowery shows the Bowery Mission and the Salvation Army Memorial Hotel. For decades 225 Bowery was the street's tallest building and the largest Salvation Army (SA) shelter in the world. After the SA left in 2014, it became a boutique hotel, went belly up during the COVID crisis, and then became a homeless shelter; as of 2024, it is a hotel again. (Salvation Army National Archive.)

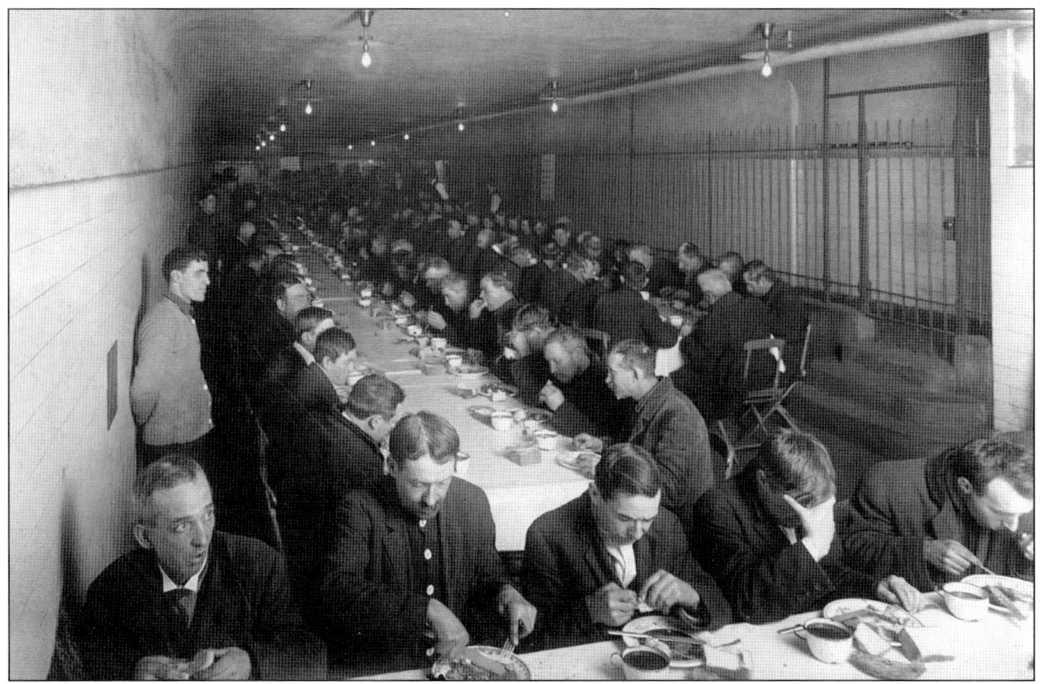

The c. 1910s Bowery Mission photograph above shows 100 men being served a free meal. Note the flatware, China plates, and enamel cups; there were no plastic or Styrofoam back then. The use of electric versus gas lighting in this windowless room must have been a vast improvement. Seen below is the Bowery Mission coffee line around the 1950s. Since 1894, the mission has run a summer camp for inner city kids and, since 1990, has provided housing for women. Recently challenged by the Covid crisis and the immigrant crisis, Pastor Jason Storbakken says these are no obstacle for an institution devoted to Matthew 25, verse 35-36: "For I was hungry and you gave me something to eat . . . I was a stranger and you invited me in." (Above, AWC; below, Bowery Mission Archive.)

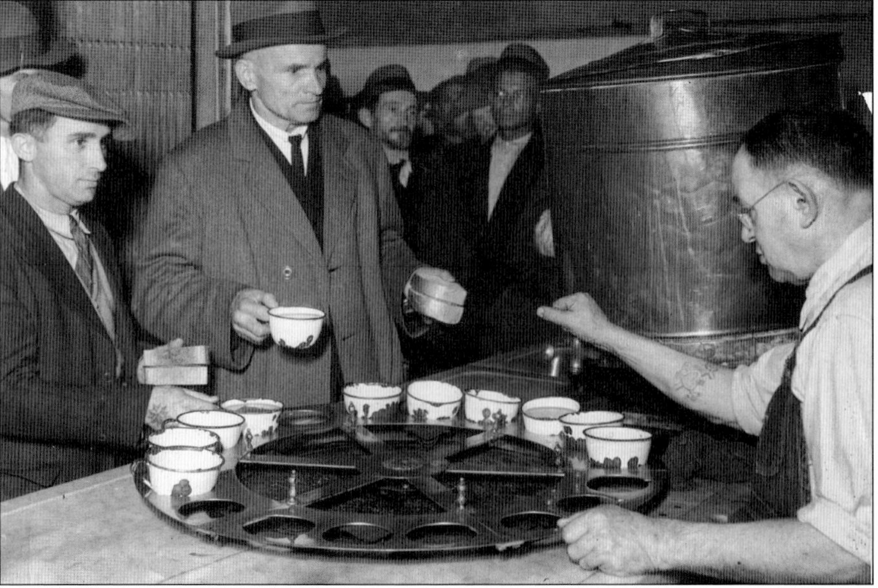

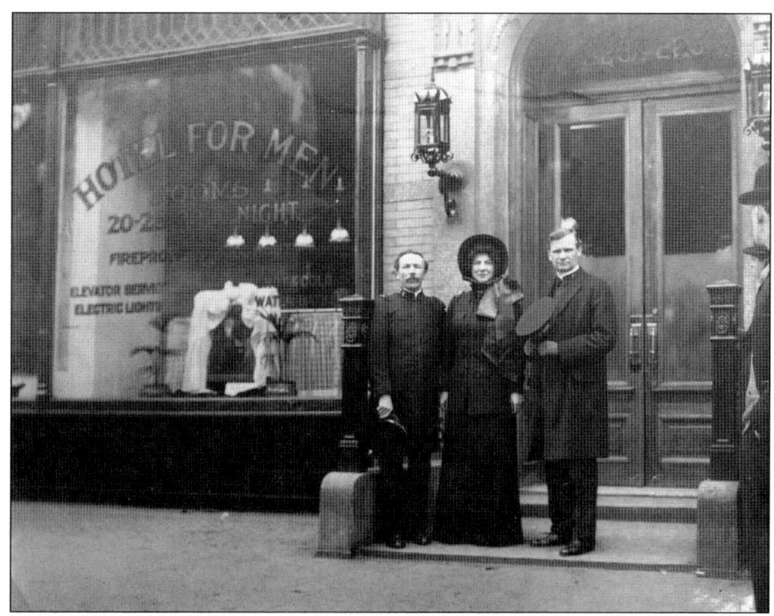

Comdr. Evangeline Booth (1865–1950) outside the Salvation Army Memorial Hotel for Men, 225 Bowery, 1912. The daughter of Salvation Army founders Catherine and William Booth, she was the SA's commander of the United States (1904–1934), their general (1934-1939), and winner of the US Army's Distinguished Service Medal for her work during World War I. (SANA.)

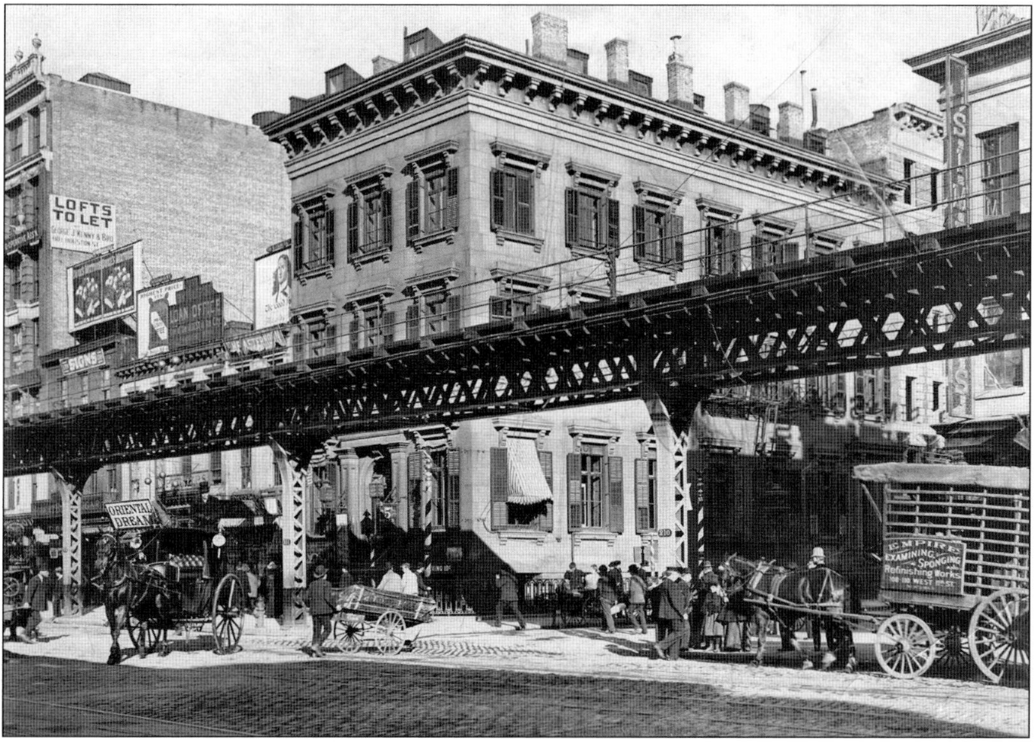

This YMCA mission opened at 153 Bowery on September 1, 1889, offering 5¢ meals, shelter, and gospel services. Over the years, the organization operated shelters at 134 and 243 Bowery, its enormous Bowery Branch at 8 East Third Street, and the Young Men's Institute at 222 Bowery, which offered a gym, library, vocational courses, and uplifting speakers like Theodore Roosevelt. Its goal was to save young men from Bowery hedonism. (Kautz Family YMCA Archive.)

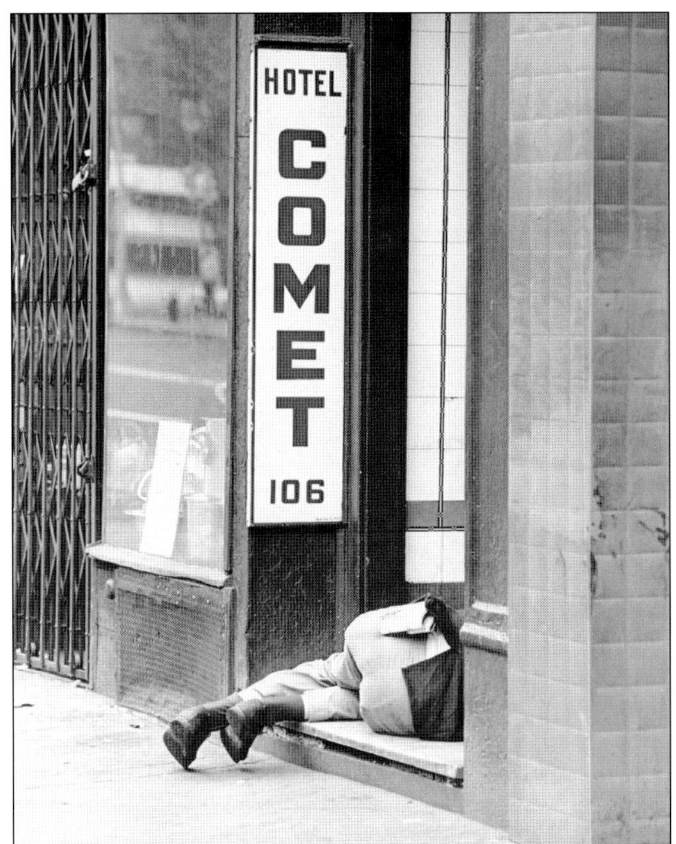

This c. 1970 photo by Joseph C.A. Mercurio shows a man passed out at the entrance of the Comet Hotel lodging house at 106 Bowery. (© Joseph C.A. Mercurio.)

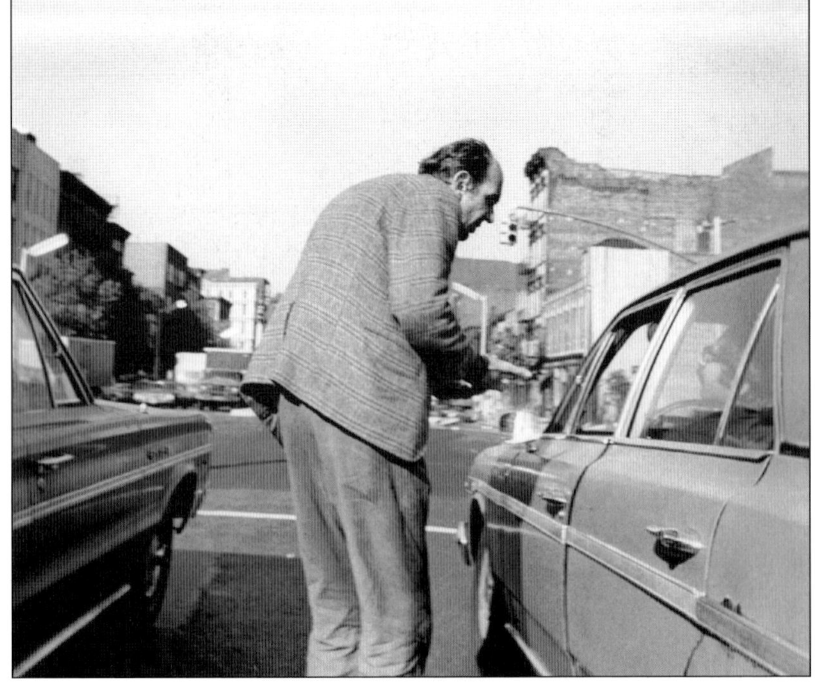

This photograph of a panhandler at the corner of Bowery and Houston Street was taken by world photographer Ed Grazda. It appears in his study of the street, *On the Bowery: NYC 1971.* (Ed Grazda.)

Photographer Cynthia MacAdams's extensive work on the Bowery includes shots of its street life and denizens, including this unusual 1980 shot entitled "Joy." (Cynthia MacAdams/NYPL-PC.)

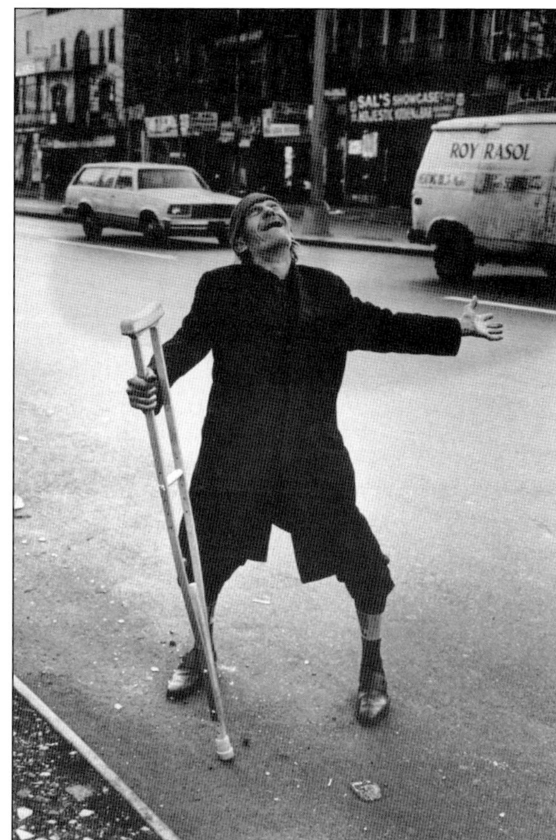

German-born photographer Carin Drechsler-Marx has likewise studied the architecture and people of the street, including this shot of homeless men from 1974. Her work was published in the book *Bowery* (1984). (CDM.)

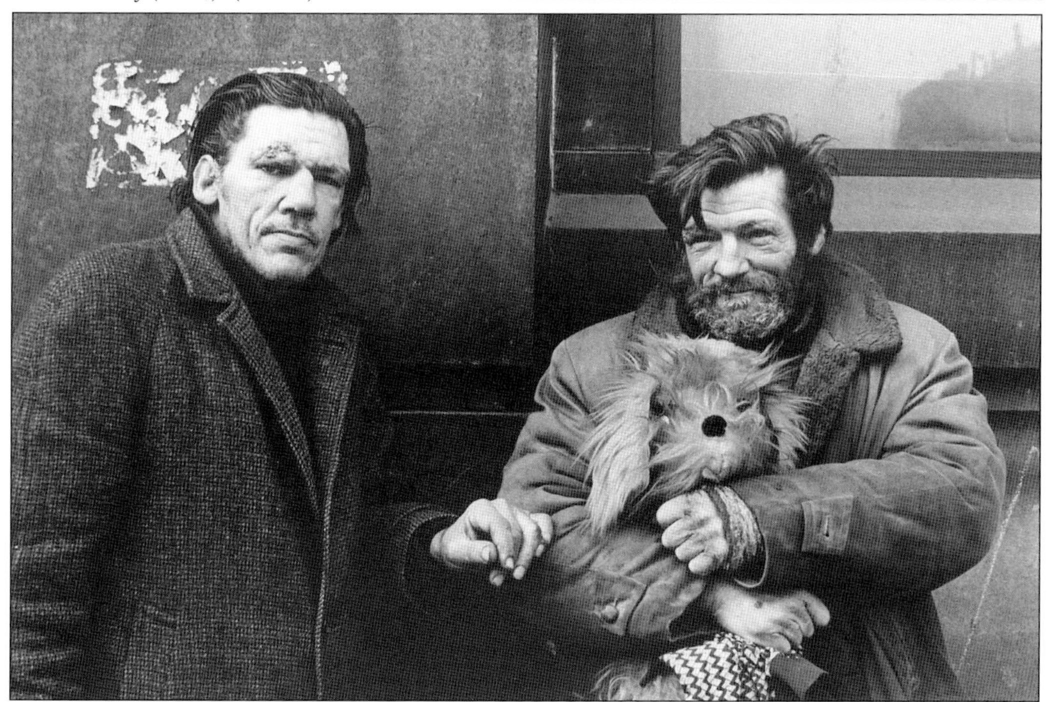

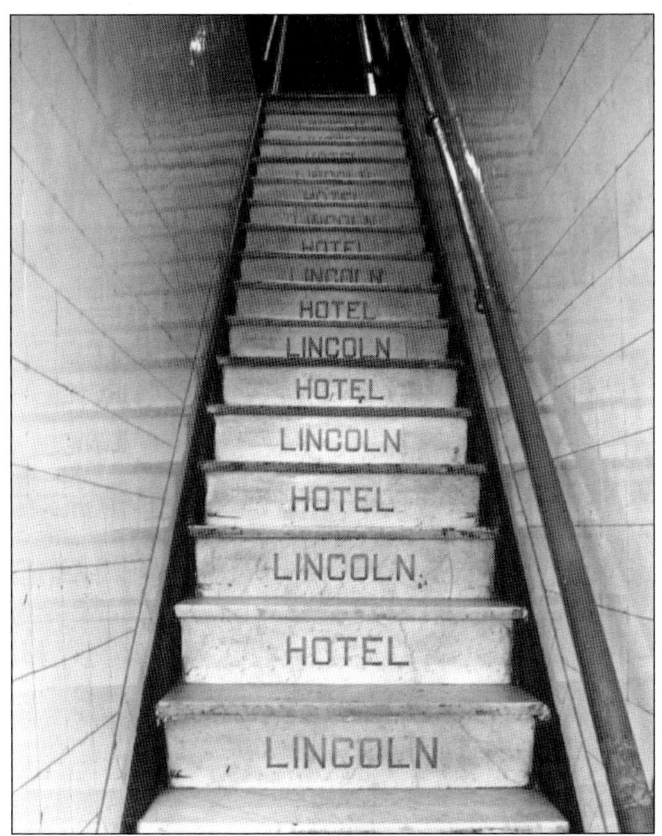

As one ascended the staircase in these lodging houses, it was not uncommon to see the hotel's name on every step. Whether as an advertisement or to assure woozy lodgers they were indeed in the right place, the repetition was hard to miss. These Lincoln Hotel stairs, at 184 Bowery, were photographed in 2015. (© MBTFC.)

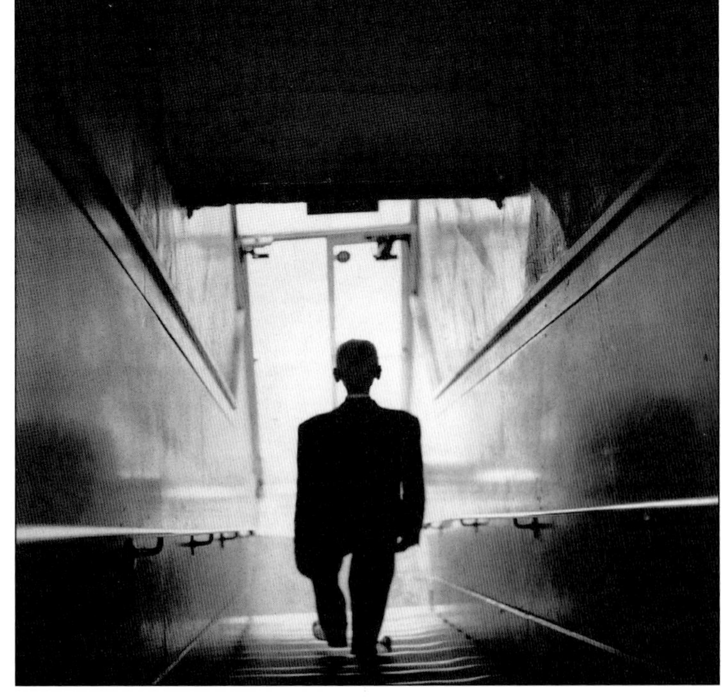

This photograph from 2000 shows an elderly resident descending the staircase at the Andrews Hotel, 197 Bowery. Known today as the Andrews, it is operated by Breaking Ground, which offers mental health and substance abuse assistance, and helps residents transition to permanent housing. Harvey Wang's photographs appear in the book *Flophouse: Life on the Bowery*, with text by David Isay and Stacy Abramson. (© Harvey Wang.)

Four

Bowery in Literature, Song, Film, and the Imagination

In the 1890s, H.C. Bunner wrote that "properly speaking," the Bowery "is a place rather than a street or avenue." Indeed, how many street names include "the"? As reflected in songs, literature, films, and the imagination, it is an iconic place and existential symbol.

While some 19th-century chroniclers disparaged the world-famous street, others, like poet Walt Whitman—"the Bowery Boy of literature"—were inspired by its verve and expressive character. Its mix of immigrants, gangs, hustlers, and the poor gave us Bowery-esque vernacular and idiomatic terms like "chum," "pal," "joint," "so long," "blow-out," "have a yen for," "going on a bender," and "kick the bucket." A titillating subject in the movies' peepshow days, 30-second films like *How They Do Things on the Bowery* (1897) showed people drinking, smoking, kissing, and rolling on the floor. Mae West's hilariously salacious *She Done Him Wrong* (1933), a Bowery homage, shocked censors, but enthralled audiences. Tony Pastor's rousing song "In the Bowery" (1873) contrasted Bowery's fun-loving common folks with the waxwork stiffs of Fifth Avenue. The song "Sidewalks of New York" premiered on the Bowery, and America's first great songwriters—Stephen Foster and Irving Berlin—have important Bowery links within one block of each other.

The sing-along sensation "The Bowery" (1891) was a sarcastic, cautionary tale about greenhorns getting fleeced there. Its refrain—"I'll never go there anymore"—widened the street's ill-repute. Both from the pulpit and in literature, it became an archetypal symbol of dead-end dissipation and ruin. In Theodore Dreiser's *Sister Carrie* (1900), Hurstwood asphyxiates himself in a Bowery lodging house. The Bowery down-and-out were shown by painter Reginald Marsh and photographers Jacob Riis, Lewis Hine, Weegee, and Berenice Abbott. Owen Kildare chronicled his life as a newsboy, boxer, and criminal in *My Mamie Rose* (1903, filmed as *Regeneration* in 1915). Horatio Alger's *Ragged Dick* (1868) described the hard life of its bootblacks. The book (1928) and film (2002) *Gangs of New York* depicted the 1800s gangsterdom, including the real-life "Bowery Boys." The street's desolation was captured in Lionel Rogosin's semi-documentary *On the Bowery* (1956), referenced in Allen Ginsberg's epic poem *Howl* (1956), and in poems or songs by Jack Kerouac, Bob Dylan, Jim Croce, and others. Woody Guthrie was playing in Bowery bars during the weeks he wrote "This Land Is Your Land" (1940).

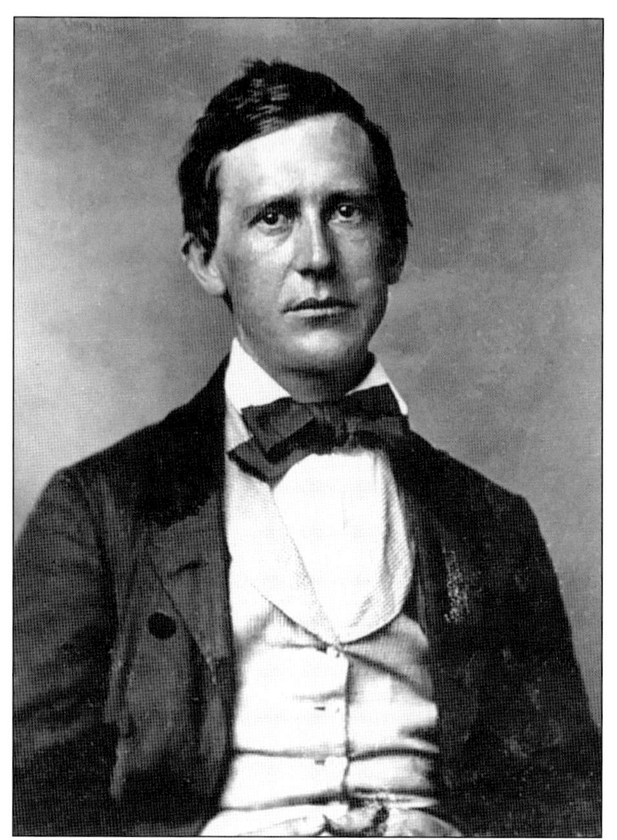

America's first great songwriter, Pennsylvania-born Stephen Foster (1826–1864), is remembered for songs including "Oh! Susanna," "Beautiful Dreamer," and "Hard Times Come Again No More." Controversial because many works were written for minstrel shows, he was defended by Frederick Douglass who generously wrote that Foster's songs were "heart songs" that humanized African Americans: "The finest feelings of human nature are expressed in them. . . . They awaken sympathies for the slave, in which anti-slavery principles take root and flourish." Foster's last residence was the New England Hotel, at 30 Bowery, seen here in about 1869. He died at age 37 with less than a dollar in his pocket. Forty years later, just one block away at 12 Pell Street, America's second great songwriter, Irving Berlin, age sixteen, wrote his first song. (Left, LOC; below, AWC.)

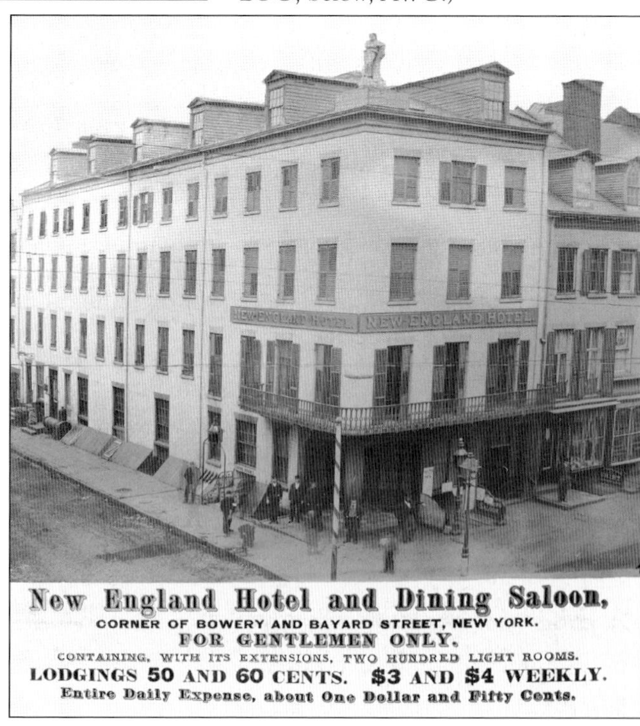

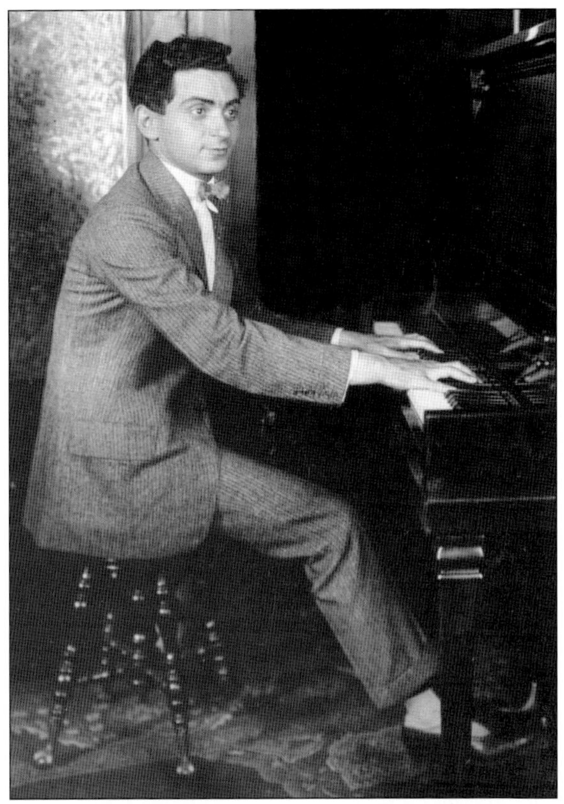

According to Irving Berlin (1888–1989), America's second great songwriter, "I got my musical education on the Bowery." After his father died in 1901, thirteen-year-old Russian Jewish immigrant Izzy Balin left school and ran away from home, working as a Bowery newsboy and sleeping in a homeless shelter for boys. He earned additional revenue by singing as he sold newspapers, including inside saloons, where customers tossed him coins. He later became a busker, singing for small change on street corners. In 1904, the famous Bowery denizen Chuck Connors recognized Balin's talent and got him a singing waiter job at the Pelham saloon and dance hall at 12 Pell Street, just off Bowery. He wrote his first song there, changed his name to Irving Berlin, and later wrote "God Bless America" and "White Christmas." (Right, NYPL-Pic; below, RMC.)

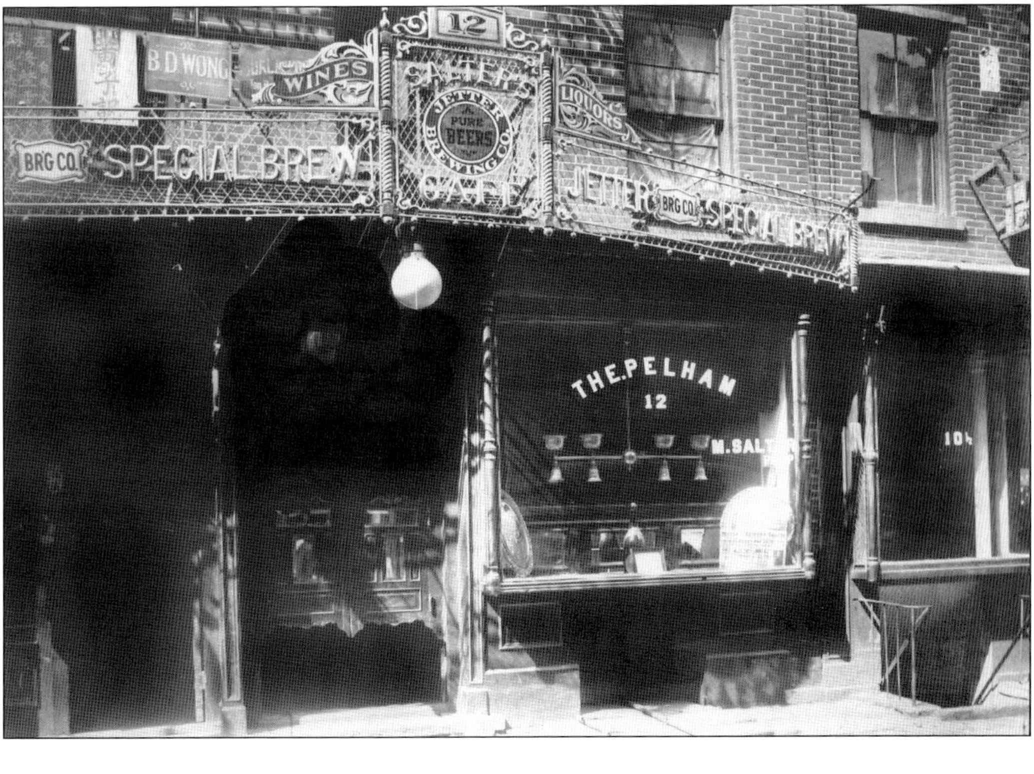

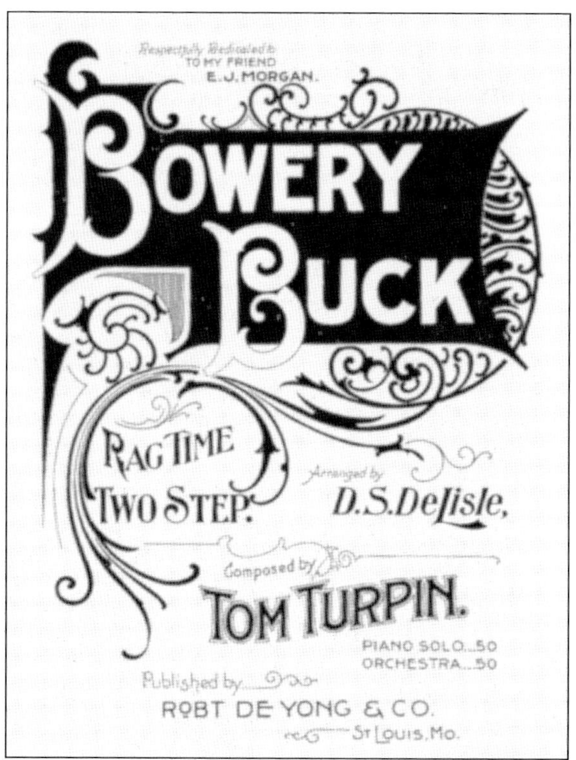

"Bowery Buck" (1899) was a popular ragtime piece by African American composer Tom Turpin (1873–1899). Because the Bowery, like Coney Island, was synonymous with fun and edgy adventure, it is unsurprising that scores of songs were written about it: "In the Bowery," "The Bowery Grenadiers," "My Pearl's a Bowery Girl," "Only a Bowery Boy," "The Bowery Crawl," and "Bowery Gals," the earlier version of the classic "Buffalo Gals." (LOC.)

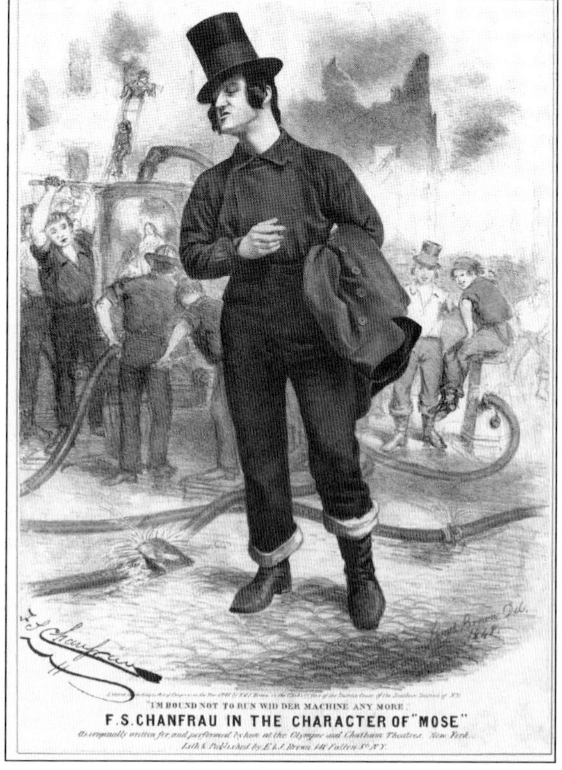

According to theatrical legend, in 1848, when actor Frank Chanfrau first walked out on stage as Mose, the brawny firefighting Bowery Boy, the audience gasped. Dressed in a red shirt, rolled-up pants, stovepipe hat, and a cigar butt in his mouth, he spoke and moved with Bowery-esque swagger. He received thunderous applause. The play, *A Glance at New York*, and Chanfrau's larger-than-life caricature were sensations, especially with working-class audiences. (HTC.)

Herbert Asbury called the Bowery Boys "the strutting peacock of gangland." They had a much-emulated style of dress, speech, walk, and a badass reputation for fights with other gangs, especially foreign-born ones. Though they were less violent by the time of this 1880 illustration, this Bowery B'hoy still has the swagger, and a dandyish flash well matched by his G'hal. The setting is the Atlantic Garden, near the boys' old 40 Bowery clubhouse. (AWC.)

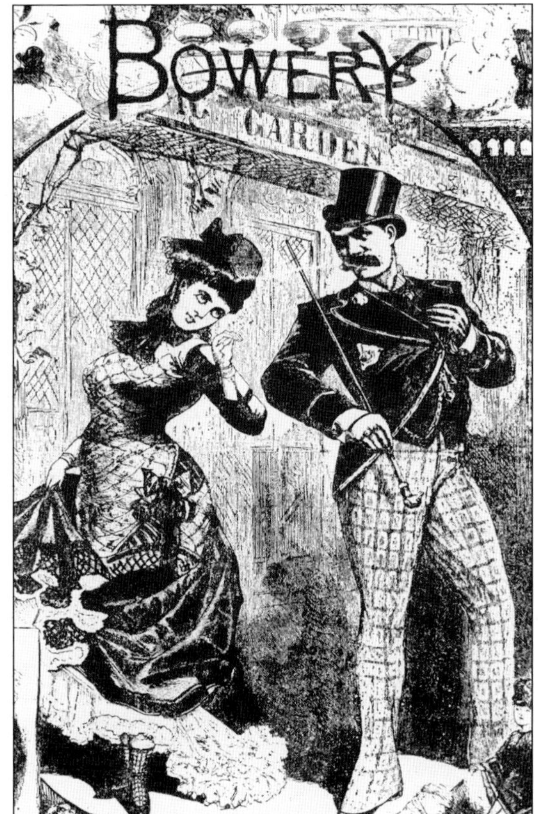

A far cry from the original firefighting Bowery Boys, who were genuinely roughneck, these comical, tough-talkin' movie goofballs are the archetype most people associate with the term. One of the most popular movie series ever, the Bowery Boys appeared in dozens of films from the late 1930s until the last one, in 1958. (DM.)

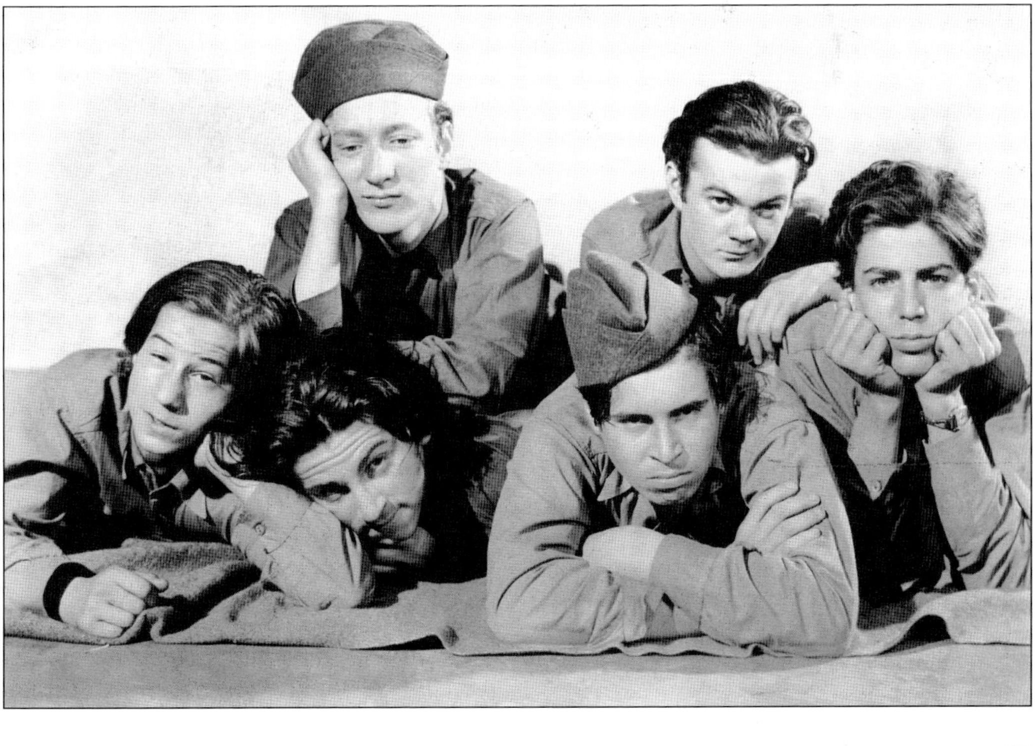

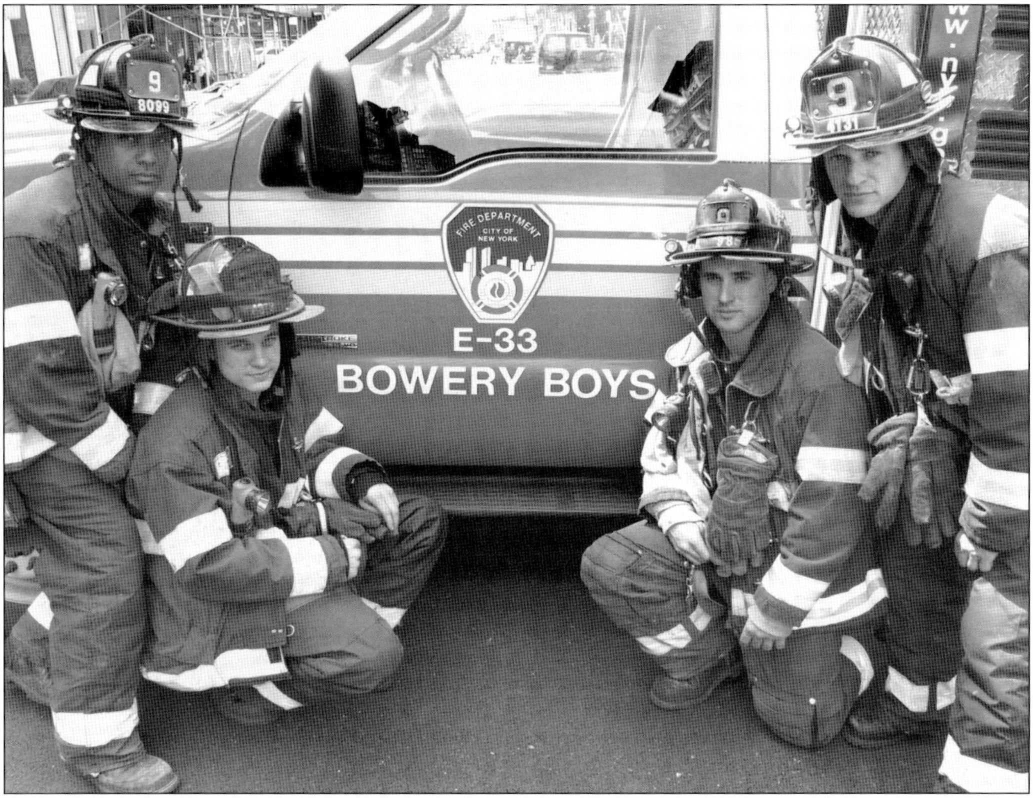

The Bowery Boys of today have, poignantly, returned to their roots, with the name blazoned on the firetrucks of Engine Company 33, Ladder 9 on Great Jones Street, just off Bowery. Photographed next to one of their trucks in 2015 are, from left to right, Marlon Sahai, Andrew Tanzi, James Walker, and Anton Shipman. (DM.)

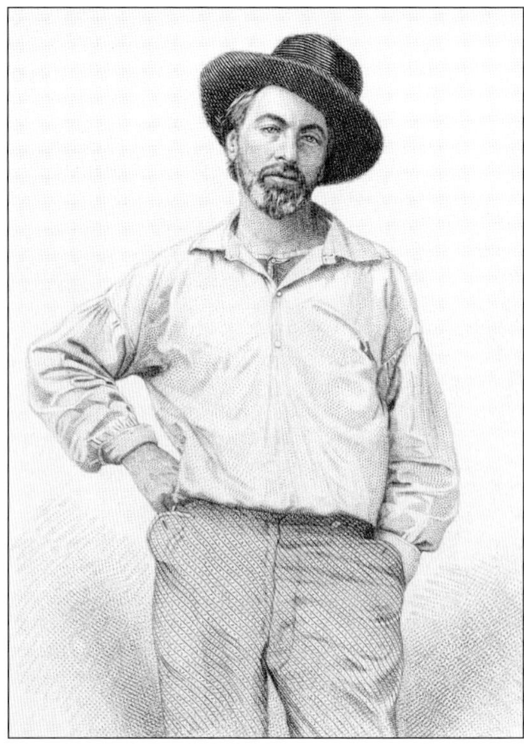

Poet Walt Whitman was sometimes referred to as "the Bowery Boy of literature" because of his earthy, expressive use of the vernacular. He frequented the street as a young man, as well as the Bowery Theatre. On seeing Junius Brutus Booth there, he wrote, "His genius was to me one of the grandest revelations of my life, a lesson of artistic expression." This engraving of Whitman by Samuel Hollyer is based upon a lost 1854 daguerreotype. (NYPL-MD.)

Writer Stephen Crane (1871–1900), who influenced realism and impressionism in American fiction, set several works in the Bowery, including *Maggie: Girl of the Streets*, written at age 21. Like a method actor, he spent nights in dive bars and flophouses. Returning home nearly frozen, a friend asked why he had not worn extra undergarments. "How would I know what the poor devils felt if I was warm myself?" (WC.)

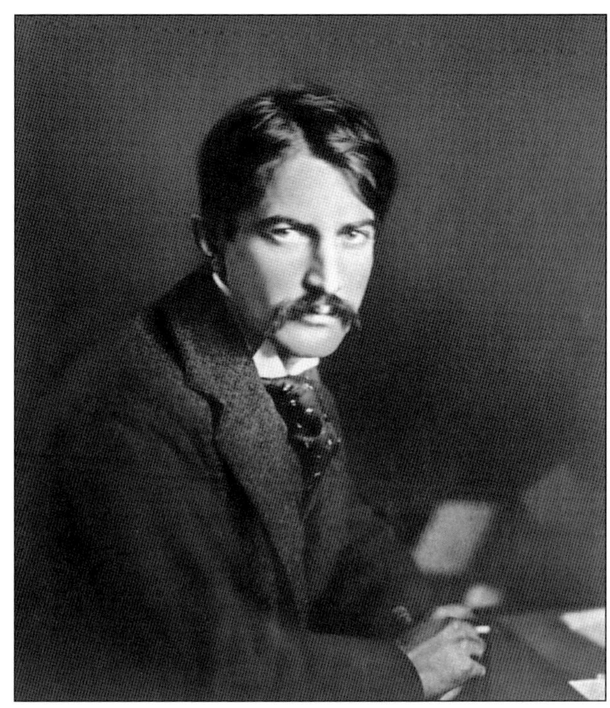

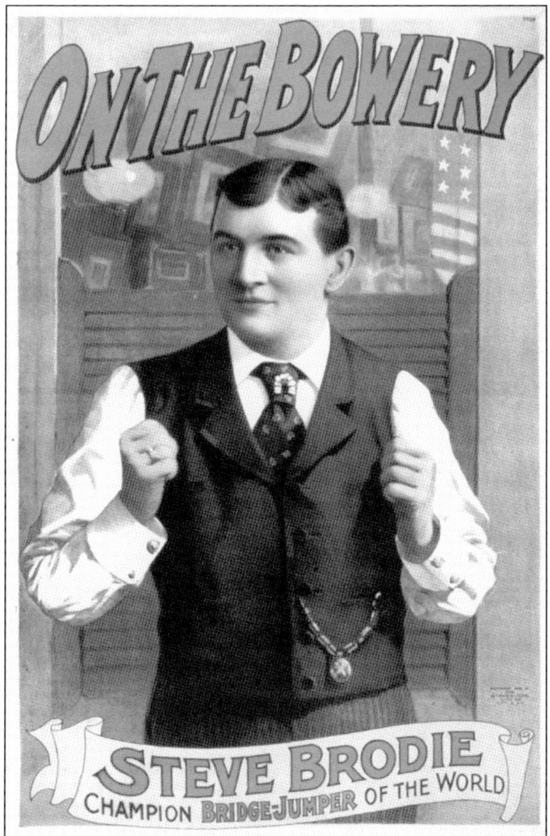

One Bowery character who caught the imagination of Americans was daredevil Brooklyn Bridge jumper Steve Brodie (1861–1901). The term "to do a Brodie" meant taking a dangerous leap or chance. Brodie appeared as himself in this 1896 play, recreating the jump and singing the songs "The Bowery" and "My Pearl's a Bowery Girl." He was depicted in the film *The Bowery* (1933) and the Bugs Bunny cartoon *Bowery Bugs* (1949). Another Bowery folk hero who played himself on stage was raconteur Chuck Connors, who appeared in the 1907 scenic extravaganza *From Broadway to the Bowery*. (LOC.)

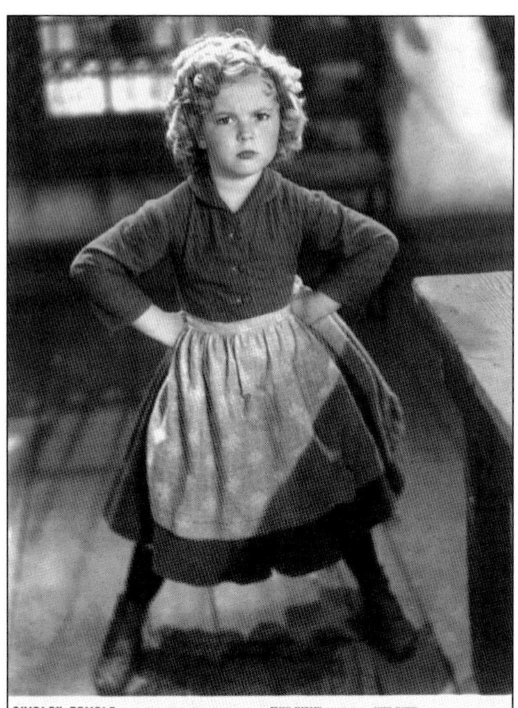

The Bowery Princess was the original title for the popular Shirley Temple film *Dimples* (1936), in which she played a busker (street entertainer) who wows the crowds while her grandfather picks their pockets. There is, of course, a moral turnaround in the story, but just before release 20th Century-Fox changed the title to avoid advertising "America's sweetheart" in alignment with a boulevard famous for its vice. (DM.)

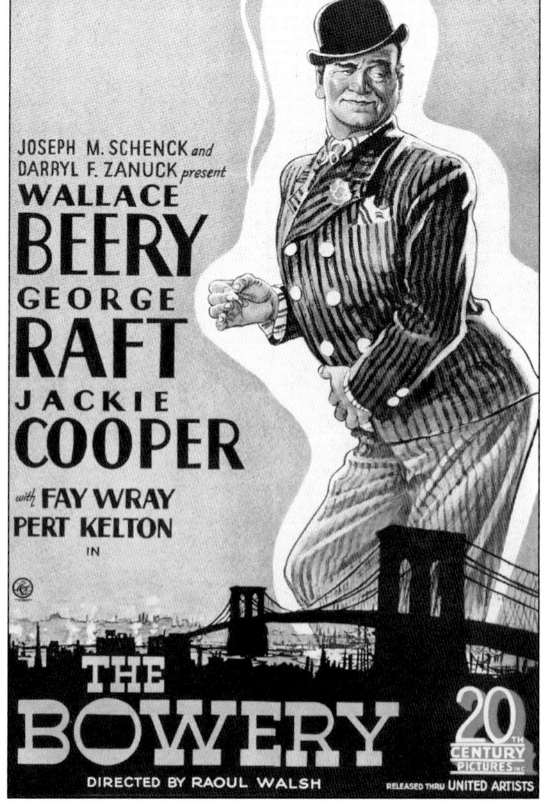

A lively 1933 pre-Code film with something to offend everyone, Raoul Walsh's *The Bowery* was a fictional hokum built around a supposed rivalry between real-life Bowery legends Chuck Connors and Steve Brodie. Wallace Beery's body language in this poster mimics the Bowery dance move, the Hard Walk, in which the dancer imitated a tough guy strutting down the avenue. (PD.)

This publicity shot of Ed Brady (1889–1942) personifies a Bowery tough from old Hollywood's central casting. Whether a murderer, thief, pickpocket, or just an all-around bum, you would not want to meet this guy in a dark alley. A character actor who slid into the ranks of extra work, when he died in 1942, he had almost 400 movie credits. (IMBD.)

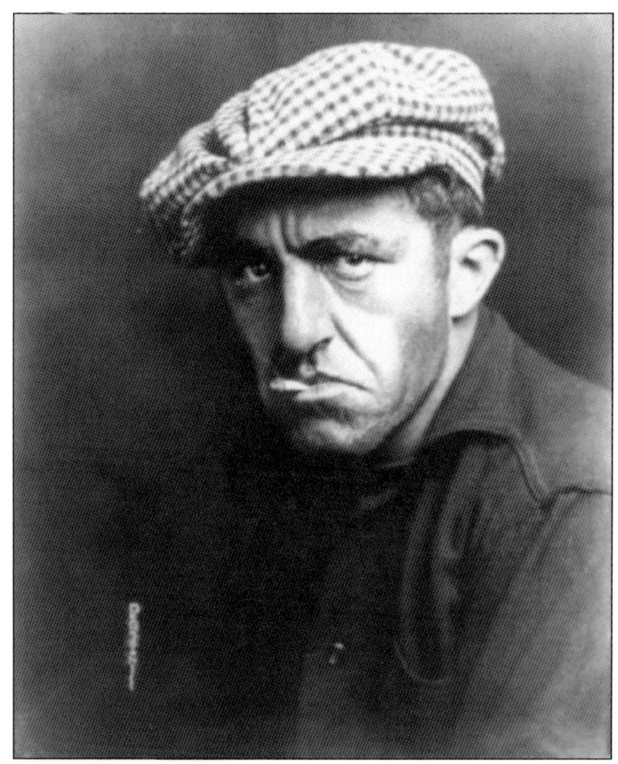

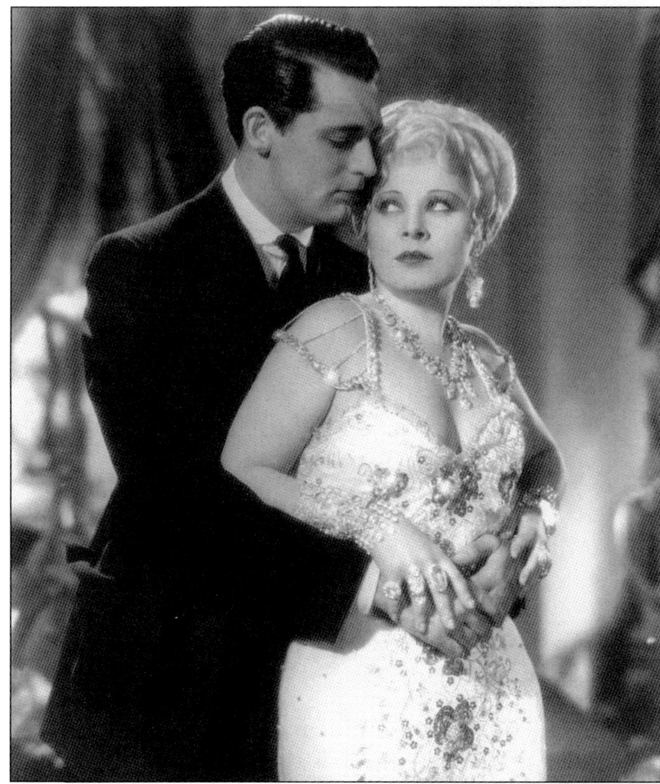

Mae West's *She Done Him Wrong* (1933), a raunchy homage to the Gay Nineties Bowery, contains the cinema's most famous seduction line: her command to mission worker Cary Grant to come up and see her sometime. The film was a smash hit. It saved Paramount from bankruptcy, but enraged the Catholic Legion of Decency, and helped usher in a heavy censorship regime in Hollywood. (Bruce Goldstein.)

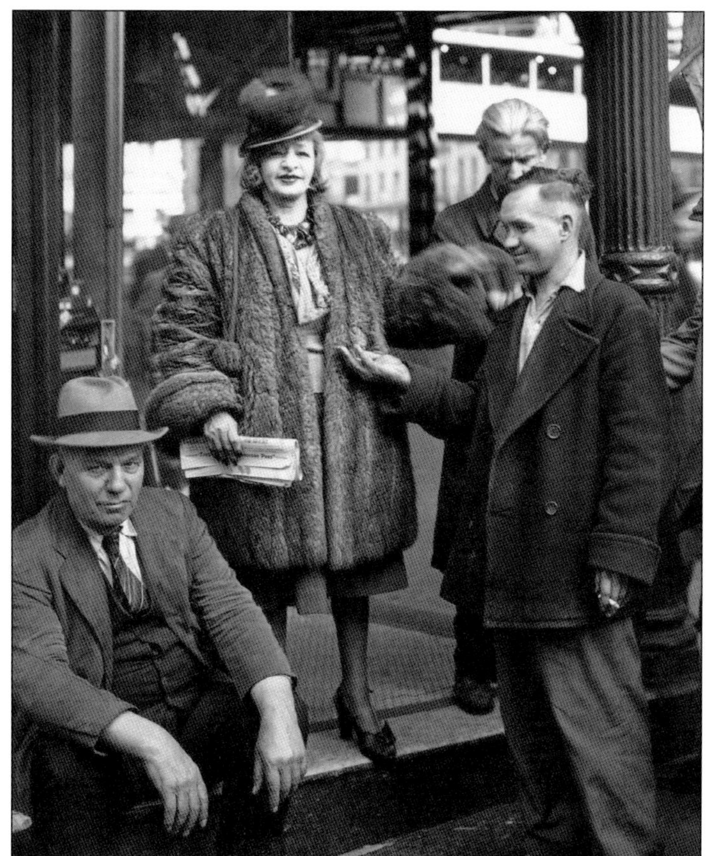

A short, bosomy peroxide blonde who wore lots of makeup and jewelry, Mazie Phillips (1896–1964) was the "Queen of the Bowery." Made famous by journalist Joseph Mitchell, she was a bouncer, ticket cage cashier, and co-owner of the Venice movie theatre on Chatham Square. Also known as "Saint Mazie," she generously gave the down-and-out money for meals, drinks, or a bed in a flophouse. This image was captured by Todd Webb in 1946. (© Todd Webb Archive.)

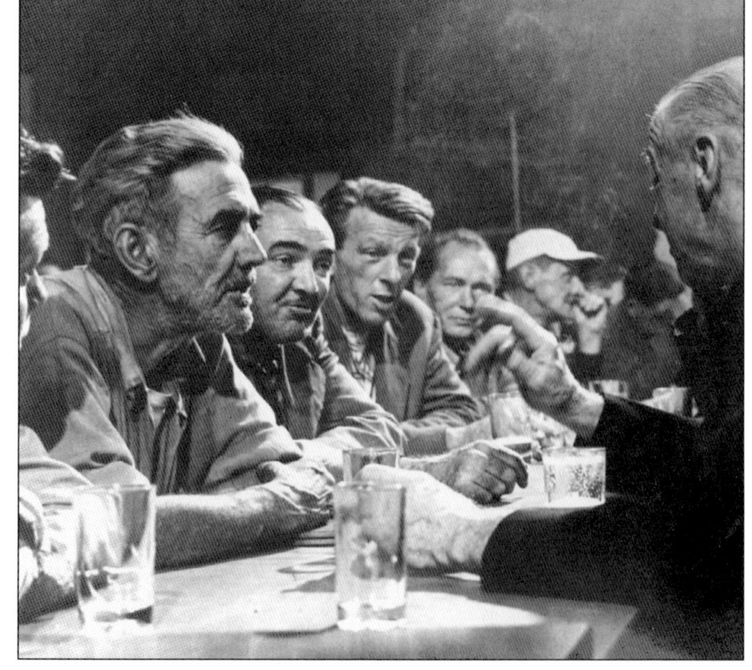

Filmed just before the elevated train came down, Lionel Rogosin's semi-documentary *On the Bowery* (1956) chronicles three days on skid row, centering on the drinking and working life of Ray Salyer, a drifter. Filmed on real locations, including the Bowery Mission, the film uses actual Bowery denizens as actors in a narrative they help craft. A Venice Film Festival winner, it had a major impact on the independent film movement. (RHI.)

Five

Bowery Arts and Artists from the 1950s to the Present

Despite its lingering ill-repute as America's skid row, during the second half of the 20th century, the Bowery quietly rose like a phoenix to again nurture American arts and culture. In the 1950s, at the Five Spot jazz club on Cooper Square, Billie Holiday gave some of her last performances, and Ornette Coleman shook things up with his improvisational approach to jazz. Since 1958, cutting-edge theater and dance have thrived on East Fourth Street between Bowery and Second Avenue, the epicenter of off-off-Broadway, including La MaMa and New York Theatre Workshop. Nearby, the Bouwerie Lane Theatre presented avant-garde shows inside a cast-iron former bank building, and grand opera was performed inside the matchbox-sized Amato Opera. In the 1970s, the grungy club CBGB birthed punk rock and became a laboratory of musical experimentation, featuring early performances by the Ramones, Patti Smith, Blondie, and Talking Heads. Other music venues included the Tin Palace and Great Gildersleeves. Today, music thrives at Bowery Electric and the Bowery Ballroom, with creative wordplay at the Bowery Poetry Club.

When the elevated train came down in 1956, the Bowery's cheaper real estate and spacious upper floors—former industrial or lodging house lofts—began attracting a bohemia of painters, sculptors, writers, filmmakers, photographers, and musicians, all seeking elbow room in which to live and create. Their impact on American culture has been significant, including painters Mark Rothko, Roy Lichtenstein, and Jean-Michel Basquiat; sculptors Eva Hesse and Maya Lin; musician Debbie Harry; photographers Robert Frank, Nan Goldin, Jay Maisel, and Stephanie Chernikowski; writers William Burroughs, Diane di Prima, Hettie Jones, Kate Millet, Bob Holman, John Giorno, and Amiri Baraka, founder of the Black Arts Movement.

In 1973, a vacant lot at Bowery and Houston was transformed by the Green Guerillas into Liz Christy Garden, the city's first community garden. Across the street, a 1982 Keith Haring mural made the Bowery Wall a famous spot for street art. Today's Bowery is home to the New Museum, Grey Art Museum, Howl Arts, Westwood Gallery, Sperone Westwater, and many other galleries, though few up-and-coming artists can afford the rent and many Bowery artists' lofts have been lost to gentrification.

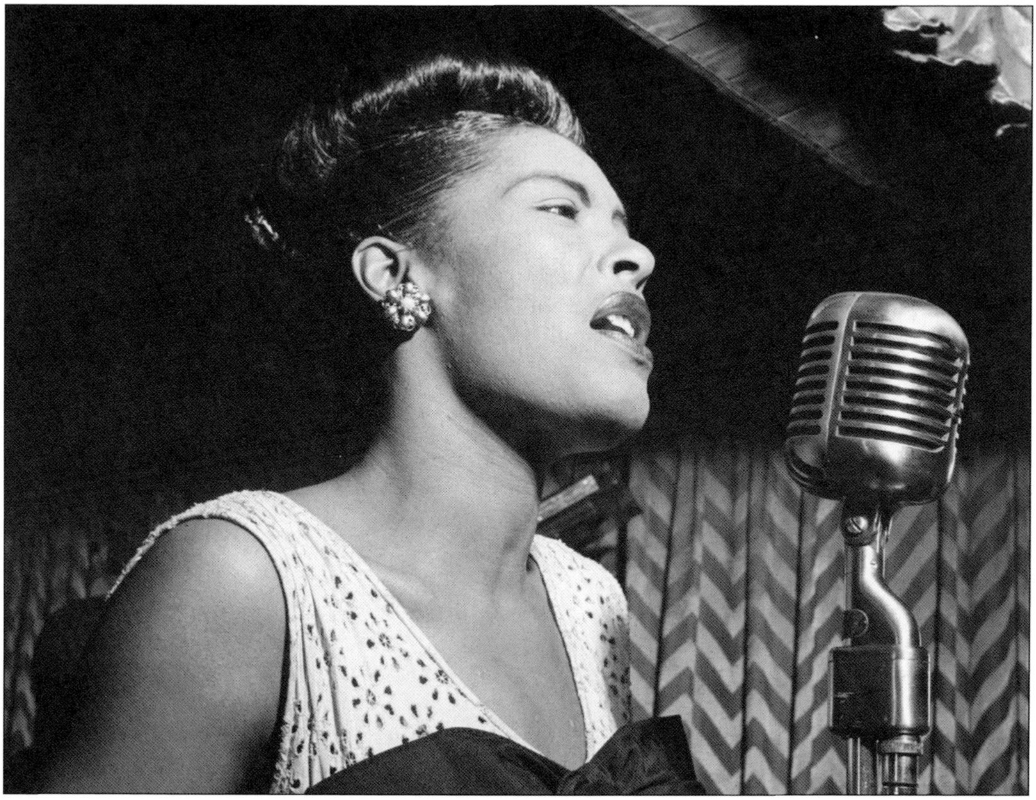

Jazz and blues legend Billie "Lady Day" Holiday gave some of her last performances at the Five Spot jazz club at 5 Cooper Square. Her cabaret license was revoked due to a drug charge, but club owners Joe and Iggy Termini hired her anyway, filling the club through word of mouth alone. Poet Frank O'Hara recalled that "while she whispered a song along the keyboard . . . I stopped breathing." This 1947 photograph is by William Gottlieb. (LOC.)

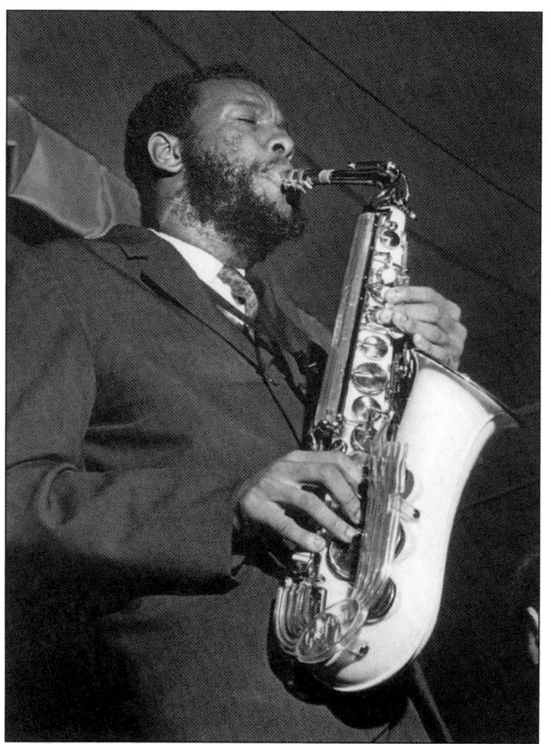

In 1959, during gigs at the Five Spot, saxophonist Ornette Coleman (1930–2015) broke musical ground when he introduced "free jazz," an improvisational approach that championed ensemble experimentation. In the 1950s and 1960s, the Five Spot was a premier place for serious, cutting-edge jazz, including Thelonious Monk, Cecil Taylor, Eric Dolphy, David Amram, Charles Mingus, and John Coltrane. This 1960 photograph was taken by Robert Parent. (Dale Parent.)

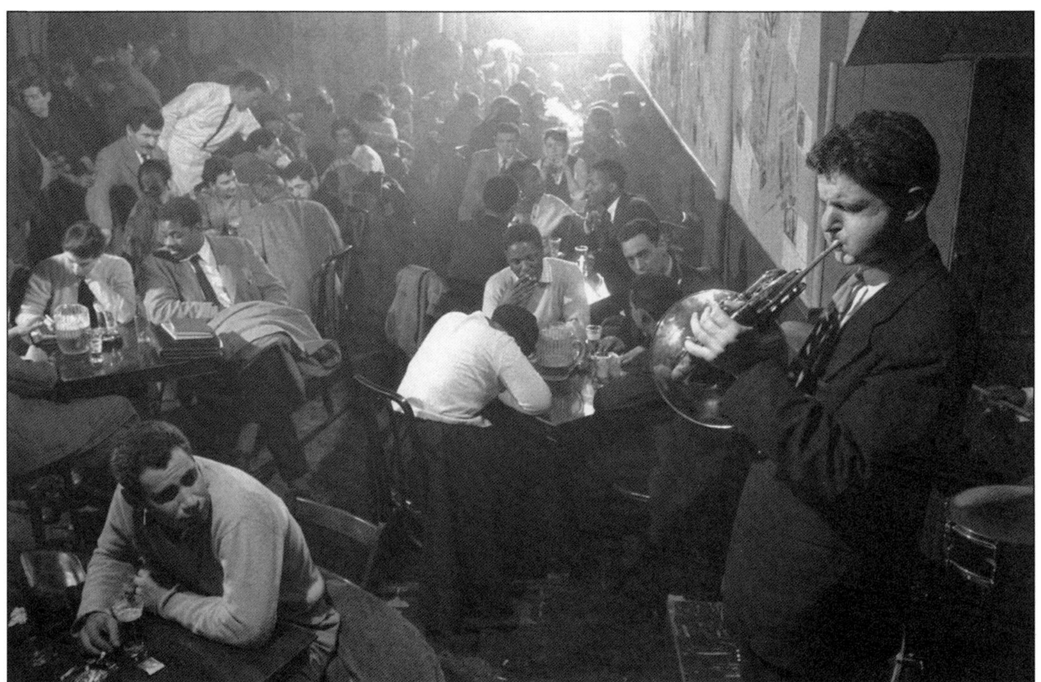

Burt Glinn took this photograph of composer-musician David Amram (born 1930) playing before a bustling Five Spot crowd in 1957. Patrons included Leonard Bernstein, Willem de Kooning, James Baldwin, Jack Kerouac, Norman Mailer, and Allen Ginsberg. Sometimes, there were late-night poetry readings. Writer Dan Wakefield recalled that it was an informal, inexpensive, no-frills place where one could sit for hours nursing a beer and listening to music. (David Amram.)

The gateway to the epicenter of off-off-Broadway is Bowery and Fourth Street. Though it lacks glitzy marquees, its theater row in the East Fourth Street Cultural District, which stretches from Bowery to Second Avenue, boasts a dozen theaters, including La Mama Experimental Theatre and New York Theatre Workshop. Phebe's Tavern, "the Sardi's of off-off-Broadway," has been a favorite since the 1960s. Germania Fire Insurance Building is at right in this 1980 photograph. (CDM.)

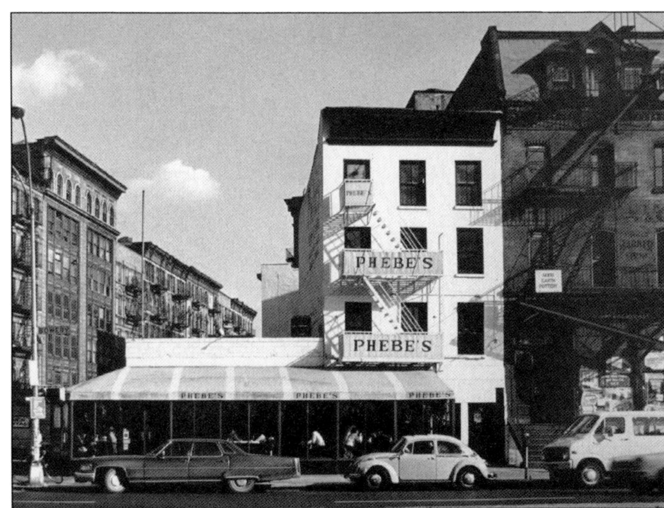

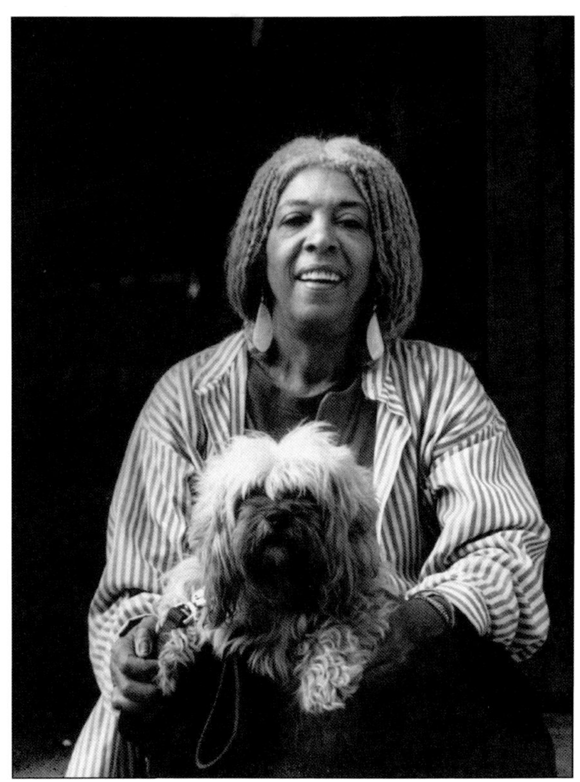

A nurturing earth mother to the experimental theatre and Off-Off-Broadway movements, Ellen Stewart (1919–2011) was a producer-director-founder of the influential La MaMa Experimental Theatre Club, which is named for her. Located at 74 East Fourth Street since the 1960s, it has witnessed work by Al Pacino, Robert De Niro, Sam Shepard, Harvey Fierstein, Lanford Wilson, Philip Glass, Robert Wilson, Richard Foreman, Meredith Monk, and Ping Chong. This 1985 photograph is by Cynthia MacAdams. (CM.)

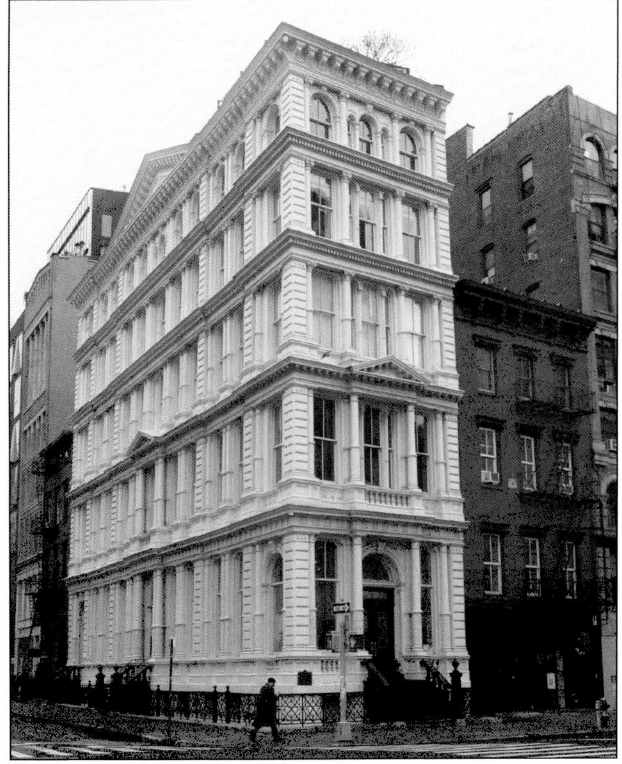

Though this cast-iron NYC Landmark at 330 Bowery began life as the Henry Englebert–designed Bond Street Savings Bank; in 1963, it became the cutting-edge Bouwerie Lane Theatre. Shows included Frank Langella in Andre Gide's *The Immoralist*, the Cockettes in *Palm Casino Review*, Bernadette Peters in *Dames at Sea*, and countless productions by the Jean Cocteau Repertory Company, including a Tennessee Williams premiere. The photograph is from 2024. (DM.)

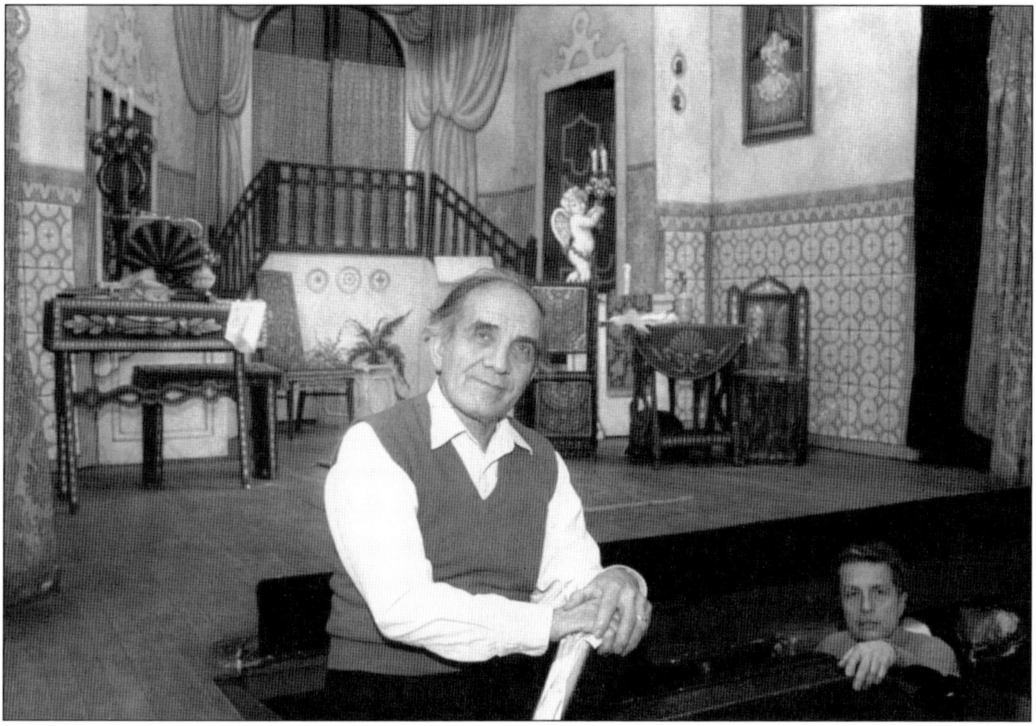

Built inside an 1899 structure that once housed a cigar-rolling factory, from 1964 to 2009, the Amato Opera House was located at 319 Bowery. With only 107 seats, it was "the world's smallest opera house," but consummate sets, direction, orchestra, and players gave audiences a riveting experience. The company was founded in 1948 by Anthony and Sally Amato. Ruby Washington's 1989 photograph shows Anthony and the Amato's tiny stage. (*New York Times*/Redux.)

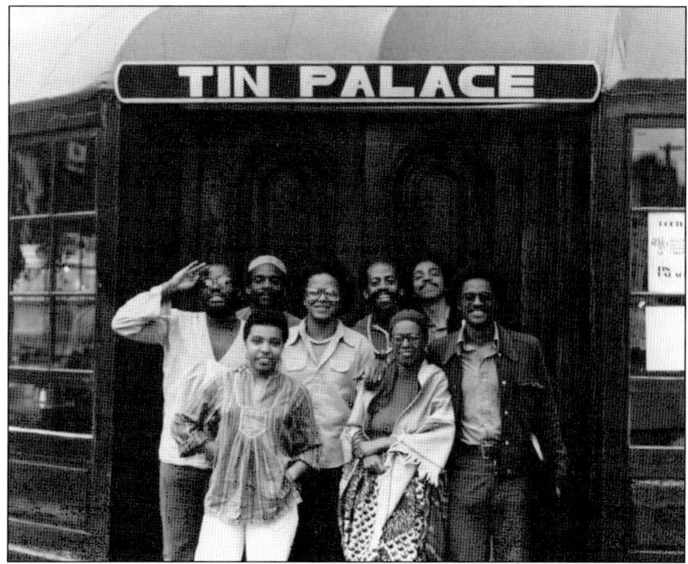

Another cutting-edge jazz club was the Tin Palace at 325 Bowery, a reputed former site of a speakeasy run by mobster Meyer Lansky. The brainchild of writer Paul Pines, it lasted only from 1970 to 1980. Performers included Eddie Jefferson, Shelia Jordan, Roscoe Mitchell, Paul Bley, James Blood Ulmer, and the debut of the World Saxophone Quartet. This 1976 Amos Rice photograph shows Stanley Crouch, Patricia Spears, David Murray, Philip Wilson, Bobo Shaw, and others. (Carol Pines.)

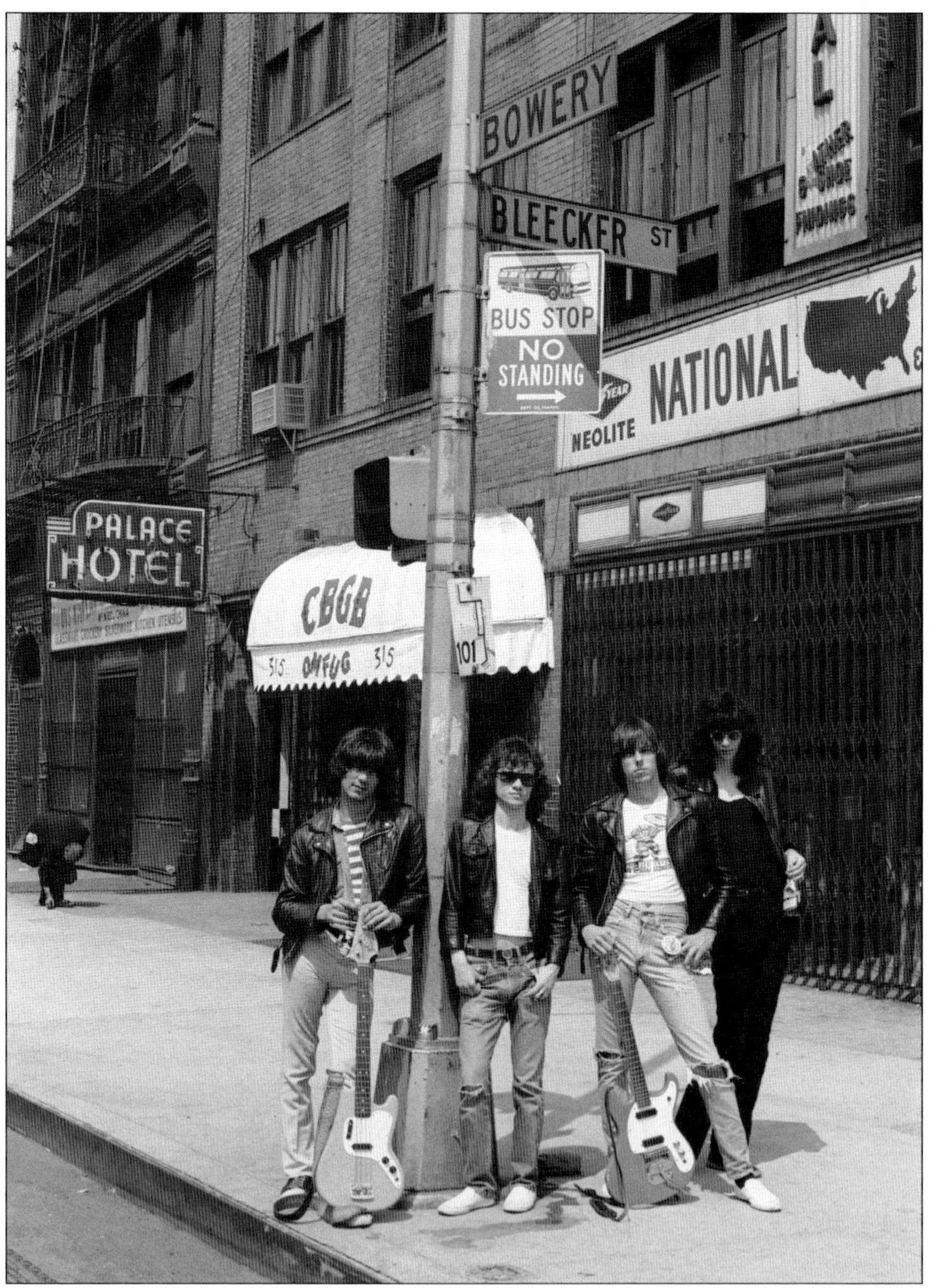

This 1975 Bob Gruen photograph shows the Ramones, the first punk rock band, outside CBGB, the club where it all began. Located at 315 Bowery, its initials reference the original plan of club founder Hilly Kristal (1931–2007) to offer country, bluegrass, and blues. Its famously grungy interior was a nurturing space for new songs and new bands, even fledgling teenage bands. Performers included Patti Smith, Talking Heads, Blondie, Richard Hell, Living Colour, John Cale, Dead Boys, Joan Jett, Iggy Pop, Alan Jackson, and the B-52s. After a long legal dispute with his landlord, and a public campaign to save it, CBGB closed on October 15, 2006. The street sign at Bowery and Second Street reads, "Joey Ramone Place." (© Bob Gruen.)

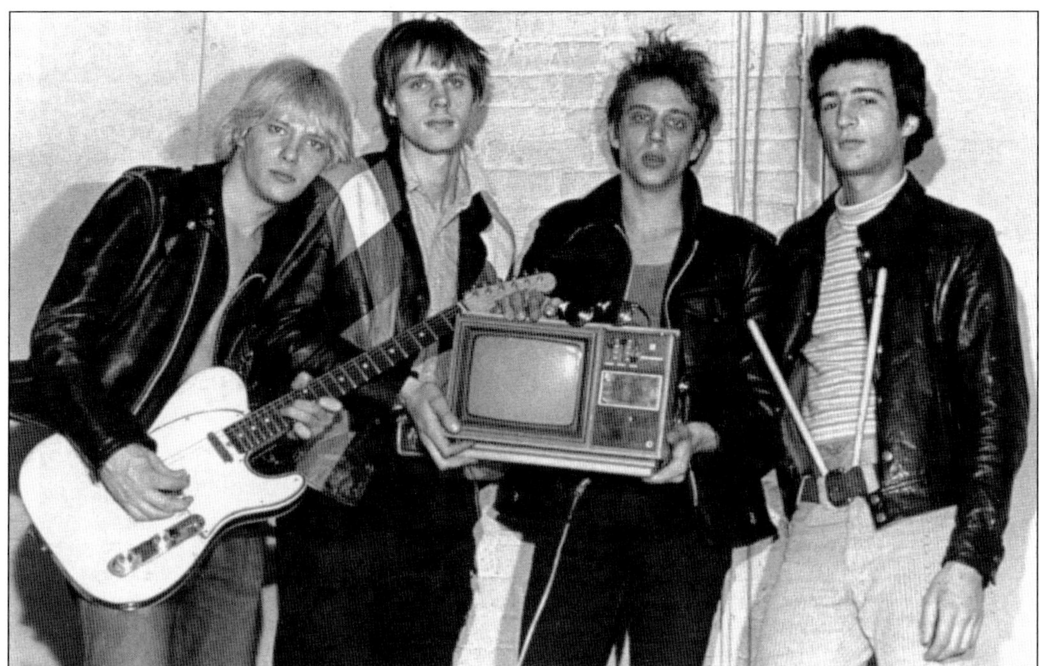

An important influence on punk rock, Television was the first band to receive intense media attention at CBGB shortly after it opened in 1974. The original members, pictured here in 1974, are (left to right) Richard Lloyd, Tom Verlaine, Richard Hell, and Billy Ficca. (© Richard Hell.)

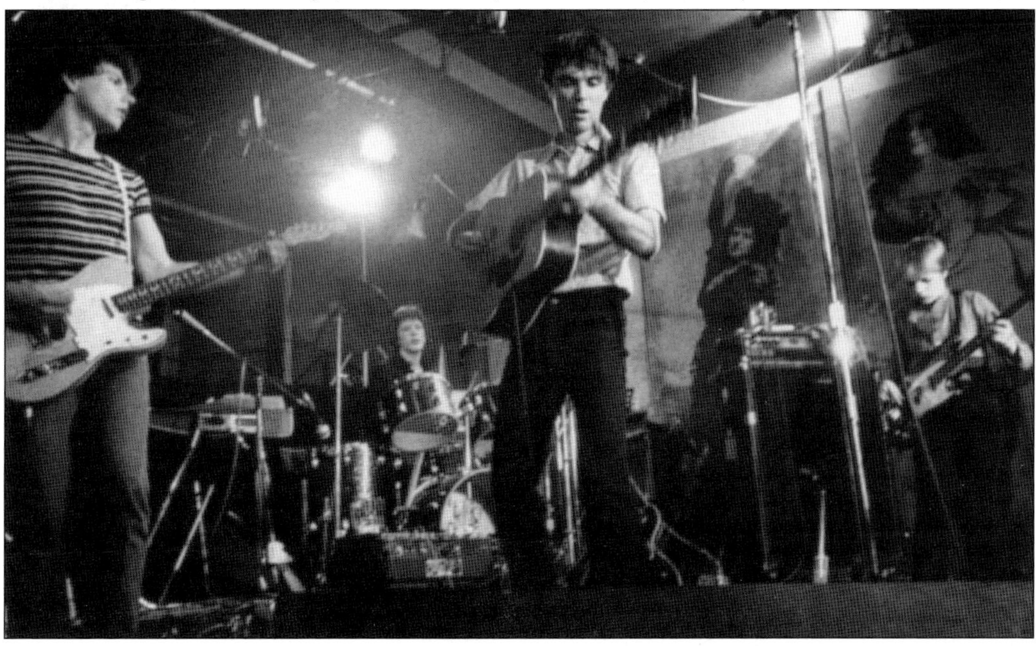

Legend has it that when the new wave band Talking Heads first appeared at CBGB, on June 20, 1975, as the opening band for the Ramones, there were only 10 people in the audience. That night they performed "Psycho Killer," the song that later became their first hit. This 1977 David Godlis photograph shows (left to right) Jerry Harrison, Chris Frantz, David Byrne, and Tina Weymouth at CBGB. (© David Godlis.)

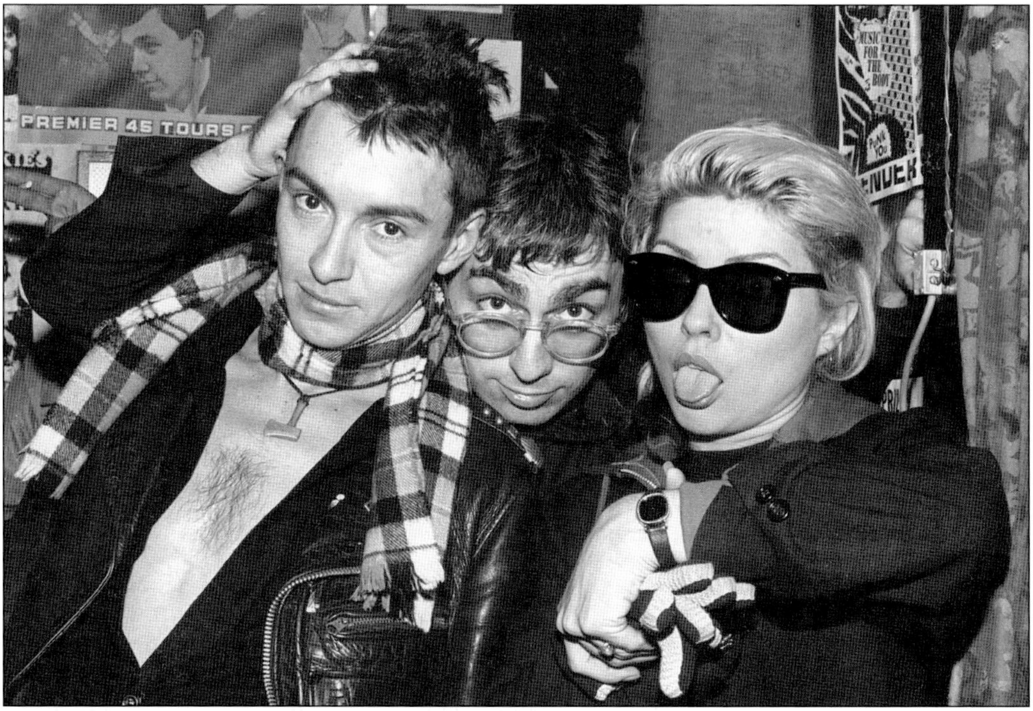

Artist Arturo Vega, graphic designer for the Ramones, is clowning with Blondie's Chris Stein and Debbie Harry at CBGB's 1978 benefit for Dead Boys drummer Johnny Blitz, hospitalized after being knifed in the East Village. A much-loved figure, Vega died in 2013, but inspired Howl! Happenings: An Arturo Vega Project, which presents art exhibitions, music, and events at 250 Bowery and 6 East First Street. This 1978 image was captured by Lisa J. Kristal. (© LJK.)

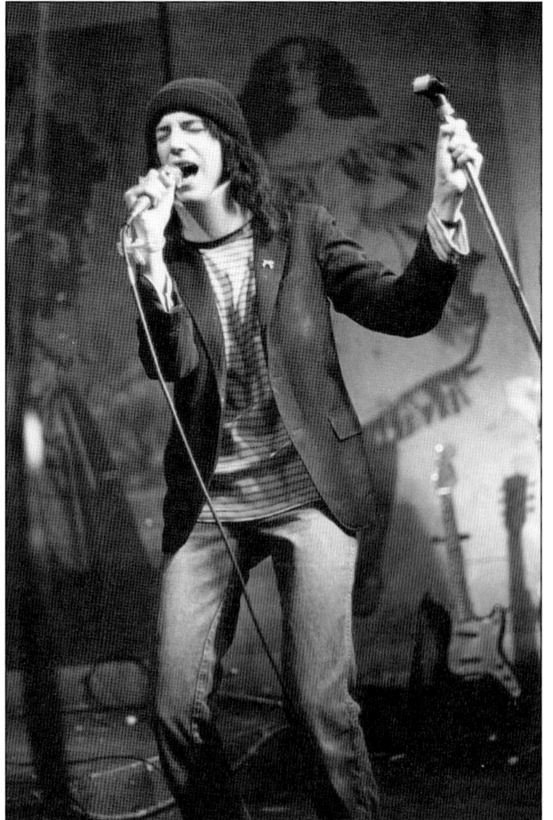

Singer-songwriter-poet-author Patti Smith first ventured inside CBGB in 1974 to see the band Television. She has recalled its "smell of piss and beer" but immediately felt at home: "The absence of glamour made it seem all the more familiar, a place we could call our own." Smith gave an elegiac three-and-a-half-hour performance at the club the day before its doors closed for good. This 1977 photograph is by Lisa J. Kristal. (© LJK.)

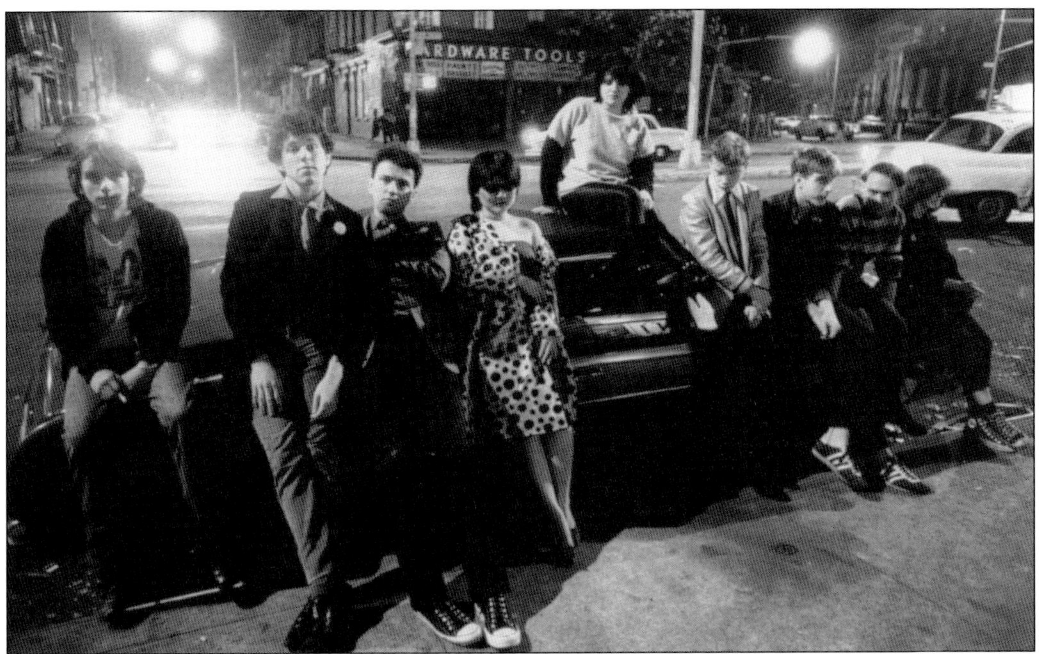

This 1978 David Godlis photograph of "No Wave Punks" shows (left to right) Harold Paris, Kristian Hoffman, Diego Cortez, Anya Phillips, Lydia Lunch, James Chance, Jim Sclavunos, Bradley Field, and Liz Seidman. "They were just standing there outside CBGB when I walked out. They were all core people in the No Wave scene." No Wave was a short-lived, but influential, rebellious approach to music, art, filmmaking, fashion, and performance that rejected conformity and commercialism, and flourished in Lower Manhattan from the mid-1970s through the mid-1980s. CBGB was an artistic anchor for that movement, inspiring collaborations between filmmakers and musicians, with rockers behind and in front of the camera, and on soundtracks. The 1997 photograph below, also by Godlis, shows independent filmmakers Jim Jarmusch and Sara Driver arriving at CBGB to celebrate the launch of Jarmusch's Neil Young documentary. (Both, DG.)

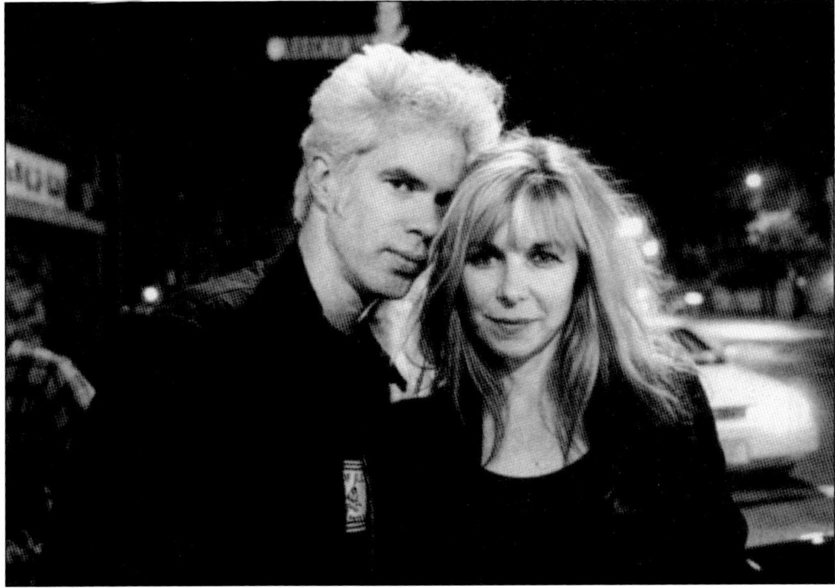

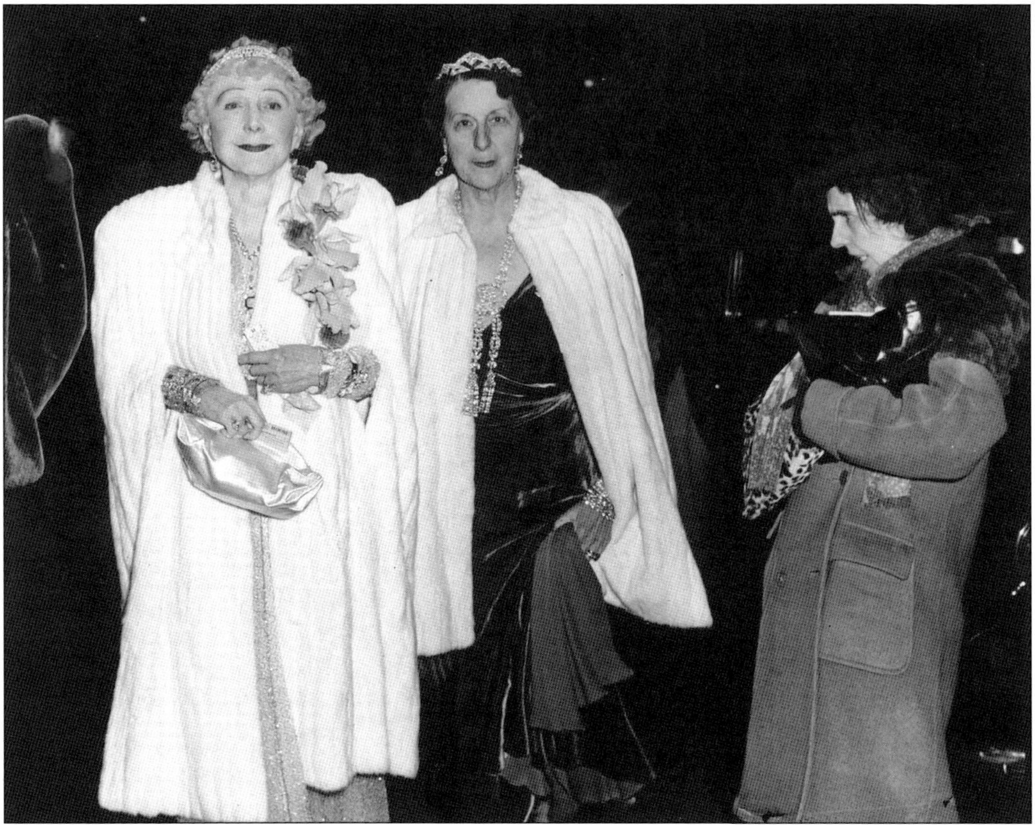

The Bowery was a muse for Ukrainian-born photographer Weegee (Arthur Fellig, 1899–1968), known for crime scenes and raucous shots inside Sammy's Bowery Follies. His famous 1943 photograph "The Critic," taken outside the Metropolitan Opera, was indirectly a Bowery scene. As bejeweled socialites arrive, a spectator disapproves. It appears spontaneous, but Weegee had brought along a Bowery inebriate, his assistant unleashing her from the taxicab at just the right moment. (Toledo Museum of Art.)

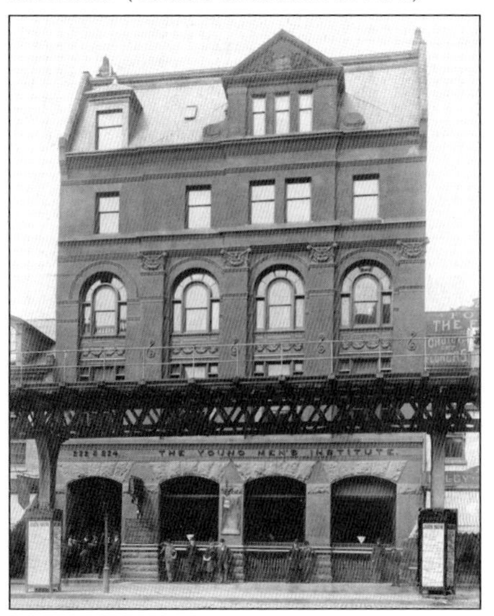

Though this 1884 Queen Anne–style landmark at 222 Bowery (designed by Bradford Gilbert) started life as the uplifting Young Men's Institute, by the mid-1900s, it reinvented itself as a live-work space for artists, including painters Fernand Leger, Mark Rothko, Michael Goldberg, Lynn Umlauf, Lynda Benglis, writer William Burroughs, and poet John Giorno. The photograph is from around the 1890s. (Kautz Family YMCA Archive.)

Latvian-born Mark Rothko (1903–1970) was one of the most influential Abstract Expressionist painters. Some of his most important work was created at his 222 Bowery studio, including the murals produced in 1958–1959 for the Seagram Building's ultra-exclusive Four Seasons restaurant. Detesting the place, he stated privately, "I hope to ruin the appetite of every son of a bitch who ever eats in that room." This photograph was taken in 1961. (Christopher Rothko.)

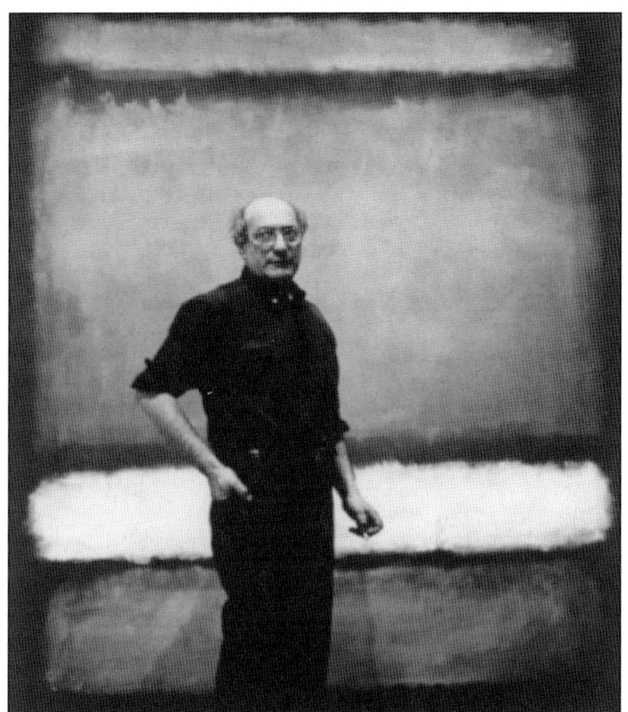

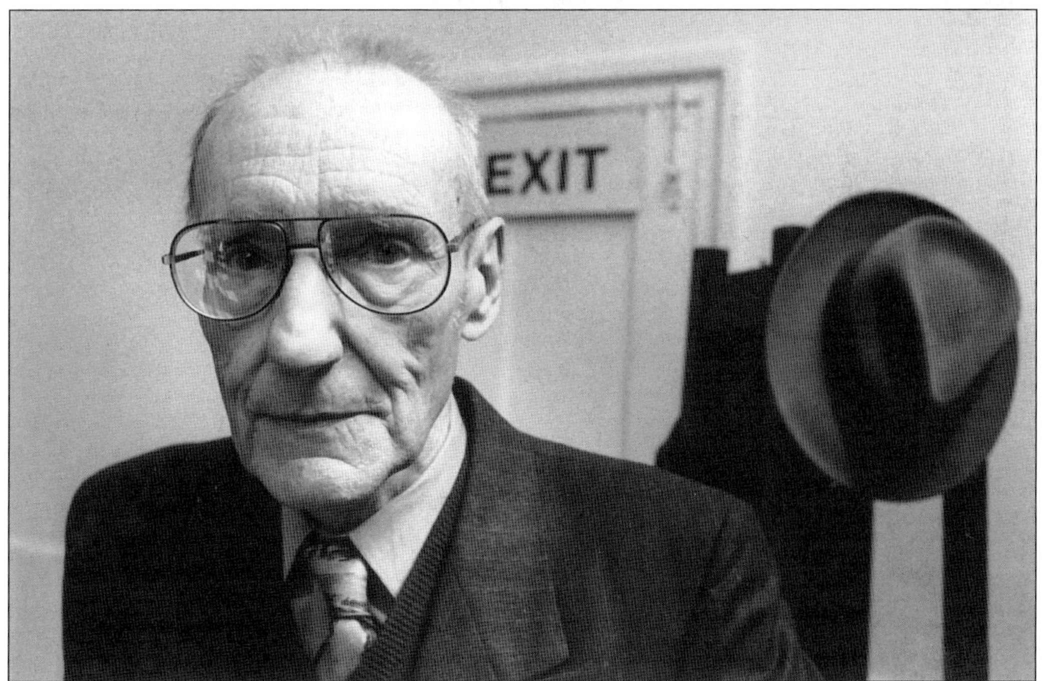

Beat Generation writer William S. Burroughs (1914–1997), author of *Naked Lunch*, lived and worked for several years at 222 Bowery, occupying a stark, windowless former locker room space. Patti Smith recalled him as "simultaneously old and young. Part sheriff, part gumshoe. . . . He camped in 'the Bunker' with his typewriter, his shotgun, and his overcoat." This 1989 photograph is by John Minihan. (John Minihan.)

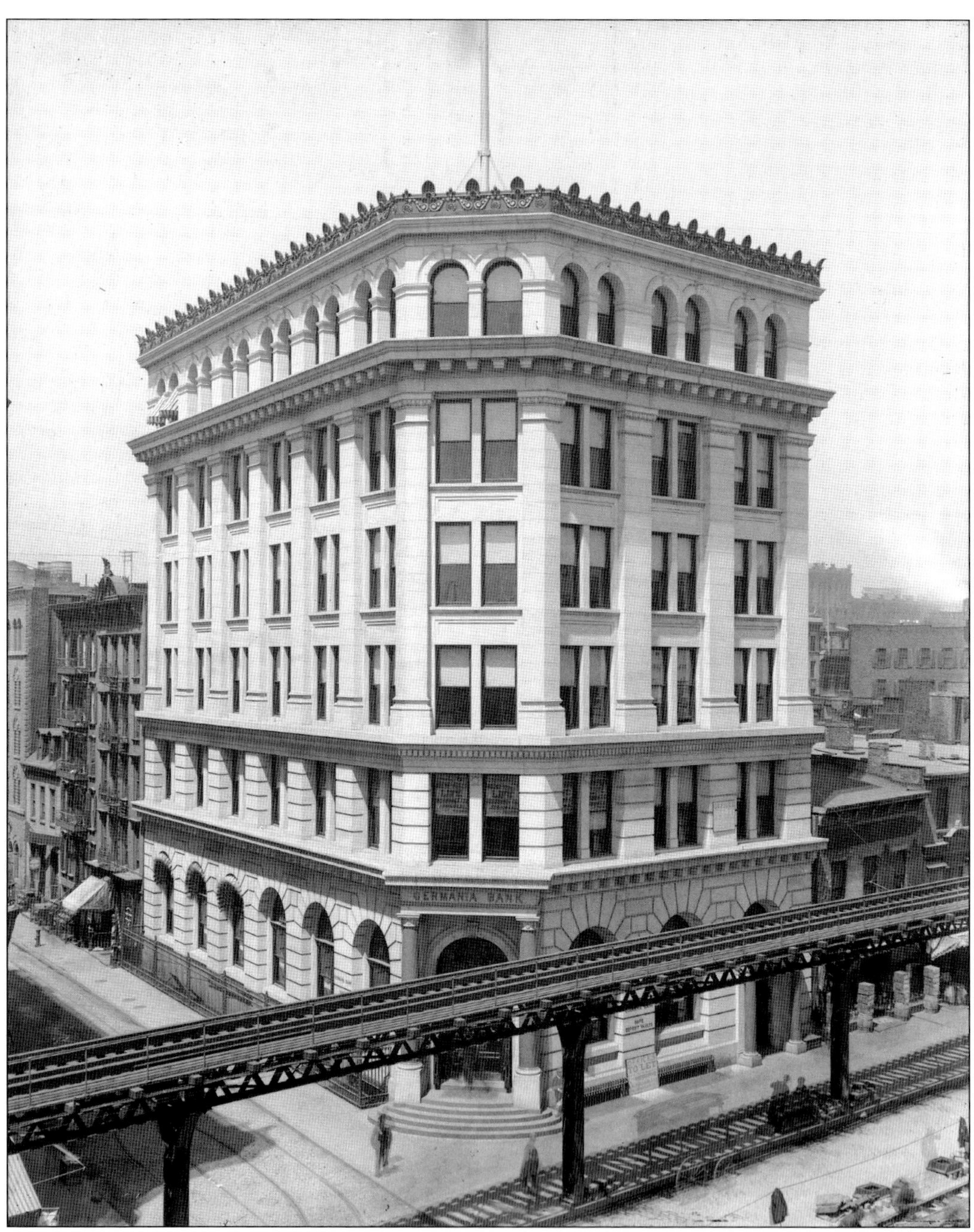

Another landmark building turned incubator for art was the 1898 Beaux Arts–style Germania Bank Building (designed by Robert Maynicke) at 190 Bowery, seen here in about 1905. For a time the studios of Abstract Expressionist painter Adolph Gottlieb and pop artist Roy Lichtenstein, from 1966 to 2014 it was Jay Maisel's home and photography studio/school. Bought for $102,000, Maisel sold it in 2014 for $55 million. It now houses a skateboarding boutique. (MCNY.)

Influential pop artist Roy Lichtenstein (1923–1997) made the third floor of the Germania Bank Building his studio home from 1966 until 1973. Best known for his sardonic use of comic strip elements, this painting, produced in his 190 Bowery studio in 1967, is entitled *Modern Painting with Classic Head*. (Estate of Roy Lichtenstein and GRAY Chicago/New York.)

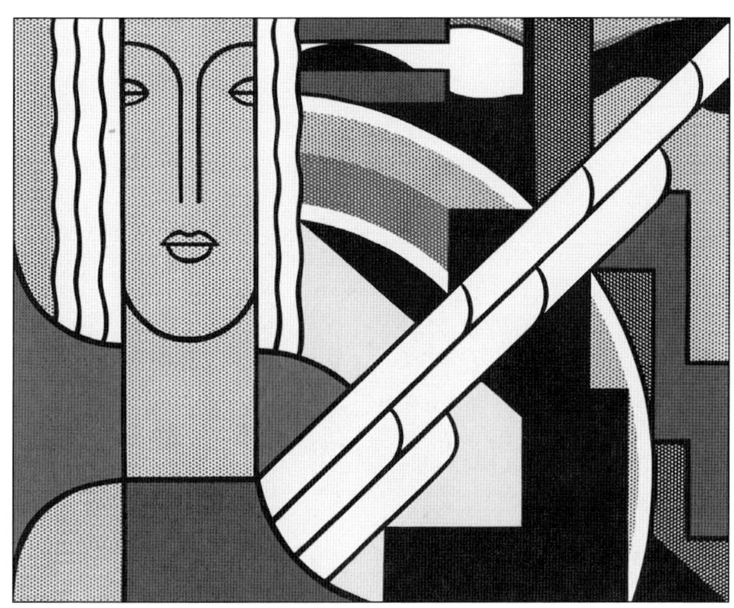

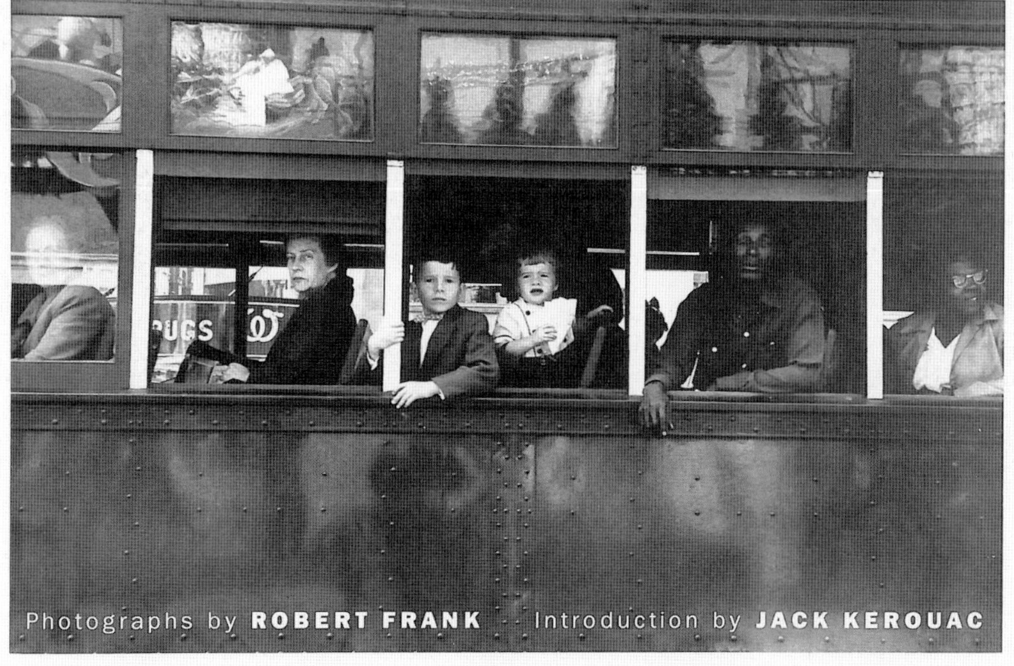

Swiss-born photographer-filmmaker Robert Frank (1924–2019) lived at 184 Bowery and on Bleecker Street for over 50 years. According to critic Sean O'Hagan, Frank's *The Americans* "changed the nature of photography, what it could say and how it could say it . . . it remains perhaps the most influential photography book of the 20th century." His films include *Pull My Daisy* (1959), a Beat Generation collaboration. (Steidl Books.)

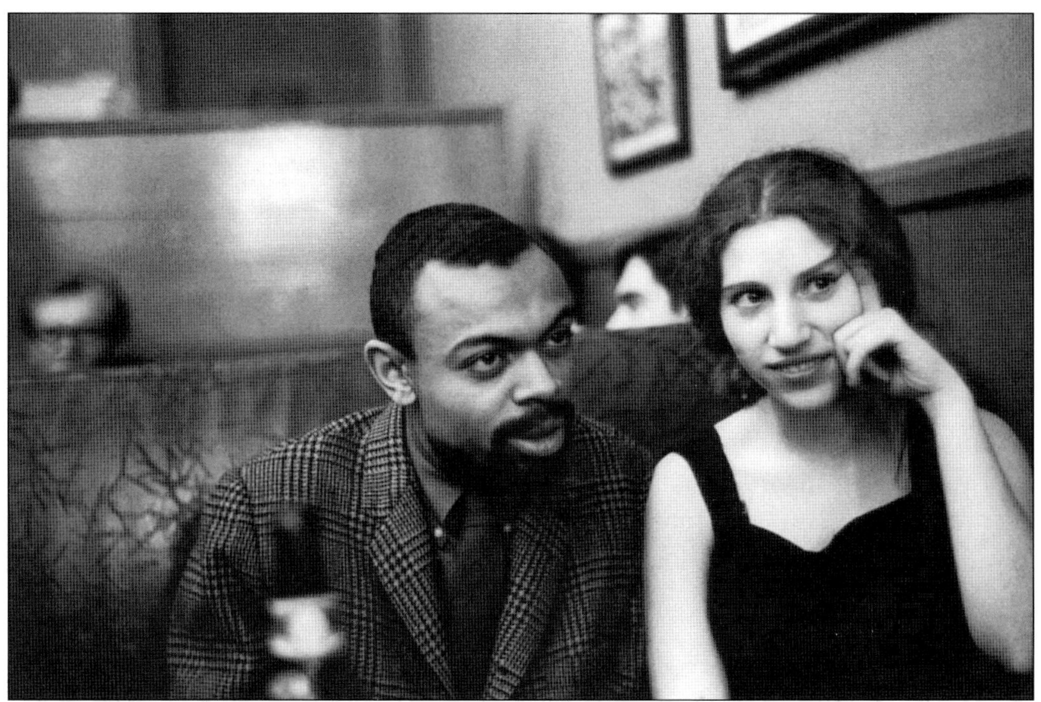

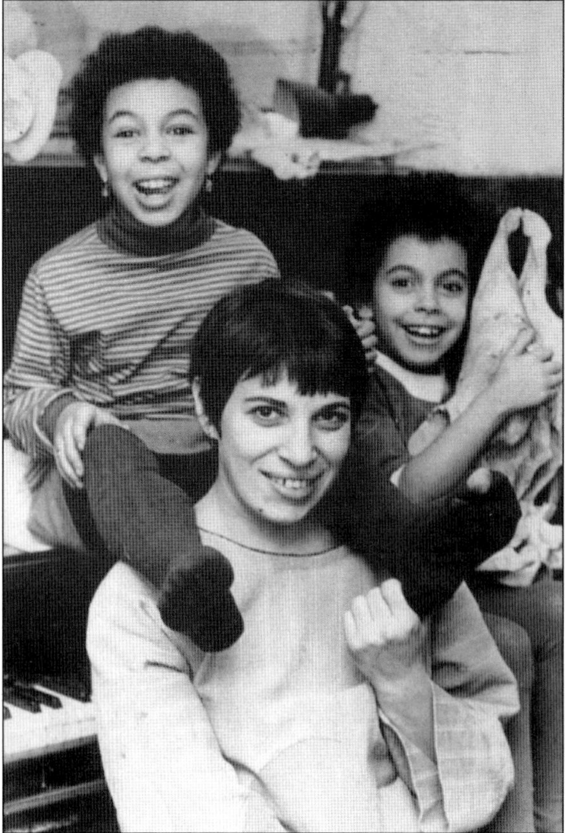

In the mid-1960s, while living at 27 Cooper Square, poet-playwright LeRoi Jones (better known as Amiri Baraka, 1934–2014) germinated both the name and initial ideas for the influential Black Arts Movement. In the early 1960s, he coedited with Beat poetess Diane Di Prima (1934–2020) *Floating Bear*, an influential mimeographed journal of new literary work. Many issues were prepared at Di Prima's apartment at 35 Cooper Square. This 1960 photograph is by Fred W. McDarrah. (McDarrah/Getty Images.)

This late-1960s photograph shows poet-editor-teacher-activist Hettie Jones (1934–2024) with daughters Kellie Jones (left) and Lisa Jones inside 27 Cooper Square, an 1844 building she occupied for over 60 years and helped save in 2007. Her revealing autobiography covers the Beat Generation, the Civil Rights era, her biracial marriage to LeRoi Jones (Amiri Baraka), and the bohemian whirl of writers, artists, and jazz musicians that passed through her building. (Hettie Jones.)

This c. 1966 photograph shows German-born sculptor Eva Hesse (1936–1970) inside her studio at 134 Bowery. One of the most prominent women in a field dominated by men, she broadened the concept of sculpture by introducing unorthodox materials including fiberglass and ephemeral matter like rope, latex, and fabrics, things that do not have a long shelf life. According to Hesse, "Life doesn't last; art doesn't last." (Estate of Eva Hesse.)

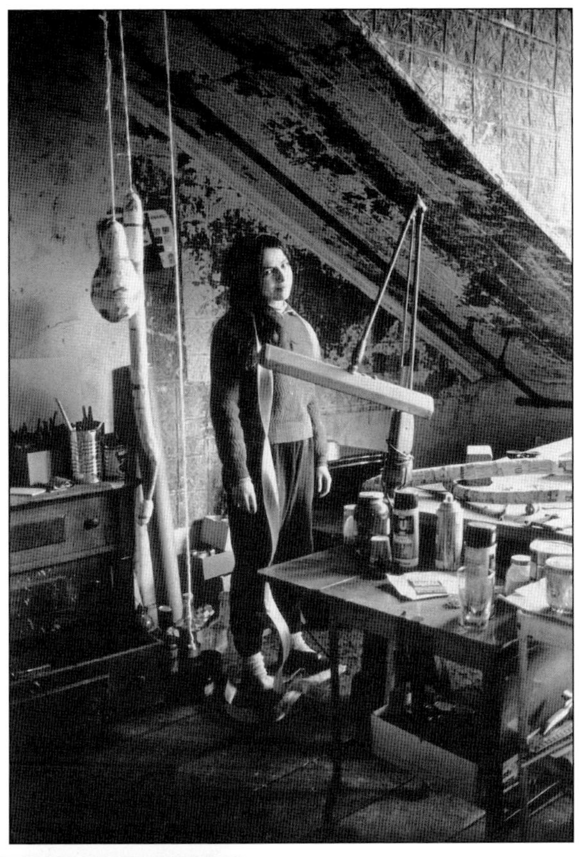

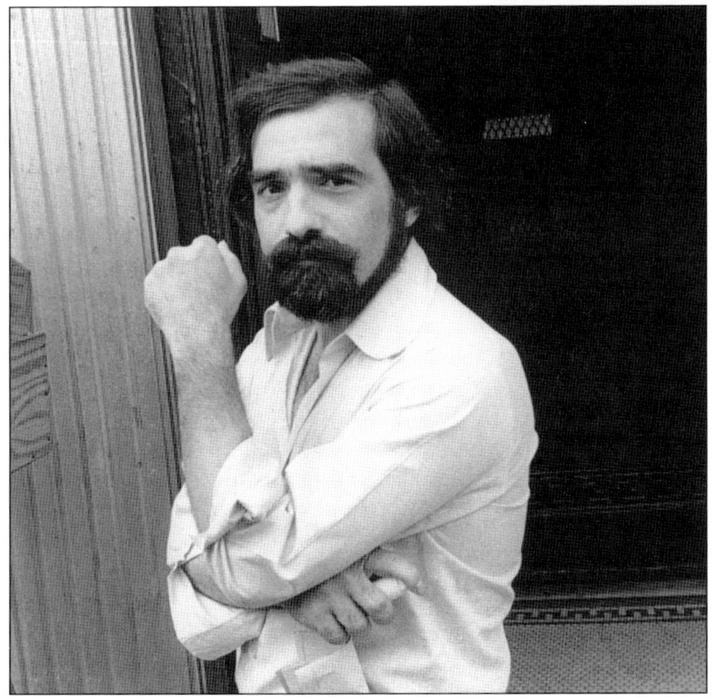

Filmmaker Martin Scorsese (born 1942) grew up near the Bowery, on Elizabeth Street. In a 2013 letter to city planning urging protective zoning for the street, he stated, "The neighborhood and residents of the Bowery became clear catalysts for turning me into a storyteller. Whether it's *Mean Streets* or *Gangs of New York*, the influence of The Bowery—the grittiness, the ambiance, the vivid atmosphere—is apparent." This 1979 photograph was taken by Godlis. (DG.)

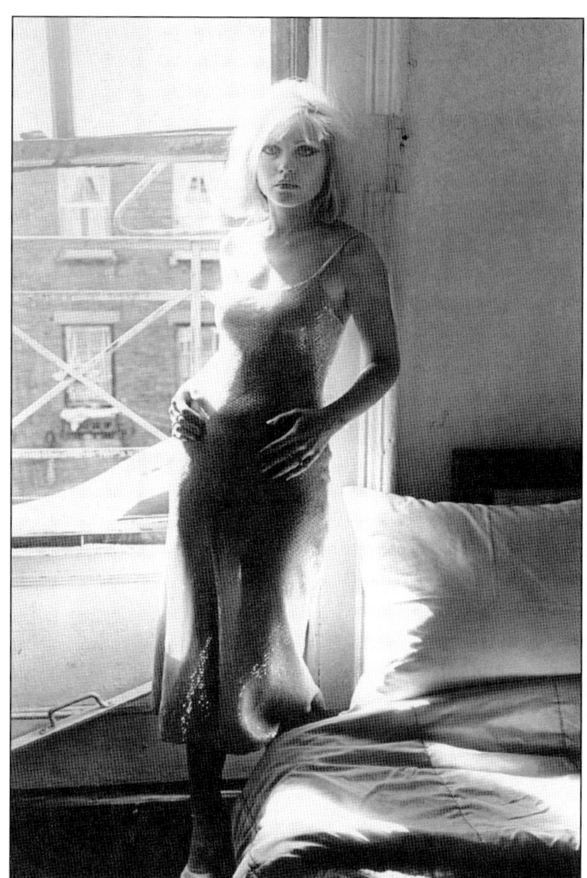

In the 1970s, tiny 266 Bowery was home to Debbie Harry and Chris Stein. The band Blondie rehearsed and made initial recordings here. A fireplace was the heat source, and the kitchen and bathroom were shared by the building; Harry remembers poltergeists and a urine smell from the street below. Globe Slicers kitchen supply store has been there since 1947. Stein's 1977 photograph shows Harry in a dress designed by neighbor Stephen Sprouse. (© Chris Stein)

Sculptor-designer Maya Lin (born 1959) lived and worked at 98 Bowery from 1988 to 1998. She rose to prominence at age 21 after winning the design competition for the Vietnam Veterans Memorial. Initially controversial because of its modernist approach—and because Lin was young, female, inexperienced, and Chinese American—the powerful result was widely embraced. Works designed here include Alabama's Civil Rights Memorial. This 1988 photograph at 98 Bowery was taken by Michael Katakis. (© Michael Katakis/the British Library.)

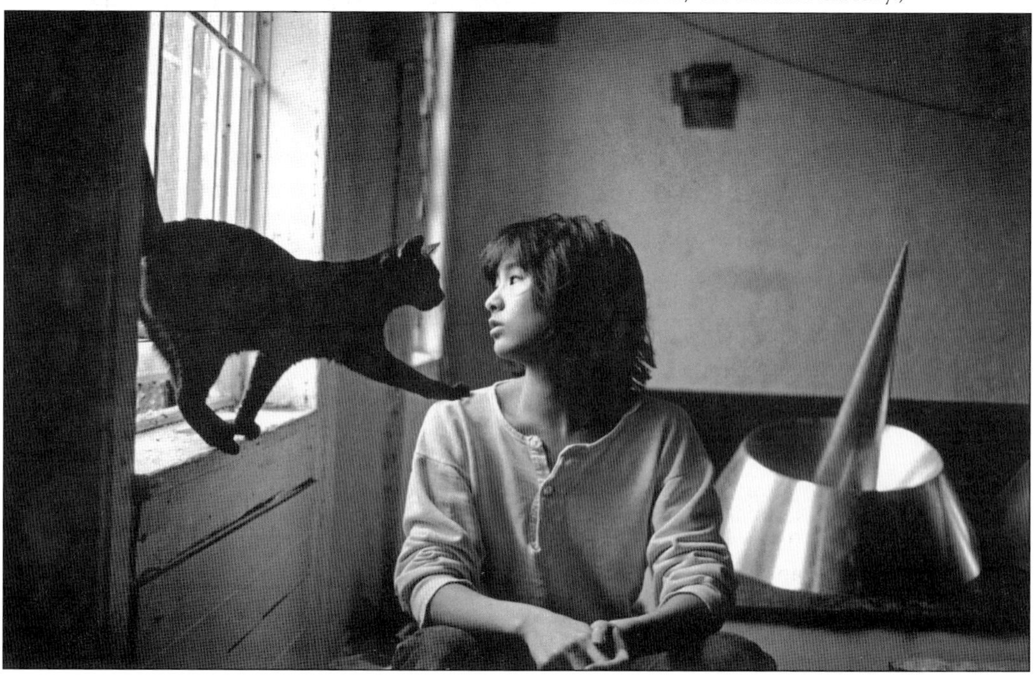

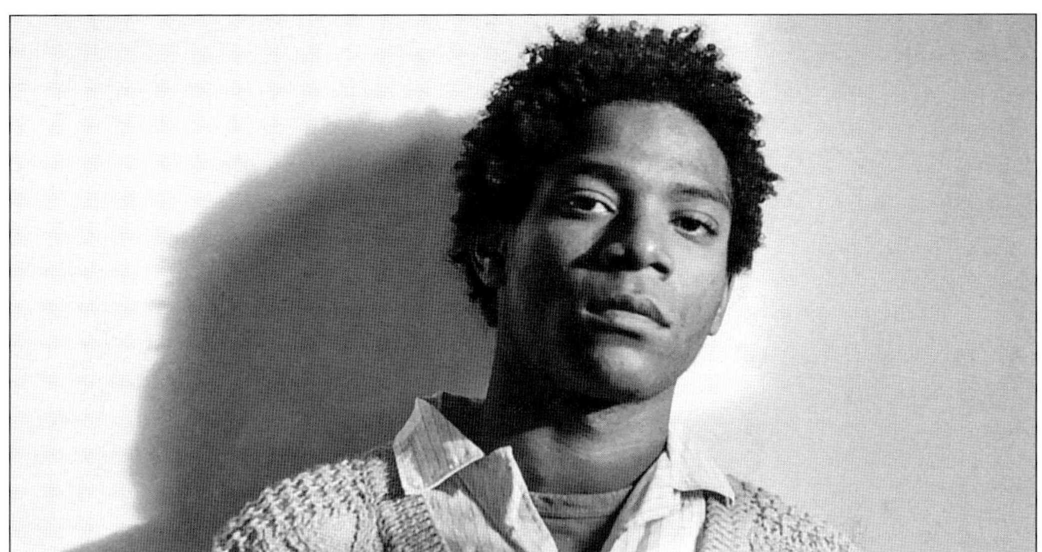

During his tragically brief, meteoric career from street artist to an internationally recognized painter, Jean-Michel Basquiat (1960–1988) lived and worked at 57 Great Jones, off the Bowery, in an 1860s stable and former clubhouse of mobster Paul Kelly. Born in NYC to Afro-Caribbean parents, his provocative works used painting, drawing, written text, and neo-Expressionist figures, often containing a sociopolitical critique of racism and injustice. This 1984 photograph is by Lee Jaffe. (© Lee Jaffe.)

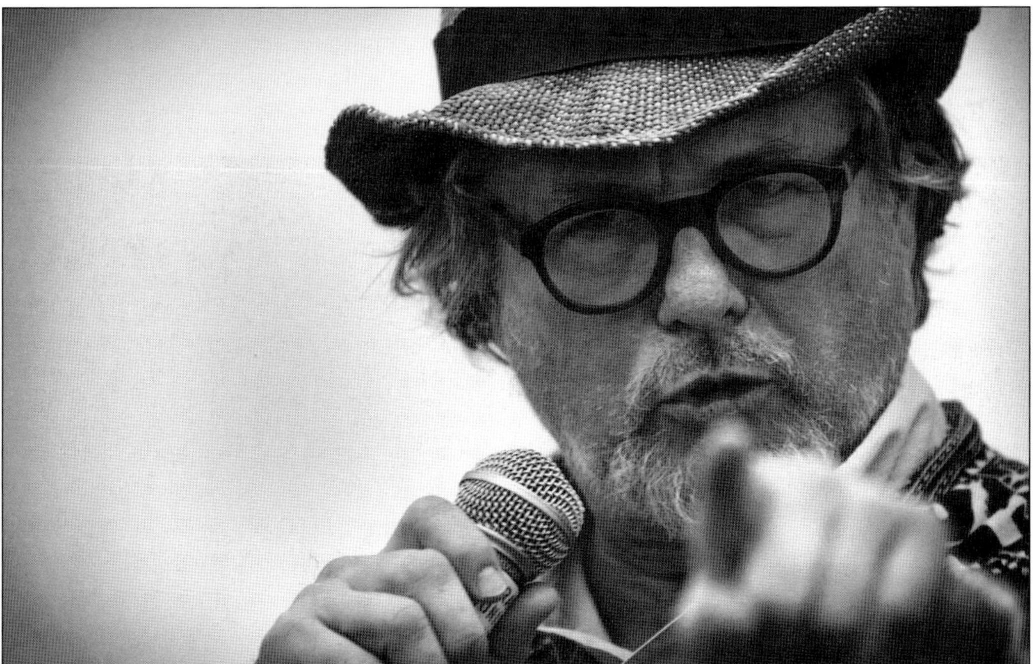

Poet-founder of the Bowery Poetry Club at 308 Bowery, Bob Holman embodies the street's tradition of wildness and creativity, particularly via spoken word performances and poetry slams. According to Henry Louis Gates, he "has done more to bring poetry to cafes and bars than anyone since Ferlinghetti." Kentucky-born Holman, seen here in 2015, has lived on the Bowery for over 40 years. (Bob Holman.)

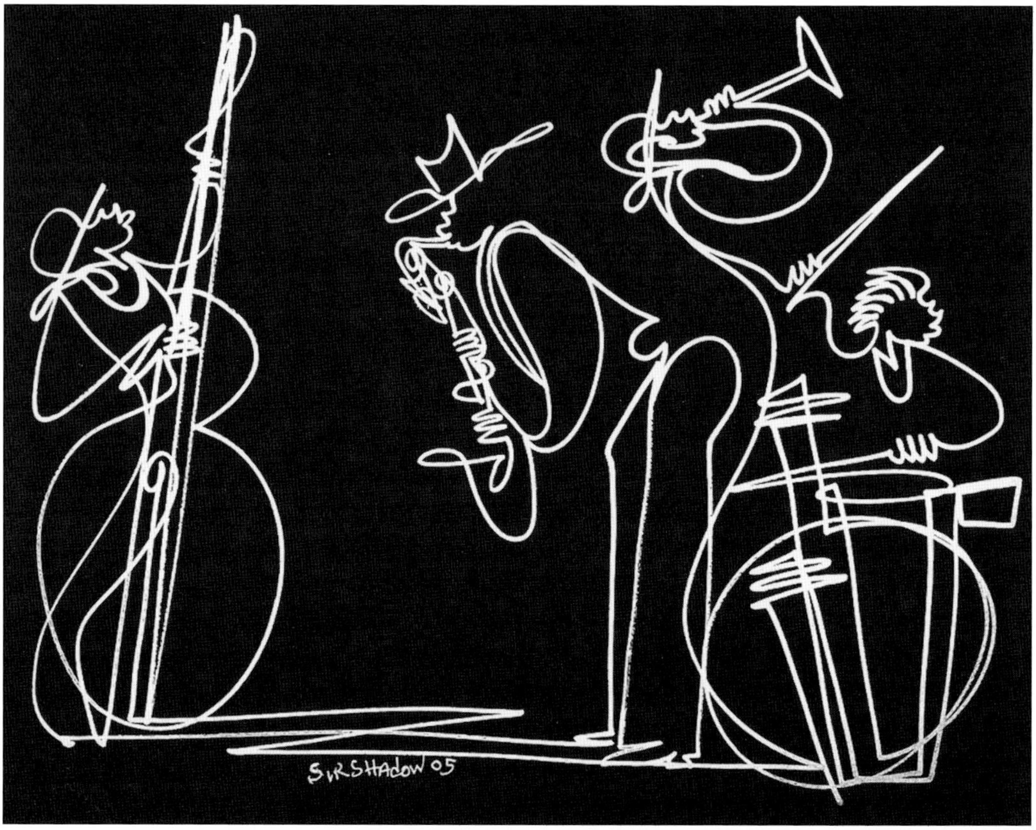

Unlike Bowery artists who dwell in spacious lofts, six-foot-four artist-poet Sir Shadow (born 1949) has lived and worked in a cramped SRO cubicle inside the Whitehouse Hotel at 340 Bowery since 1995. A master of positivity, he insists his tiny space keeps him free. His popular jazz musician drawings are rendered in one continuous line, a style he calls "flowetry." The hotel is being converted to a "boutique micro hotel"; Sir Shadow will continue living there. (Sir Shadow.)

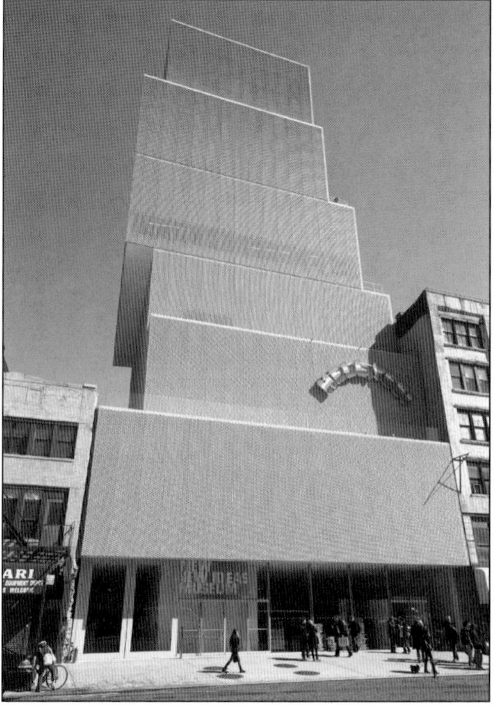

When it arrived at 235 Bowery in 2007, the New Museum of Contemporary Art was controversial. While many welcomed the increased arts activity on the Bowery, others saw the 180-foot tower as a harbinger of overdevelopment. Perhaps anticipating this, a sign reading, "Hell, Yes!" was installed on its façade. The building design is by Japanese architects Kazuyo Sejima and Ryue Nishizawa of the firm SANAA. (Lonely Planet.)

Six

Social, Political, and Intellectual Ferment

In addition to its impact on American popular culture, the Bowery has often been a scene of social, political, and intellectual ferment. In the 1800s, there were labor marches and gatherings of socialists, anarchists, unionists, religions, and fraternal organizations inside its meeting halls and saloons. Military Hall, at 193 Bowery, witnessed the founding of the Tinsmiths, the first sheet metal workers union (1863), the founding of the Benevolent and Protective Order of Elks (1868), and the Metropolitan Police's organization into a professional, uniform-wearing law-enforcement agency (1840s). It also saw the first American worship services of the Primitive Methodists (1829) and Saint Bartholomew's Episcopal Church (1835). An 1899 strike at the People's Theatre spawned America's first actors' guild, the Hebrew Actors' Union. Since its founding in 1859, Cooper Union, America's first free university, has accepted all, regardless of race, religion, or gender. A bastion of free speech and progressive thought, its Great Hall has witnessed anti-slavery speeches by Lincoln and Frederick Douglass, Clara Lemlich's strike call for 20,000 shirtwaist workers (1909), and the NAACP's first public meeting (1909).

Given the Bowery's diversity, it is unsurprising that race, class, and national identity issues have been strongly felt here. The venerable townhouses at 134-136 Bowery were hotbeds of Abolitionist activity, and a violent 1854 incident on a Park Row/Bowery streetcar triggered legal challenges that eventually ended segregation on NYC public transportation. Class conflict and anti-British fervor helped spark the deadly 1849 Astor Place Riot. Though controversial, Tammany boss turned Congressman "Big Tim" Sullivan built one of America's first multi-ethnic political organizations, supported labor and women, and passed the gun-control Sullivan Law. Wallace and Burrows's *Gotham* credits an 1890s club at 392 Bowery as America's first homosexual rights organization. In 1973, the Green Guerillas transformed a vacant lot at Bowery and Houston into the city's first community garden.

During the past 50 years, ideas and issues have continued to be debated at Cooper Union, and the community continues to speak out on tenants' rights, gentrification, and the preservation of affordable housing, small businesses, green spaces, and the neighborhood's historical context, scale, and character.

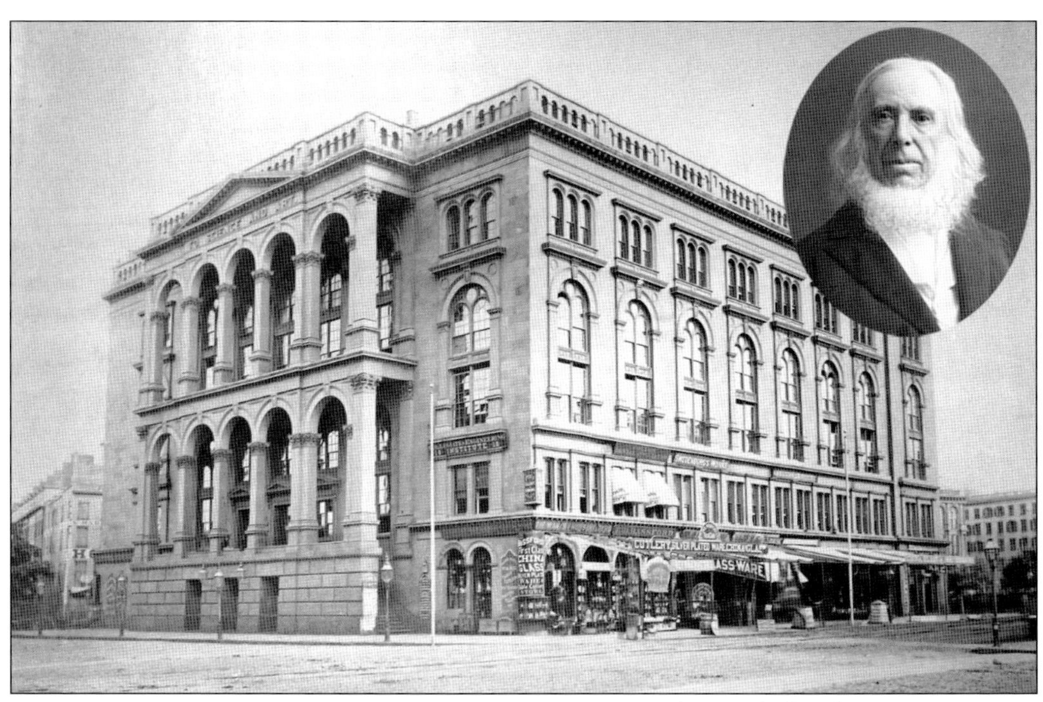

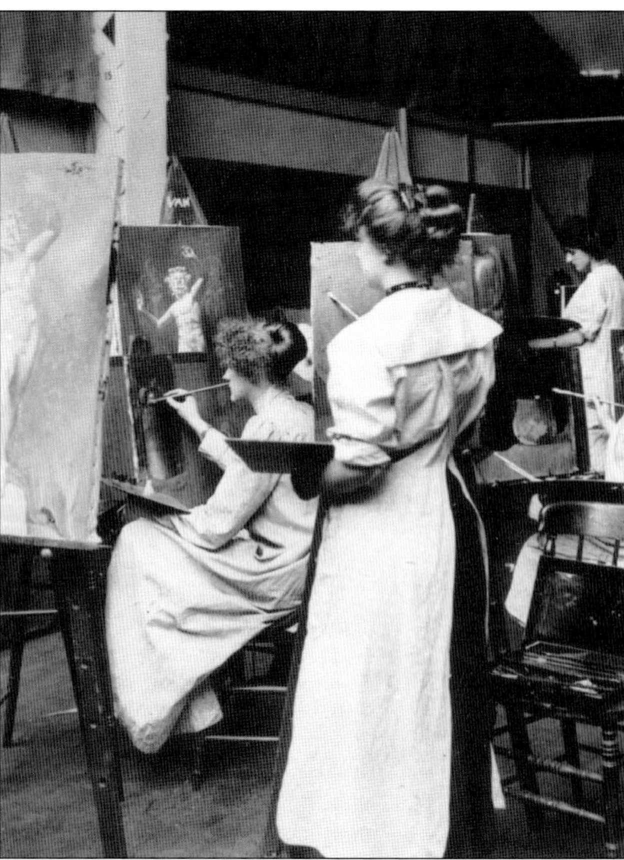

America's first free university, the Cooper Union for the Advancement of Science and Art began life in 1859 with doors open to all regardless of race, class, religion, or gender. It was founded by philanthropic industrialist Peter Cooper, who designed America's first steam locomotive, invented powdered gelatin, and helped fund the first transatlantic telegraph cable. He was a progressive thinker who opposed slavery and supported rights for women, workers, and Native Americans. The landmark Anglo-Italianate-style Foundation Building, designed by Frederick A. Peterson, was the first to use rolled iron I-beams. In 1859, it was the city's tallest building. Ground-level businesses during the early years helped pay off the construction debt. This c. 1870s photograph of the Foundation Building includes an inset of Peter Cooper. The 1921 photograph to the left is of a women's painting class. (Both, CUA.)

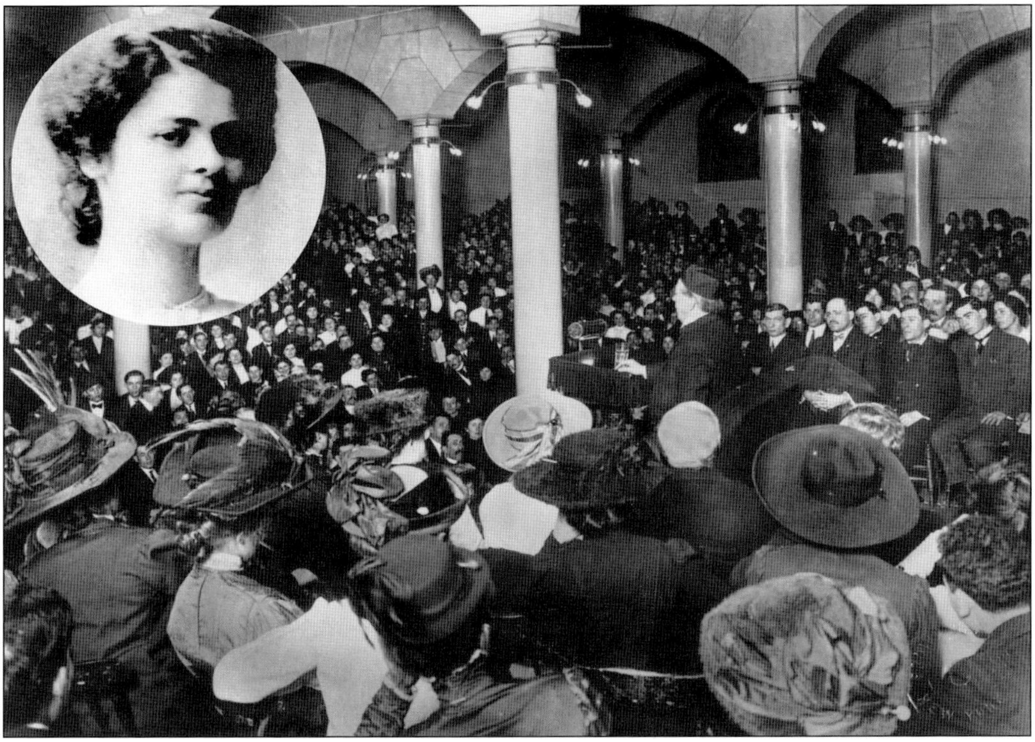

Cooper Union's Great Hall has long been a bastion of free speech, a place where ideas and issues are discussed or debated, even when controversial. Topics have included women's rights, workers' rights, Native American rights, socialism, atheism, and even Victoria Woodhall espousing free love. Speakers have included Mark Twain, P.T. Barnum, Chief Red Cloud, Frederick Douglass, Susan B. Anthony, Mother Jones, Eugene Debs, Nikola Tesla, William Randolph Hearst, Andrew Carnegie, Robert Oppenheimer, and many US presidents. This November 22, 1909, photograph shows American Federation of Labor (AFL) president Samuel Gompers addressing garment workers. Later that night, Ukrainian-born garment worker Clara Lemlich (inset) galvanized the crowd with a call for a general strike, which brought on the Uprising of 20,000 shirtwaist workers. The February 5, 1910, Bain News Service photograph below shows strike pickets during the Uprising of 20,000. (Above, CUA; below, LOC.)

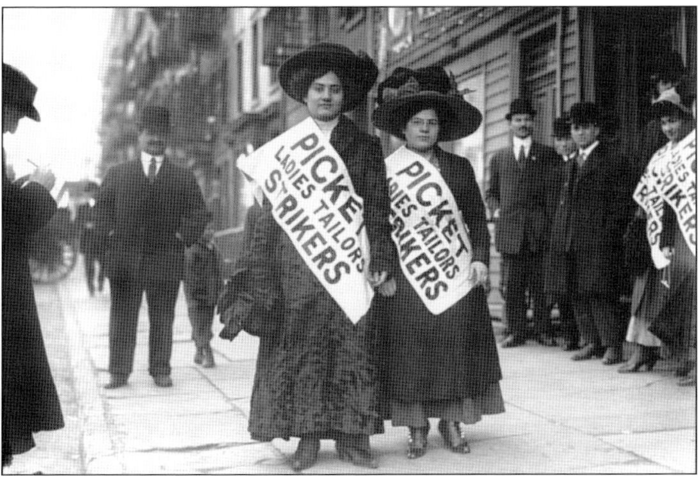

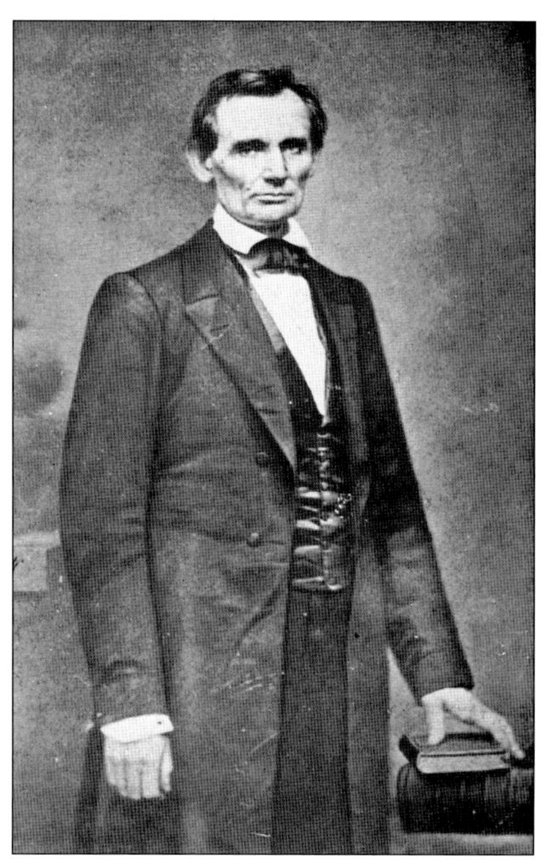

On February 27, 1860, this iconic photograph of Illinois lawyer Abraham Lincoln was taken in Matthew Brady's studio at Broadway and Tenth Street. That night, his famous anti-slavery speech electrified the audience at Cooper Union's Great Hall; three months later, he became the Republican Party's candidate for president. As he later wrote, "Brady and the Cooper Union made me president of the United States." (LOC.)

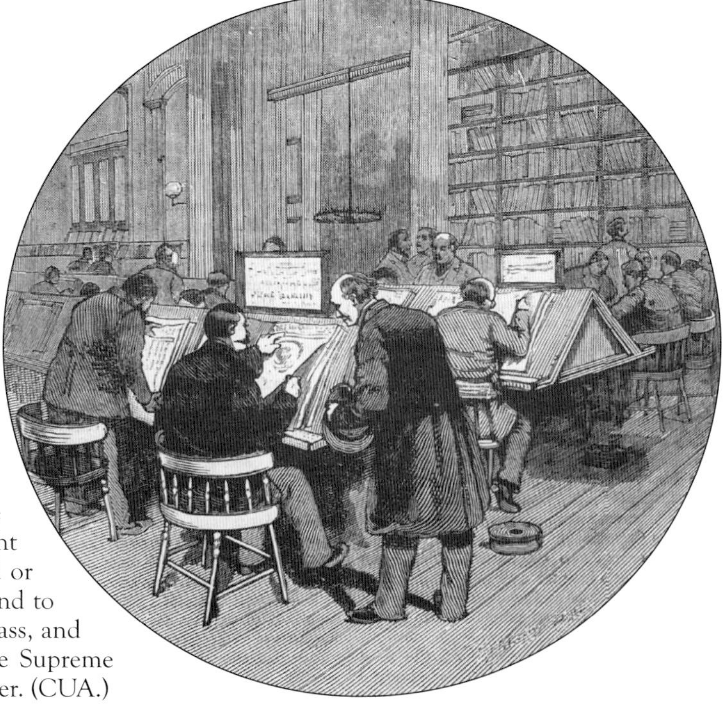

This 1883 illustration from *Frank Leslie's Popular Monthly* shows newspaper racks inside Cooper Union's Reading Room. Decades before New York Public Library was founded, this open-to-all facility offered books and periodicals from around the world and kept late hours to accommodate workers coming in from night shifts. Especially during cold or rainy weather, it was a godsend to the homeless, the working class, and immigrants, including future Supreme Court Justice Felix Frankfurter. (CUA.)

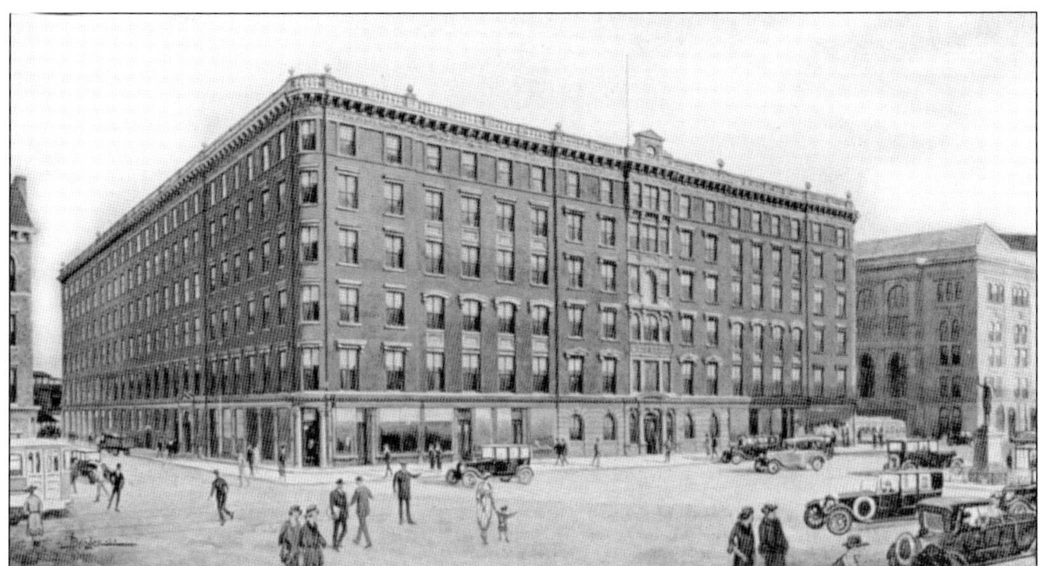

While Cooper Union was the Bowery's intellectual anchor, its spiritual anchor was the immense six-story Bible House, located just north of Cooper Union on Astor Place. The city's first cast-iron building, it was erected in 1853 and famously printed and distributed millions of Christian bibles in multiple languages around the world. It was demolished in 1956. (CUA.)

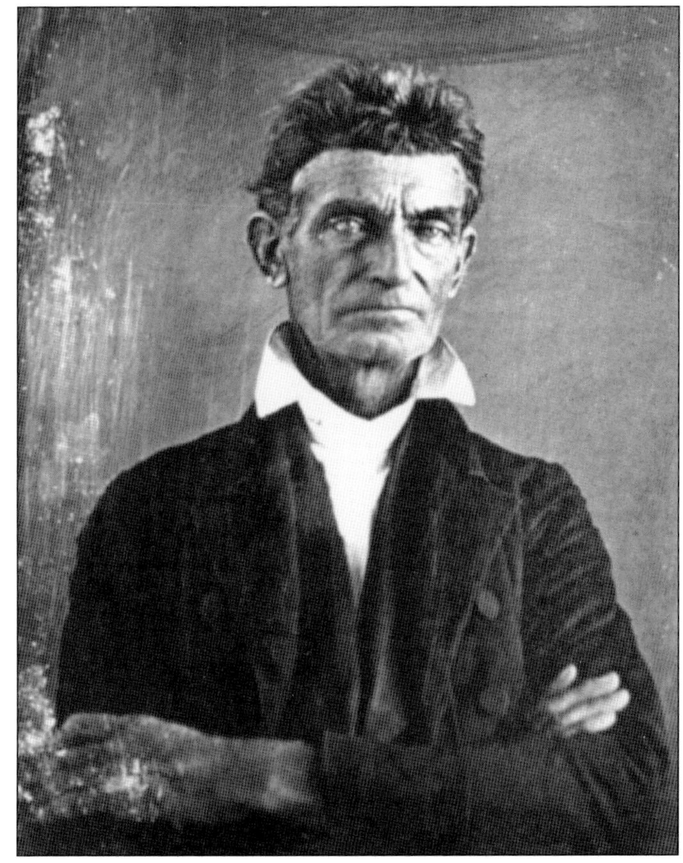

Executed for the raid on the federal armory at Harper's Ferry, Virginia, anti-slavery firebrand John Brown (1800–1859), with the rope still around his neck, was put on a train bound for an upstate New York burial. Detoured in darkness to 163 Bowery, he was embalmed by Quaker undertaker Jacob Hopper. A father of 20, Brown's commitment to "All men are created equal" and Christianity's "Golden Rule" made him an Abolitionist martyr. This photograph is from 1856. (Louis DeCaro.)

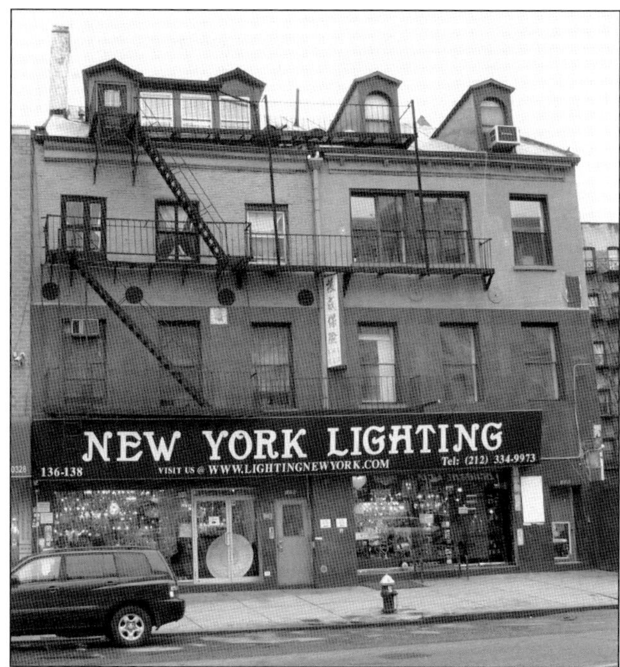

Among NYC's oldest structures, these 1790s Federal-era townhouses at 134-136 Bowery were for 60 years a center of anti-slavery activity. Seen here in 2016, they were built by Samuel Delaplaine, a devout Quaker who also donated land for a Negro cemetery on nearby Chrystie Street. Anti-slavery literature was printed and sold here, and a Quaker-owned rooming house here is believed to have likely been a stop along the Underground Railroad. (DM.)

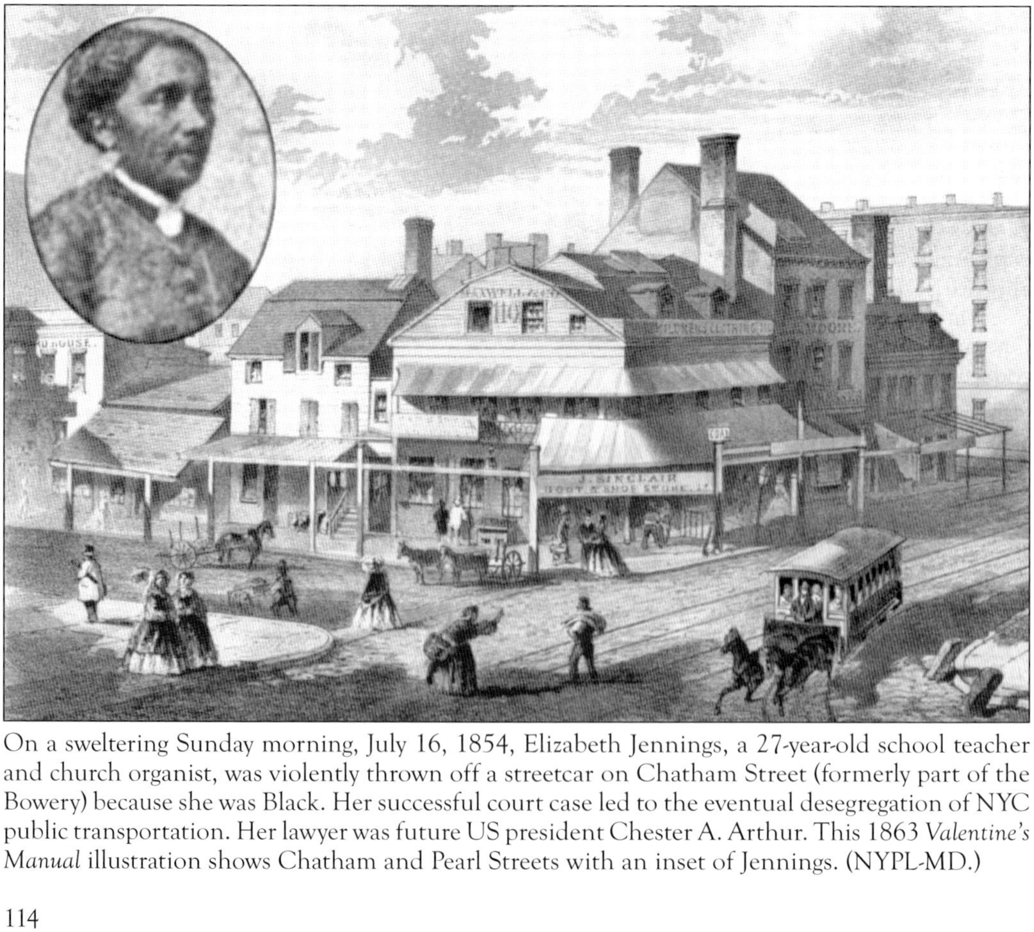

On a sweltering Sunday morning, July 16, 1854, Elizabeth Jennings, a 27-year-old school teacher and church organist, was violently thrown off a streetcar on Chatham Street (formerly part of the Bowery) because she was Black. Her successful court case led to the eventual desegregation of NYC public transportation. Her lawyer was future US president Chester A. Arthur. This 1863 *Valentine's Manual* illustration shows Chatham and Pearl Streets with an inset of Jennings. (NYPL-MD.)

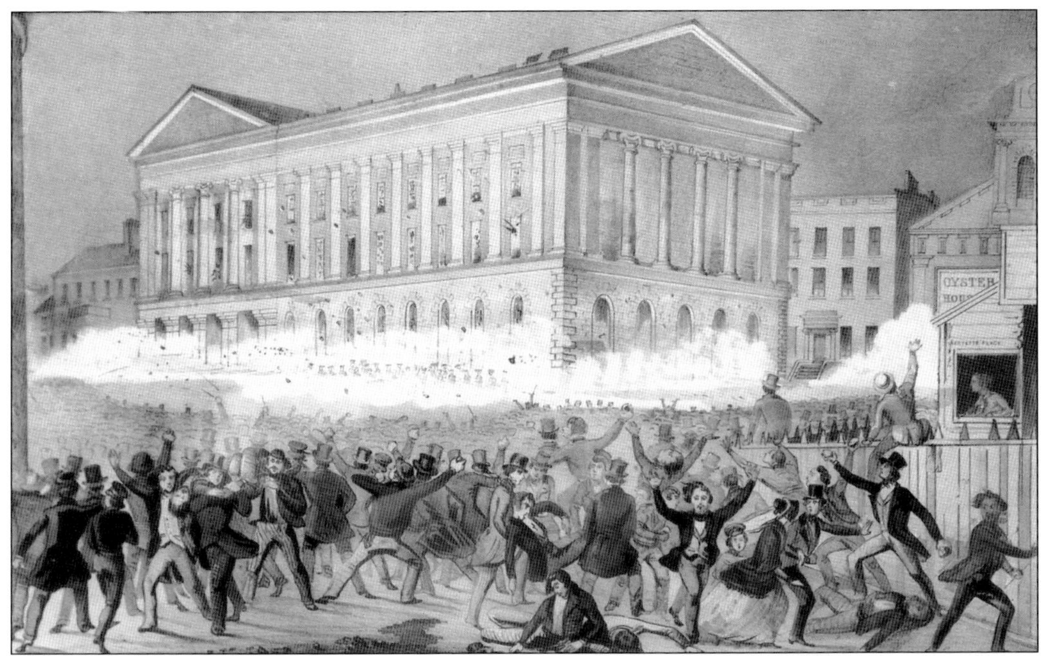

The Astor Place Riot on May 10, 1849, was one of early NYC's bloodiest tragedies. It ostensibly involved the long rivalry between brawny American Shakespearean actor Edwin Forrest—loved by commoners, the Bowery Boys, and the Irish—and genteel British Shakespearean actor Charles Macready, adored by the city's Anglophile elite. It also involved anti-British fervor, class conflict, resentment of the new Astor Place Opera House's exclusionary dress code, and newspapers whipping people into a polarized frenzy. While Forrest portrayed *Macbeth* further downtown, Macready's *Macbeth* was at the opera house. As an anti-British mob assembled outside the opera house, others got cheap seats inside and began hurling insults, vegetables, and even a chair at the actor. Things escalated outside, and the militia fired into the crowd of thousands, killing at least 26. As a consequence of the tragedy, theatres would cease being the democratic gathering places Whitman had admired. (Both, AWC.)

WORKING-MEN
SHALL
AMERICANS
OR
ENGLISH RULE!
IN THIS CITY!

The crew of the British Steamer, have threatened all Americans who shall dare to express their opinions this night at the

ENGLISH ARISTOCRATIC!
OPERA HOUSE!

We advocate no violence but a free expression of opinion to all public men.

WORKINGMEN! FREEMEN!!
STAND BY YOUR
LAWFUL RIGHTS!

AMERICAN COMMITTEE.

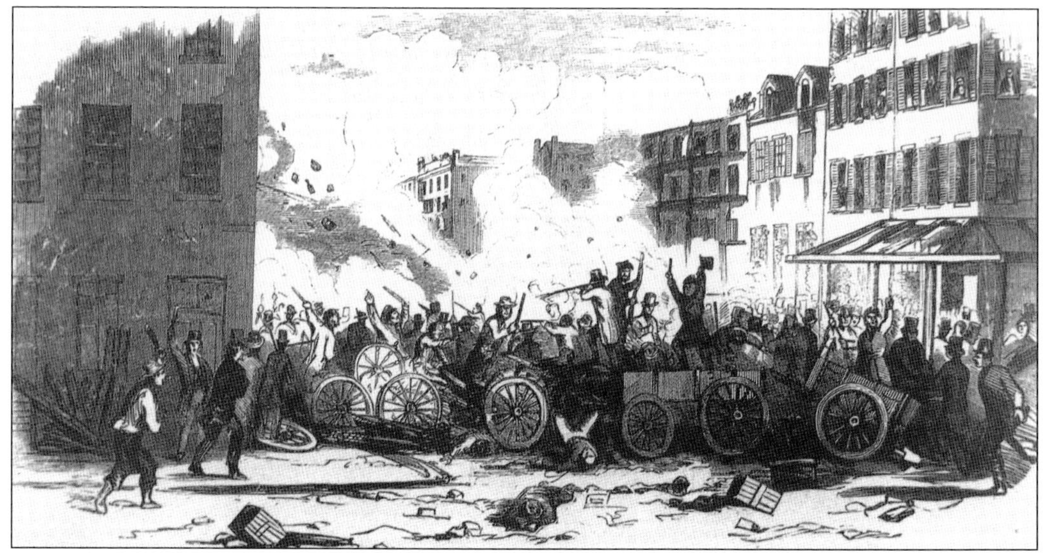

The nativist Bowery Boys' infamous two-day battle with the Irish Dead Rabbits gang, which started on July 4, 1857, inside their 40 Bowery saloon headquarters, left eight dead. Things escalated into a wider conflict, involving other gangs and criminal elements citywide, causing looting and property damage. This image is from *Frank Leslie's Illustrated Newspaper*, July 18, 1857. (LOC.)

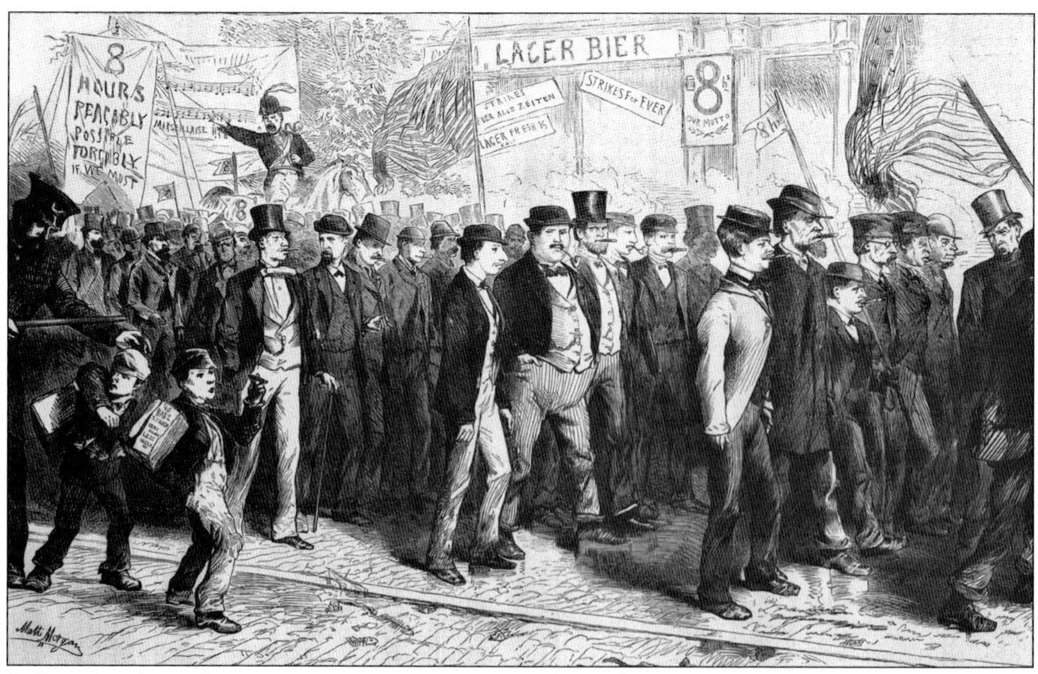

Before the elevated train went up in 1878, the working-class Bowery was a logical site for labor marches, including this 1872 procession calling for a shorter workday. Some 100,000 unionists rallied for an eight-hour day in the Great Strike of 1872, the largest labor uprising the city had ever seen. The illustration is from *Frank Leslie's Illustrated Newspaper*, June 10, 1872. (NYPL-MD.)

Children working in factories and mines and on the street selling newspapers and shining shoes were common in 1910 when Lewis Hine took this photograph outside a Bowery saloon. Labor leaders saw child labor as a consequence of workers' inability to bring home a living wage. With families in dire straits, many children chose to live and work on the streets. Education for them was not an option. (LOC.)

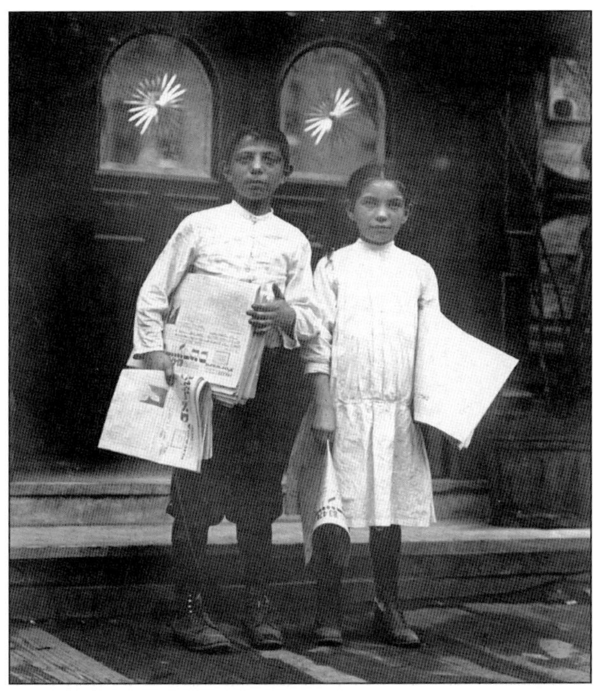

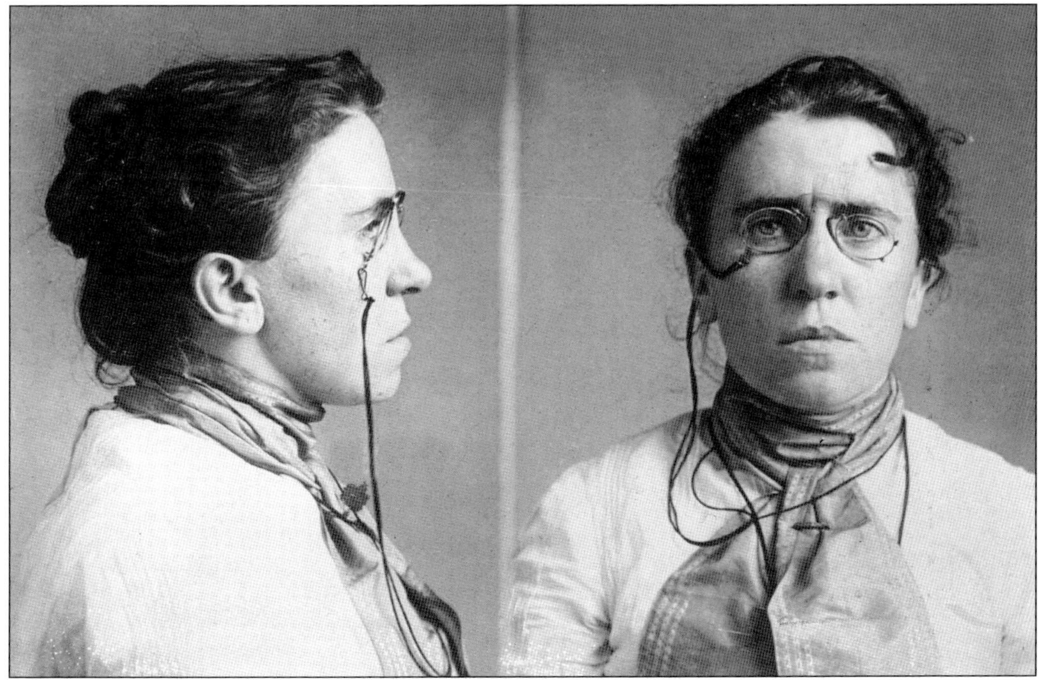

One of the biggest names on the Gilded Age lecture circuit was anarchist firebrand Emma Goldman (1869–1940). Always provocative and always getting arrested but always articulate, the Lithuanian Jewish immigrant spoke before thousands at the Bowery's Thalia Theatre, People's Theatre, Military Hall, and Cooper Union. Topics included women's rights, birth control, capitalism, militarism, labor rights, prisons, atheism, and even homosexuality and free love. The mug shot is from 1901. (LOC.)

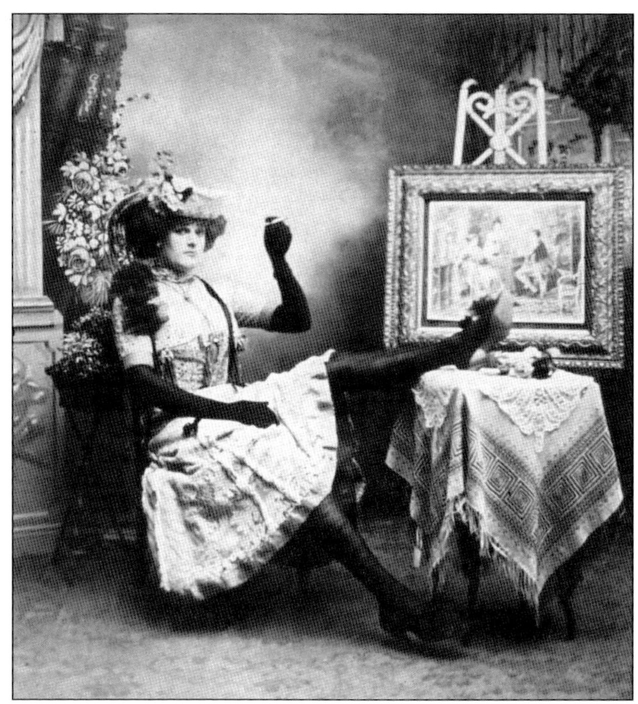

Because of its diverse crowds and anything-goes nightlife, it is unsurprising that 1890s Bowery had a dozen gay-friendly saloons, including Paresis Hall at 392 Bowery, known for its drag shows. Its upstairs was the clubhouse of Cercle Hermaphroditos, whose members sought to unite for defense "against the world's bitter persecution" of homosexual men. The Wallace and Burrows book *Gotham* considers it America's first gay rights organization. "The Bowery Queen" photo is c. 1890s. (Jonathan Katz Collection.)

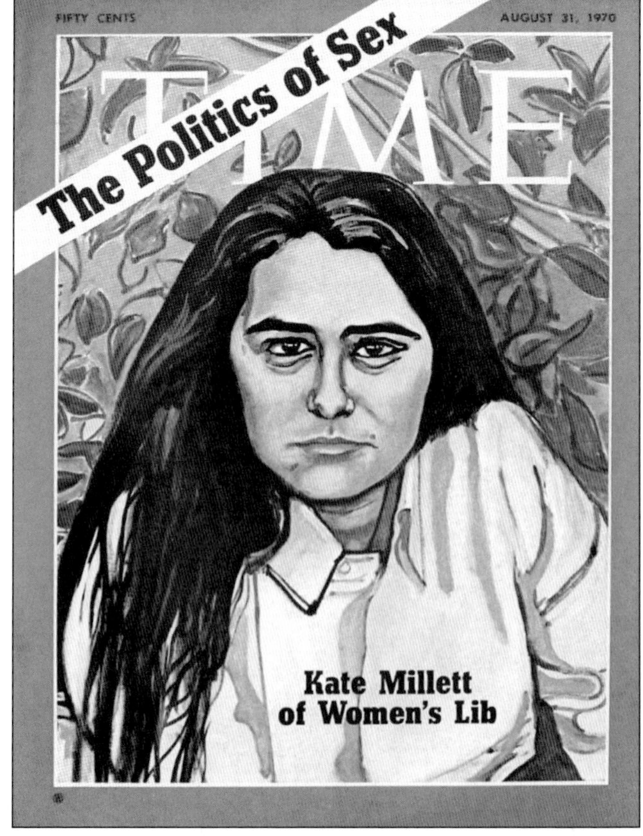

A prominent leader of the feminist movement, Minnesota-born Kate Millet (1934–2017) wrote *Sexual Politics*, which the *New York Times* called "the Bible of Women's Liberation." Millett lived and worked for over 60 years at 307 Bowery, 295 Bowery, and nearby 59 East Fourth Street. She fought to get 295 Bowery, the infamous site of McGurk's Suicide Hall, landmarked. It was demolished in 2005. The cover illustration is by Alice Neel. (Sophie Keir.)

In 1913, 75,000 lined the Bowery for the funeral of "Big Tim" Sullivan, the "King of the Bowery." An Irish American born in the Five Points ghetto in 1862, he began as newsboy and bootblack, eventually becoming a Tammany boss, state senator, US congressman, and an enterprising businessman, with holdings in theatres, saloons, and gambling. Though tainted by corrupt political and business dealings, his support for labor, women, and the poor made him popular and helped build one of America's first multiethnic political organizations. The "Sullivan Law," an early gun control measure, is named for him. He lived at the Occidental Hotel (148 Bowery), with his headquarters at 207 Bowery, where he periodically gave out food, clothing, and shoes to the needy. At right, is a c. 1900 portrait; Pictured below is Sullivan's funeral procession outside 207 Bowery, Bain News Service, September 15, 1913. (Both, LOC.)

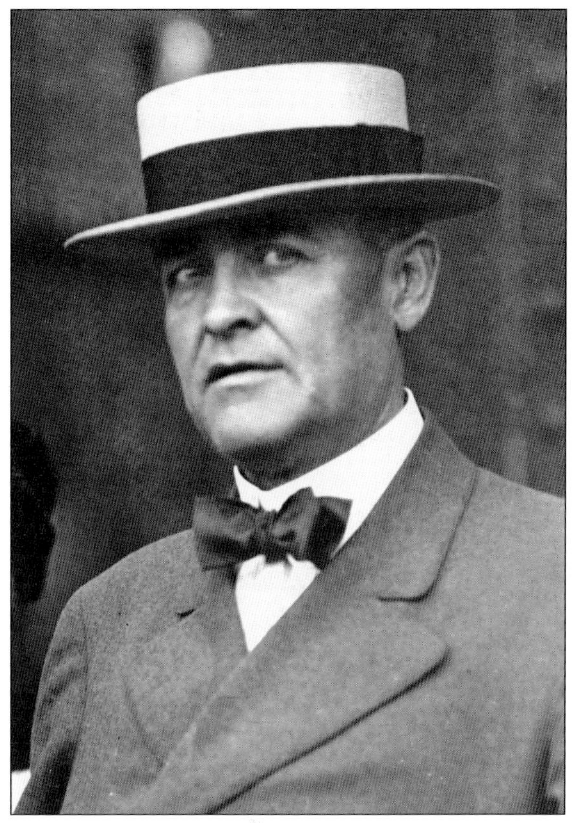

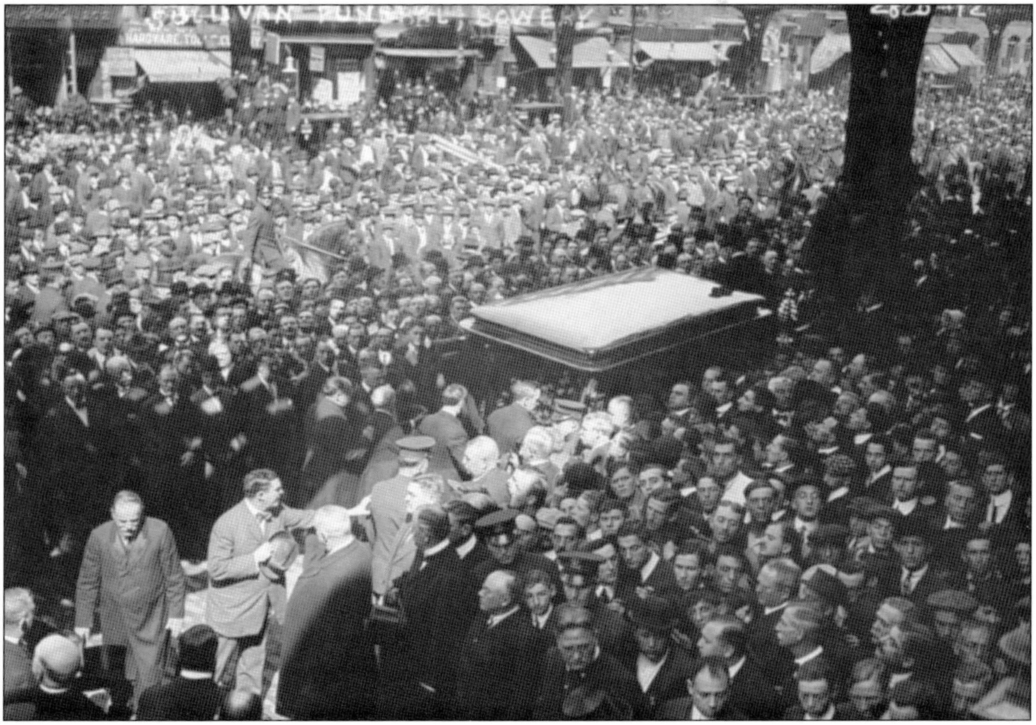

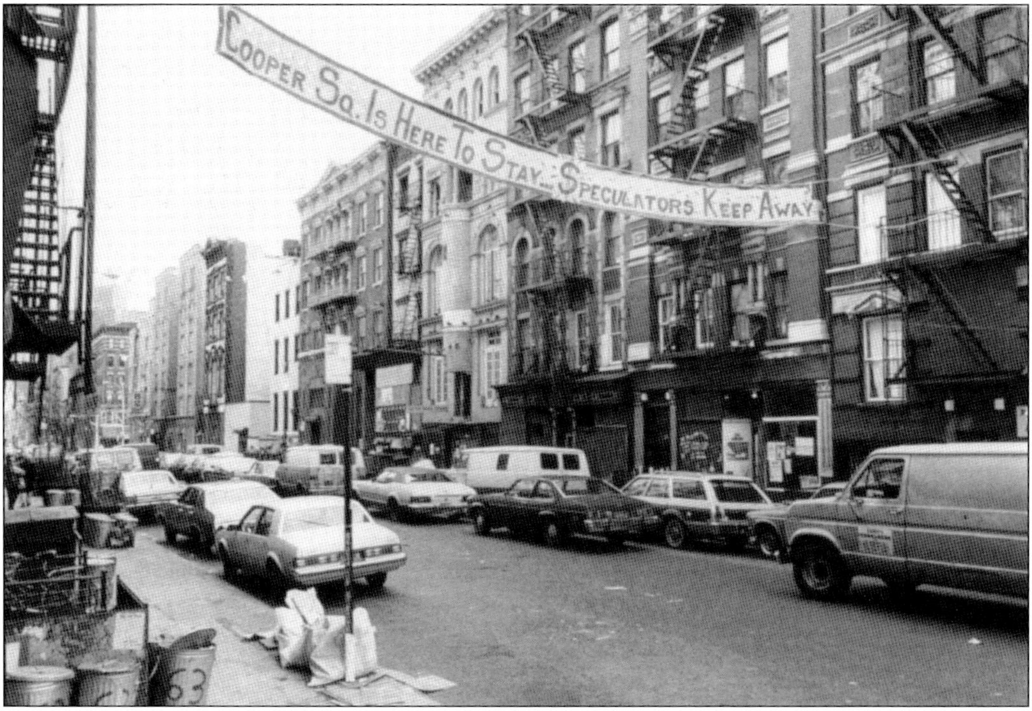

For a long time, this defiant banner graced East Fourth Street between Bowery and Second Avenue. It was raised by Cooper Square Committee, a tenants' rights group that successfully stopped Robert Moses's "slum clearance" plan, devised in 1959, to bulldoze a dozen blocks from East Ninth Street to Delancey Street, which would have displaced thousands. This 1970s photograph is by Alex Harsley. (Cooper Square Committee.)

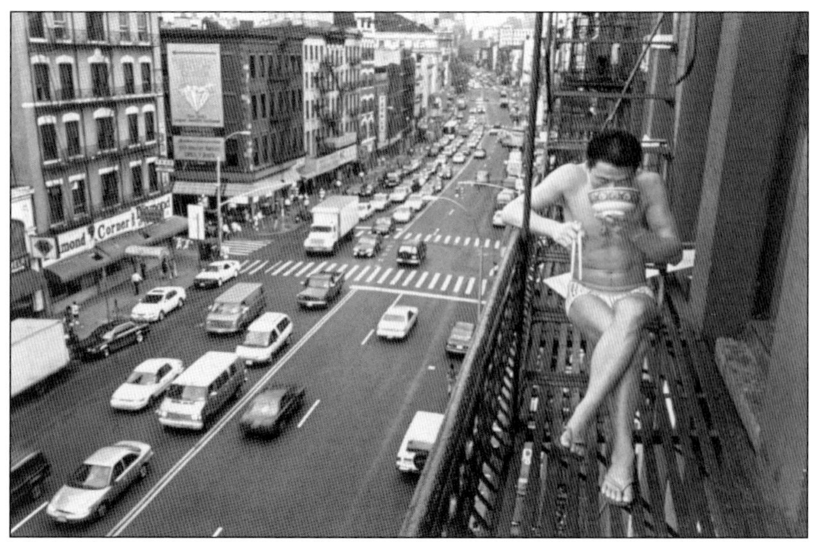

Looking north on Bowery, near Hester Street, this 1998 photograph by Chien-Chi Chang shows "a newly arrived immigrant, Tang Z, eating noodles on a fire escape." (Magnum Photos.)

As this leaflet for a 1906 mass meeting at Cooper Union makes clear, the complex, divisive issues related to immigration and immigrants go way back in our history, with the immigrants always vulnerable to the lowest salaries, precarious living conditions, and intense prejudice. (CUA.)

The New Immigrants' Protective League

MONSTER

MASS MEETING

...at...

COOPER UNION

...on...

Monday, June 11, 1906, 8 P.M.

A spirited Protest against Narrow and Unjust Restrictions of Immigration, a Menace to our Industries.

Hon. H. C. KUDLICH, Chairman

Among the speakers are:

WILLIAM L. BENNETT, M.C.
CARL HAUSER
EDWARD LAUTERBACH
LOUIS VIERECK
JOHN PALMIERI
MARCUS BRAUN
JOSEPH BARONDESS

Do not fail to come! Bring your friends along!

On May 19, 1975, shops and factories all over Chinatown closed for an enormous protest march against the brutal police beating of Peter Yew, a 27-year-old architectural engineer. An estimated 20,000 marched, calling for an end to police brutality and racial discrimination in employment, education, and housing. The photograph is by activist-photographer Corky Lee. Chinatown's Mosco Street is co-named Corky Lee Way. (Estate of © Corky Lee.)

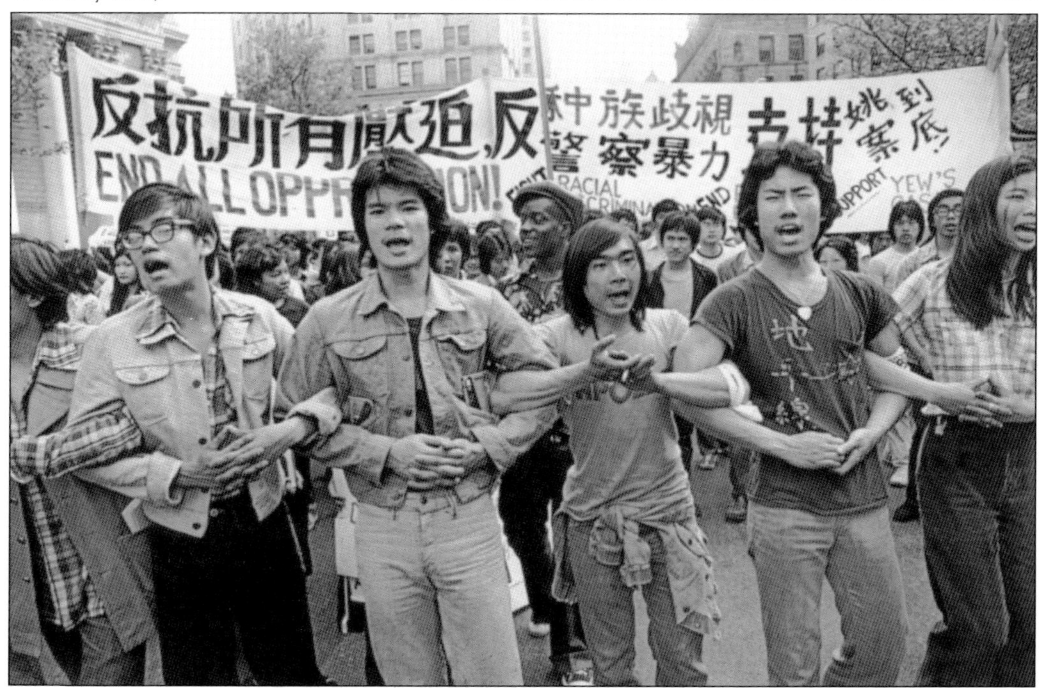

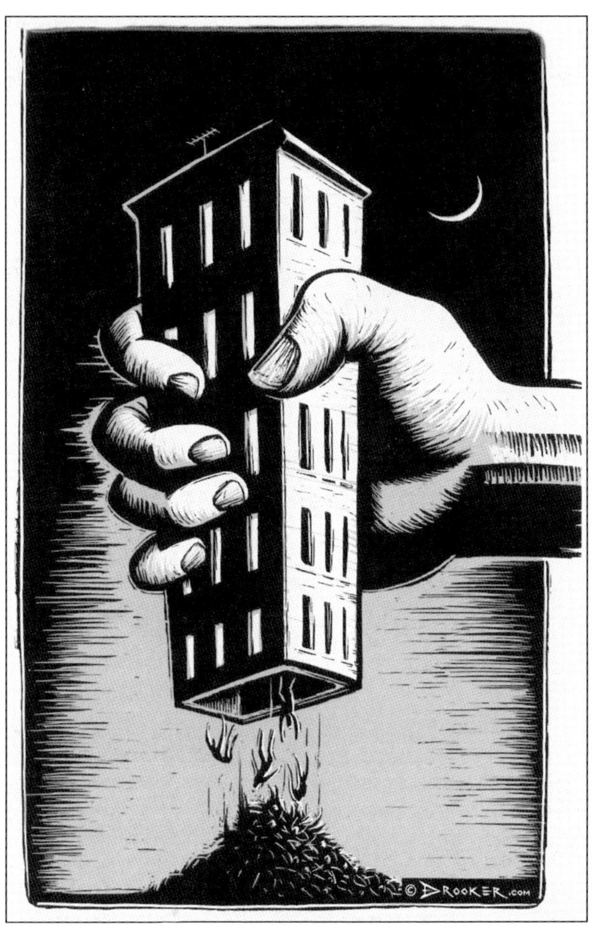

Displacement, especially among the vulnerable immigrant community, has been a recurring problem on the Bowery. In 2009, 29 low-income Chinatown residents were displaced after construction of a high-rise hotel at 91-93 Bowery caused the forced demolition of adjacent 89 Bowery and 123 Hester Street. In winter 2013, 50 tenants were mass evicted from 81 Bowery, though the Chinatown Tenants Union helped them return. On January 18, 2018, 75 low-income tenants of 83-85 Bowery were mass evicted due to landlord building code violations. The Coalition to Protect Chinatown and the Lower East Side organized pickets and hunger strikes; seven months later, the tenants returned home. Neighborhood artist-activist Eric Drooker captured the issue in this powerful piece, "The Hand that Takes." Alvin Tsang's photograph of these hunger strikers is from February 11, 2018. (Above, Eric Drooker; below, Alvin Tsang.)

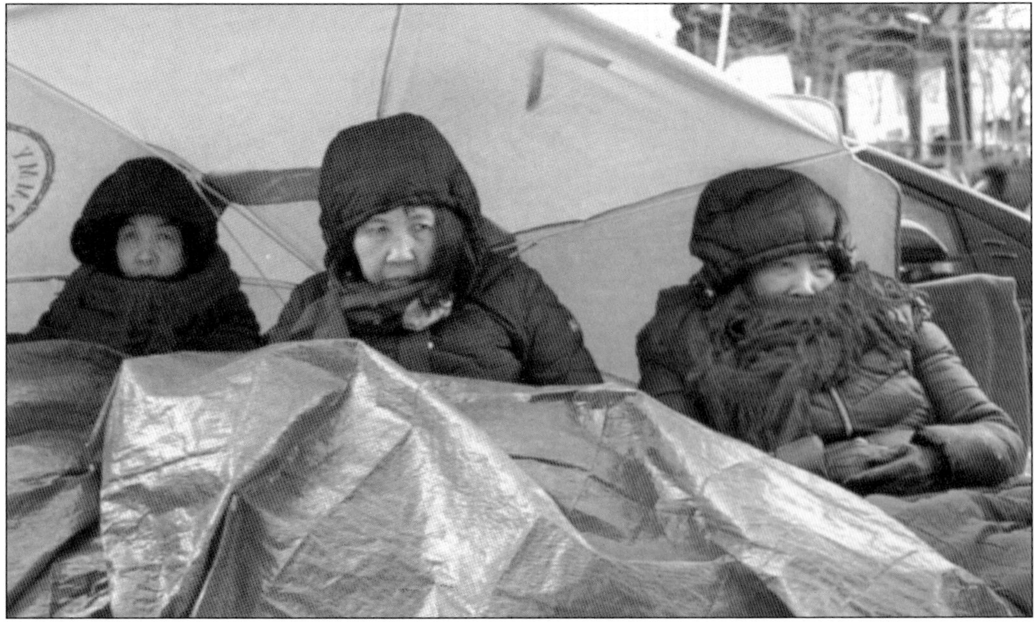

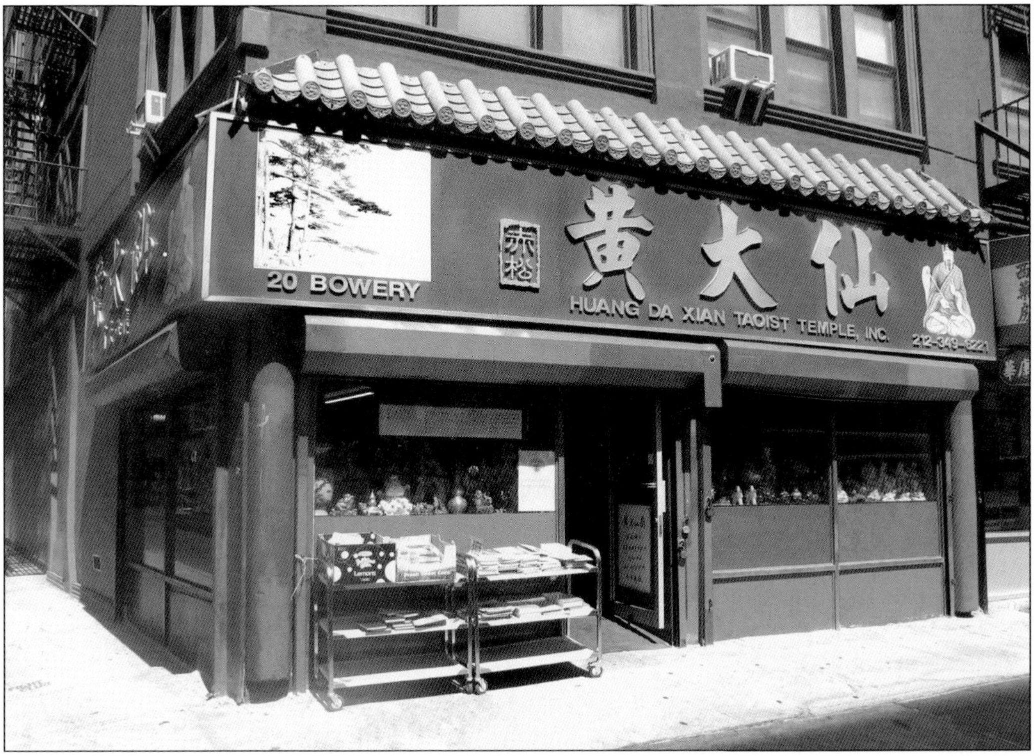

The oft-repeated statement that the Bowery has never had a church is untrue. In the early 1800s, it housed a Presbyterian church, a Baptist congregation, and America's first Primitive Methodist congregation. The Carmel Chapel opened at 134 Bowery in 1872, and the extant Bowery Mission Chapel opened in 1909. There have been Jewish shuls, Buddhist temples, and Taoist temples on the Bowery, including this one, seen in 2023. (DM.)

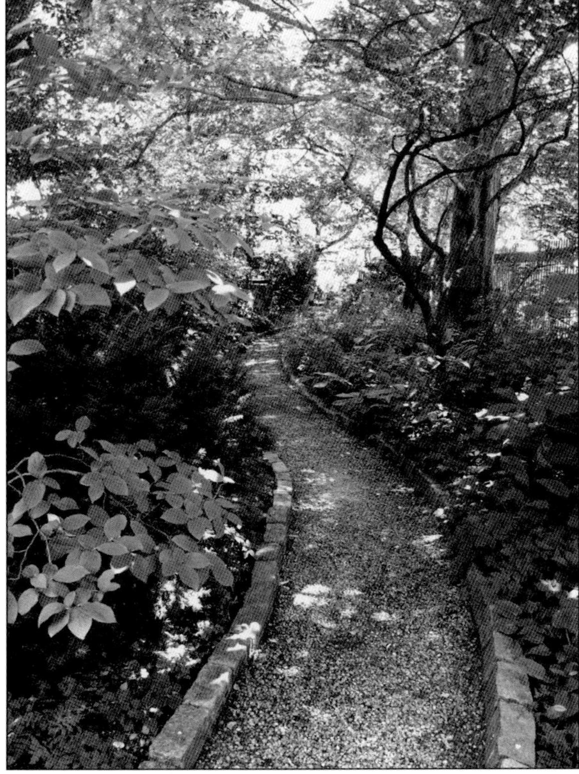

In 1973, a garbage-strewn vacant lot at Bowery and Houston was transformed into Liz Christy Garden, the city's first community garden. Its namesake was cofounder of the visionary Green Guerillas, urban gardening activists who have nurtured the creation of 600 other community gardens all over the city. Sustained by volunteers, the idyllic Liz Christy Garden, seen here in 2023, features wildflowers, birch trees, and the city's tallest dawn redwood tree. (DM.)

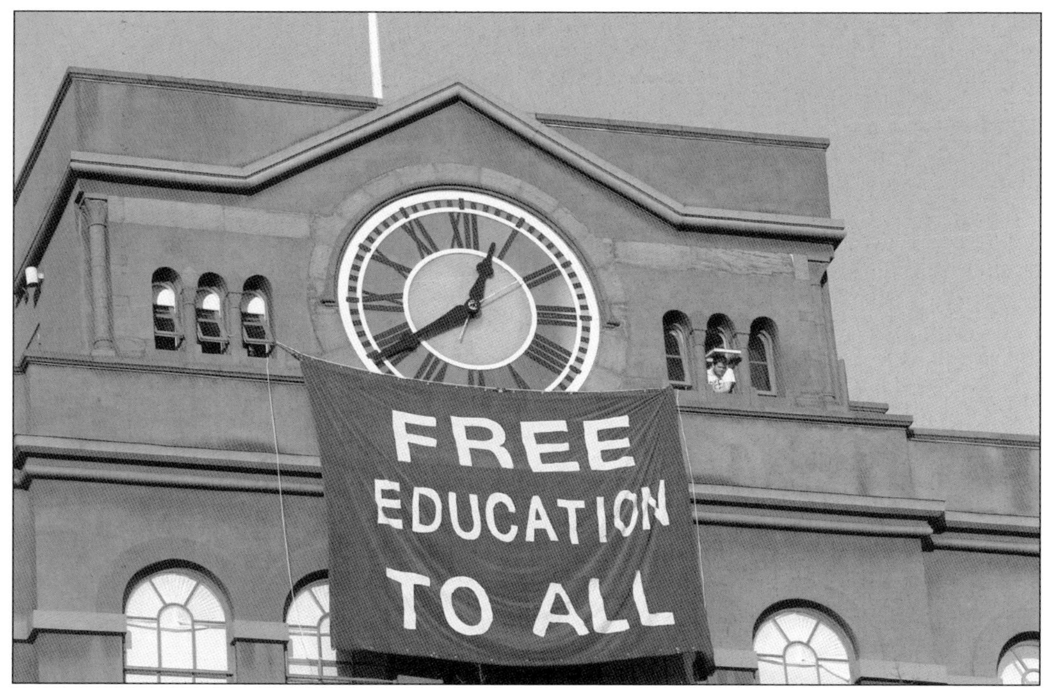

In 2012, protests and a Foundation Building occupation erupted after Cooper Union announced the elimination of its free tuition policy. The committee to Save Cooper Union blamed fiscal mismanagement and filed a lawsuit. In 2015, after the New York attorney general investigated school finances, five trustees and the president resigned. In 2018, a 10-year plan was announced to restore free tuition for undergraduates. This photograph by Michelle V. Agins was taken on December 3, 2012. (*New York Times*/Redux.)

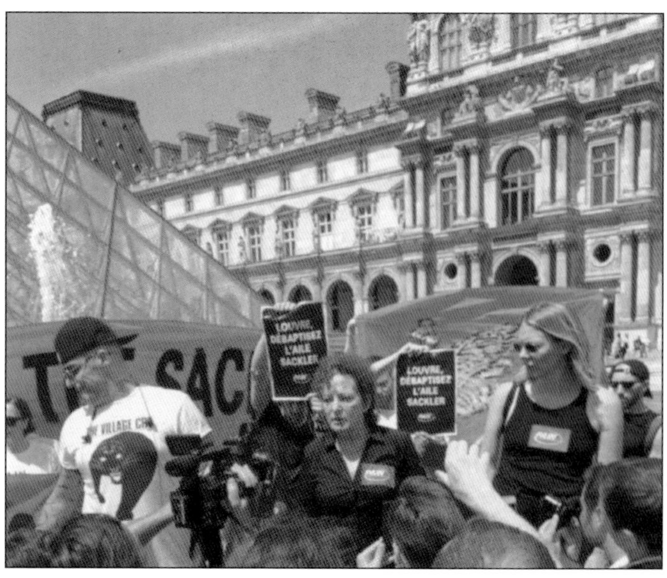

The often-autobiographical work of photographer-activist Nan Goldin (born 1953) has centered on her family, Boston's LGBT community, New York's New Wave scene, the HIV/AIDS epidemic, and the opioid crisis. Goldin's organization P.A.I.N. has successfully pressured museums and universities to remove financial and name associations with the family that aggressively marketed and profited from opioids. A former resident of 334 Bowery, Goldin is shown here protesting at the Louvre in Paris in 2019. (Sackler P.A.I.N.)

After an impassioned campaign to save it, this c. 1825 Federal-era townhouse at 35 Cooper Square (391 Bowery) was demolished in 2011. One of the last surviving links with the Bowery's earliest period of development, it was built by a descendant of Peter Stuyvesant and, at 186 years, was Cooper Square's oldest structure. Illustrious occupants included Beat poetess Diane di Prima, actor Joel (*Cabaret*) Grey, and writer Claude (*Manchild in the Promised Land*) Brown. (DM.)

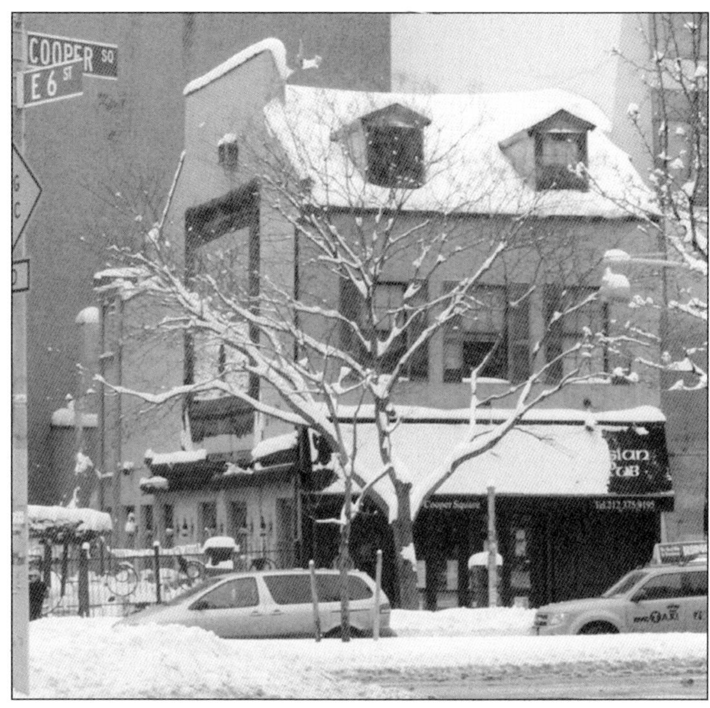

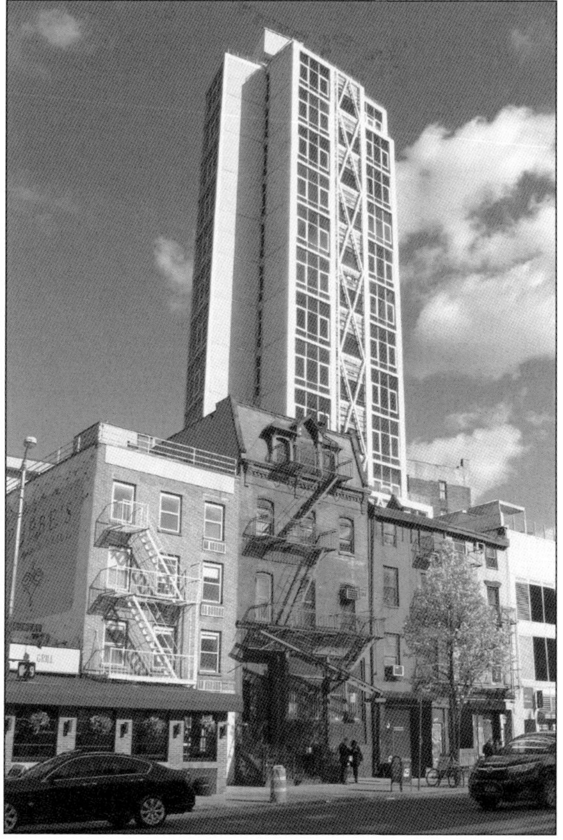

Historic preservation is a major cause downtown since out-of-scale developments are happening everywhere. The landmark 1870 Carl Pfeiffer–designed Germania Fire Insurance Building at 357 Bowery, seen here in 2015, evokes the Bowery's mid-19th century Kleindeutschland (Little Germany) era. However, its sense of historic place is jarringly disrupted by the condo tower, built in adjacent courtyards. Also jarring is the tower's iron-gated spy-cam entrance in the East Fourth Street Cultural District. (DM.)

Bibliography

Alexiou, Alice Sparberg. *Devil's Mile: The Rich, Gritty History of the Bowery.* New York: St. Martin's Press, 2018.

Anbinder, Tyler. *Five Points: The 19th Century New York City Neighborhood That Invented Tap Dance, Stole Elections, and Became the World's Most Notorious Slum.* New York: Free Press, 2010.

Bonner, Arthur. *Alas! What Brought Thee Hither?–The Chinese in New York, 1800-1950.* Cranberry, NJ: Associated University Presses, Inc., 1997.

Bowery Historic District. National Register of Historic Places. US Department of the Interior, National Park Service, 2013. Research and writing: Kerri Culhane, PhD.

Chauncey, George. *Gay New York.* New York: Basic Books, 1994.

Cliff, Nigel. *The Shakespeare Riots: Revenge, Drama and Death in 19th Century America.* New York: Random House, 2007.

DeVillo, Stephen Paul. *The Bowery: The Strange History of New York's Oldest Street.* New York: Skyhorse Publishing, 2017.

Ferrara, Eric. *The Bowery: A History of Grit, Graft and Grandeur.* Mt. Pleasant, SC: History Press, 2011.

Fields, Armand and Marc. *From Bowery to Broadway: Lew Fields and the Roots of American Popular Theater.* New York: Oxford University Press, 1993.

Freeland, David. *Automats, Taxi Dances and Vaudeville: Excavating Manhattans Lost Places of Leisure.* New York: New York University Press, 2009.

Gilfoyle, Timothy J. *City of Eros: NYC, Prostitution, and the Commercialization of Sex, 1790–1920.* New York: W.W. Norton, 1994.

Harlow, Alvin F. *Old Bowery Days.* New York: D. Appleton Co., 1931.

Isay, David, and Stacy Abramson, *Flophouse: Life on the Bowery, with* photographs by Harvey Wang. New York: Random House, 2000.

Kildare, Owen. *My Mamie Rose: The Story of My Regeneration.* New York: Baker & Taylor Co,1903.

Lott, Eric. *Love and Theft: Blackface Minstrelsy and the American Working Class.* New York: Oxford University Press, 1993.

McCabe, James D. *New York by Sunlight and Gaslight.* New York: Union Publishing House, 1882.

McNeil, Legs, and Gillian McCain. *Please Kill Me: An Uncensored Oral History of Punk.* New York: Grove Press, 1996.

Mikorenda, Jerry. *America's First Freedom Rider: Elizabeth Jennings, Chester A. Arthur, and the Early Fight for Civil Rights.* Guilford, CT: Lyons Press, 2019.

Mitchell, Joseph. *Up in the Old Hotel.* New York: Vintage Press, 1993.

Mitchell, Michael. *Monsters: Human Freaks in America's Gilded Age–The Photographs of Charles Eisenmann.* Agincourt, Ontario: Gage Publishing, 1979.

Nahshon, Edna. *New York's Yiddish Theater: From Bowery to Broadway.* New York: Columbia University Press, 2016.

Riis, Jacob. *How the Other Half Lives.* New York: Charles Scribner & Sons, 1890.

Sante, Lucy. *Low Life: Lures & Snares of Old New York.* New York: Farrar, Straus, & Giroux,1991.

Tchen, John Kuo Wei. *New York Before Chinatown: Orientalism and the Shaping of American Culture, 1776–1882.* Baltimore: John Hopkins University Press, 2001.

Trav S.D. *No Applause, Just Throw Money.* New York: Farrar, Straus & Giroux, 2006.

Wallace, Mike & Edwin Burrows. *Gotham: A History of New York City to 1898.* New York: Oxford University Press, 1998.

Welch, Richard F. *King of the Bowery: Big Tim Sullivan, Tammany Hall and New York City, from the Gilded Age to the Progressive Era.* Madison, NJ: Fairleigh Dickinson Press, 2008.

Whitman, Walt. "Old Bowery," *November Boughs.* Philadelphia: David McKay, 1892.

Windows on the Bowery: 400 Years on NYC's Oldest Street. New York: Bowery Alliance of Neighbors, 2020.

About the Organization

The oldest street in some major cities is preserved and protected; valued both as a window into the past and as an investment in the future. But in New York, where real estate rules, it is often community groups rather than city government pushing to preserve our historic fabric.

The Bowery Alliance of Neighbors (BAN) mission is to protect residents, small businesses, and the historic context and character of the Bowery. In 2007, it was shocked into existence after a 21-story tower displaced three 1830s row houses on Cooper Square. Another community wake-up call was the effort to save 35 Cooper Square, a storied 1826 Federal-era townhouse built by a descendant of Peter Stuyvesant. At a vigil there, writer Pete Hamill stated, "In order to make the present as rich as possible, you have to have a sense of the past."

In 2009, BAN commissioned the *East Bowery Preservation Plan*, which made the case for contextual zoning protections for the Bowery's most endangered east side. While the city rejected the plan, BAN helped multiple buildings get landmarked and, in 2013, was instrumental in getting the Bowery Historic District into the State and National Registers of Historic Places. Its historical signage project and book, *Windows on the Bowery: 400 Years on NYC's Oldest Street* (2020), utilizes 19 writers and historians and design work by students at Cooper Union.

In addition to illustrated talks, lobbying, and letter writing, BAN has partnered with other community groups on behalf of displaced tenants and in opposition to bulldozing public spaces like the East River Park and the Elizabeth Street Garden. In 2013, the Bowery Alliance of Neighbors received the Regina Kellerman Award for preservation work. BAN's website: www.boweryalliance.org

Former Landmarks Preservation Commission chair Kent Barwick, a key figure in saving Grand Central Station, believes that given its immense importance, the city should establish a special Bowery cultural district with protections and design regulations respecting historic context and character.

While the Tenement Museum presents the working and home life of immigrants and workers, the Bowery's narrative explores their social lives and the emergence of American popular culture. Although there is not a Bowery museum, history permeates its buildings and streetscapes. Until NYC moves to protect this irreplaceable resource, the Bowery will remain one of our most endangered historic places.